W9-BXX-832

my extraordinary

ordinary life

my extraordinary ordinary life

Sissy Spacek

with Maryanne Vollers

HYPERION

NEW YORK

With thanks to Terrence Malick and Edward R. Pressman for permission to reprint lines from *Badlands,* © 1973 Edward R. Pressman Productions, Inc.

Illustration and photo credits, beginning on p. 269, constitute a continuation of this copyright page.

Library of Congress Cataloging-in-Publication Data

Spacek, Sissy.
  My extraordinary ordinary life / Sissy Spacek with Maryanne Vollers. — 1st ed.
    p. cm.
  ISBN 978-1-4013-2436-0
  1. Spacek, Sissy. 2. Motion picture actors and actresses—United States—Biography. I. Vollers, Maryanne. II. Title.
  PN2287.S663A3 2012
  791.4302'8092—dc23
  [B]
      2011047858

Hyperion books are available for special promotions and premiums. For details contact the HarperCollins Special Markets Department in the New York office at 212-207-7528, fax 212-207-7222, or email spsales@harpercollins.com.

FIRST EDITION

10 9 8 7 6 5 4 3 2 1

THIS LABEL APPLIES TO TEXT STOCK

We try to produce the most beautiful books possible, and we are also extremely concerned about the impact of our manufacturing process on the forests of the world and the environment as a whole. Accordingly, we've made sure that all of the paper we use has been certified as coming from forests that are managed, to ensure the protection of the people and wildlife dependent upon them.

For my family

··· Contents ···

Prologue

1

TEXAS

3

NEW YORK

79

CALIFORNIA

125

VIRGINIA

197

Acknowledgments

267

Credits

269

Magic Hour: ". . . when common things are touched
with mystery and transfigured with beauty: when
the warehouses become as palaces and the tall
chimneys of the factory seem like campaniles
in the silver air."

—James Whistler, the painter, describing that
time of day when the sun is low, and light
transforms the mundane into the sublime

my extraordinary

ordinary life

··· *Prologue* ···

Little did I realize that what began in the alleys
and backways of this quiet town would end up in the
badlands of Montana.

—Holly Sargis, *Badlands*

T HERE'S NOTHING MUCH TO DO IN A SMALL TOWN ON A
warm summer morning. So I stand in the front yard, barefoot
and in short shorts, twirling my baton. The trees cast long, familiar
shadows over the carefully mowed lawns and clean-swept sidewalks.
My arms and fingertips remember the routine all on their own, years of
practice removing the effort from conscious thought, leaving only the
sensation of dancing in the soft grass, knees pumping the air, spinning.
I toss the baton and all I see is a sky so blue and clear it could swallow
me whole. A dog barks somewhere in the distance; on another street a
child is ringing his bicycle bell, but soon I hear nothing but the sound of
my own breath, and the soft impact of the baton in my hand as it re-
turns to earth. I am far away, lost in the rhythm of the spins and rolls,
until I glimpse something moving on the street.

I spin again, then snap my eyes back to the ground; a pair of fancy
black-and-white cowboy boots is walking toward me. The boots are attached to a pair of tight-fitting jeans, a dirty white T-shirt, a cute boy, much
older than me, with hair like James Dean, watching. I drop the baton to
my side, feeling suddenly exposed, uncomfortable in a new way.

"Hi, I'm Kit," the boy says. "I'm not keeping you from anything important, am I?"

I meet his gaze.

"Cut!" says Terrence Malick, from behind the camera. Suddenly the spell is broken, and I'm back on location in La Junta, Colorado, with a small crew and a smattering of bystanders watching me and Martin Sheen play the opening scene of *Badlands*, a film that would soon change all of our lives.

Little did I know, when I was growing up in my own small town in Texas, that my skills as a twirler with the marching band would come in handy in my first starring role. Or that every experience, every story I heard as a child, every person who crossed my path, was like a gift that I would carry with me for the rest of my life.

··· TEXAS ···

· · ·   I   · · ·

SOMETIMES THERE'S NO BETTER ENTERTAINMENT THAN A town dump. When we were kids growing up in East Texas, my brothers and I would ride our bikes to the dump yard over behind the high school. To us it was a treasure trove of free and wonderful things, and we spent hours there sorting through the piles. At the entrance, people would drop off the better stuff, things that weren't really trash, just used items that families had outgrown. That part was more flea market than landfill. Sometimes we would find old but perfectly good toasters, lengths of rope, used games, old toys, or boxes of paperback books. Animals were dropped off, too, in hopes that someone would give them a home.

One afternoon my brother Robbie rode home from the dump cradling a paper sack as if it was filled with diamonds. I watched as he dropped his bike in the grass and ran into the house, holding up the bag and yelling, "I found a kitten!"

My dad looked up from the news-paper.

"Can we keep it, Daddy?" he asked, still breathless.

I was just a few steps behind, chiming, "Can we, Daddy, please?"

"Yeah, we need a cat!" said Ed, our older brother.

She was a scraggly little calico, newly weaned, with six toes on each foot. After the three of us whined and pleaded for the rest of the day, our parents gave in. Our new pet had two names. Inside the house, where she was quiet and sort of mysterious, we called her Suzette. Outside, she was Cattywampus, a freewheeling mouse- and bird-hunter who roamed the neighborhood in search of adventure.

I've always thought of myself as a lot like that cat. My outside self was like Cattywampus: strong, sunny, competent, compassionate, funny, creative, and optimistic, heading out into the world wearing a smile and a bulletproof vest. My inside self was like Suzette: introspective, observant. The outside me was an open book; the inside me had secrets. Nothing earth-shattering—just the deepest thoughts I kept to myself, like the cigar box full of treasures that I had hidden under my bed. Anyone else who opened that box would have only seen a collection of ordinary objects: old cat's-eye marbles, a tiny Coke bottle, a Jew's harp, school photos of my little boyfriends with their awkward signatures scrawled across their faces. But to me each object held a special significance; they were my most precious things, talismans only I understood. I buried the cigar box in the backyard one day, hoping to preserve a time capsule of my life that I could revisit when I was older. I marked out the steps and drew a map of where I had dug the hole.

A few years later, I decided it was time to unearth the time capsule and remind myself of the past. I dug dozens of holes, but I couldn't find it. Never did. Maybe my feet had grown, or the map was wrong. No matter. I still carry that box around with me in my head, while I collect new treasures along the way. I keep them safe in a part of me that no one ever sees; a storeroom where I sort and process the events of a long and interesting life. My mother's lilting voice is there, speaking words of wisdom. So are my father's strong, capable hands that could play a banjo or build a house; my brother's trusting smile; the laughter of my children. This safe and quiet place—Suzette's world—fuels my work as an actor and filmmaker. I know it's always there within reach, inexhaustible as memory.

· · ·

ON CHRISTMAS DAY, 1949, my mother got a silver soup ladle—and me. I had green eyes and red hair, and completely ruined the holiday for my brothers. Ed was six, and Robbie was only sixteen months old when I came along. The night before, my mother had been hanging decorations on the tree when she went into labor. She insisted that my father wait until she'd finished decorating and all the presents were wrapped before she let him take her to the nearest hospital, in Tyler, Texas. Daddy's parents were visiting, and he borrowed their brand-new Chrysler for the thirty-eight-mile drive. They say he drove so fast, he burned the paint off that engine and made it just in time. I was born a few minutes after midnight. My parents named me Mary Elizabeth, but my brothers called me "Sissy," and it stuck.

We lived in Quitman, a town of 1,237 souls nestled in the rolling farmland of East Texas, about ninety miles northeast of Dallas. My father, Edwin Spacek, was the Wood County agricultural agent. My mother, Virginia, known to all as Gin, worked for an abstract office in the courthouse when she wasn't home with us. For seventeen years, Quitman was the center of my universe. I always appreciated the accident of my birth into such a wonderful world. As a child, I would lie in bed at night and think, *I'm so lucky to be born in Texas, to live in this house with these parents, and these brothers, and . . .*

All the things that are most important to me, I had before I left that little town. My values were formed in a community where material possessions didn't count for much, relationships were everything, and where waiting for something you wanted could actually be better than having it.

My brothers and I grew up together in a small ranch house that my father built on a half-acre lot along the Winnsboro Highway, a quarter mile from the center of town. The house had green clapboard siding and thick redwood trellises propping up the eaves on either side, which were perfect for climbing roses. Our dad, who came from a long line of

Czech farmers, had a degree in agriculture, and he could make anything grow. Our yard was always a wonder, manicured and lush with flower beds and persimmon trees, pears and chestnuts. Daddy could never walk by a weed. Whenever one of us kids was home sick from school, he would leave work during his 10 A.M. coffee break and stop by the drugstore to buy us a funny book. I would hear the sound of his car door slamming, and then wait for a long time before he got to the front door. I'd look out the picture window and see him in his suit and tie, pulling weeds from the lawn.

My father was a slim, handsome man with piercing almond-shaped eyes and high cheekbones. Like his father, who had owned a tailor shop, Daddy was an impeccable dresser—my favorite picture of him is as a young county agricultural agent, dressed in white linen pants, two-tone shoes, and a Panama hat, standing in a cotton field checking the crop. Our dad pretended to be strict with us. "Gin, you're going to ruin those kids!" he'd say. "Just give me one week and I'll straighten them out!" But even though he made us toe the line, he was really a soft touch. There was a time when my grandmother was sick and Mother had to leave us alone with him for a few weeks. He spoiled us rotten. One morning I woke up to see him standing over me with a dish towel draped over one arm and a breakfast tray in his hands.

He was always patient with me, even though I had quite a temper. When I was very little, there were times when I'd actually kick him in the shins, or slam my bedroom door so hard the house would shake. He told me years later that he didn't spank me because he didn't want to break my spirit. "I figured you'd need that spunk to make it in the world."

MOST SATURDAY MORNINGS I woke up to the sound of a push mower and the smell of fresh-cut grass. I would lie in bed, somewhere between awake and asleep, not wanting to open my eyes. It was getting close to summer, and by eleven o'clock in the morning, mothers who were worried about the heat would be bringing their children inside to play. But right now, the air was fresh and cool and the day was full of possibilities.

The grass in our yard was St. Augustine. I could put a blade of it between my thumbs and whistle loud enough to get the attention of all the dogs in the neighborhood. We had the best yard in town, with grass that was like a plush green carpet and so thick the blades on Daddy's mower had to be sharpened every week or two. I could tell when this needed to happen just by the sound of the effort in his pushing. Daddy's mower was the old-fashioned kind. Our neighbor, Doris Pittman—a nice man with a woman's name—had a new gas mower that didn't need pushing. One day it ran over his toes and cut some of them off. After that, Daddy didn't have to remind my brothers and me never to mow a lawn in bare feet.

Daddy had his rules. He thought that running around barefoot in the cold grass would make us sick with pneumonia. So every spring as the weather turned balmy, my brothers and I waited for him to decide when the ground was warm enough to take off our shoes and socks and go barefoot. It was a yearly ritual. All the other kids in town might be running around like wild animals, but we had to wait.

One morning, we followed Daddy out into the backyard, watched him kneel down, stretch out his arms, and feel the ground. He sank his hands into the fresh-mown grass and pondered for a moment. Then he picked up some old pecans that had fallen from a tree and cracked them in his fist. I held my breath. A ladybug landed on my sleeve, a sign of good luck. Maybe today would be the day. Daddy handed me a piece of pecan. Then he leaned down, felt the ground again, and finally gave us the nod.

The grass was soft and cool, and my feet were tender and white. Soon I would be walking up and down blistering hot oil roads that crisscrossed the town, leaving temporary footprints in the soft tar. Most of the time I ran to keep from getting burned, the tips of my toes barely touching the asphalt. By the end of summer my feet would be as tough as leather and stained black, and it was always a challenge to squeeze into my Sunday shoes. Then, sure as rain, the seasons would change and school would start, and my barefoot days would be over until spring came around again, and Daddy would give us the word.

AS FAR AS I KNOW, the first people to settle in Wood County, Texas, were Caddo Indians, who lived in small farming villages along the Sabine River. All that's left of them are the arrowheads that still turn up in the soil of freshly tilled fields. Daddy used to take us arrowhead hunting when he would drive out to look at land. I can still smell the rich dirt as we walked along the furrows, scouring the surface for glints of flint. It must have honed my skill as a spotter of lost objects, because I'm always finding things on sidewalks and gravel roads.

The white settlers who moved into Wood County in the nineteenth century planted corn and cotton in the rich bottomland, and cut and milled timber from the vast piney forests. Quitman, founded in 1850, was made the county seat, and a fine courthouse was erected in the middle of town. But Wood County's agricultural heyday ended with the Great Depression, when the timber and cotton markets went bust. Nobody could seem to keep track of how many people lost their farms and moved away. It looked like Quitman was destined to become a speck of dust on an old Texas road map until, in 1940, a couple of wildcatters struck oil about twenty miles southeast of town.

Quitman still had open sewers when my parents arrived in 1945. But before long the streets were getting fixed, fresh paint was everywhere, and the place was filling up with new faces. To me, the most exciting new additions were Ben Merritt, a physician who became our family doctor, and his wife, Susan. The first time I saw them I was eye-level with steps leading up to the Methodist church parsonage when two of the fanciest pairs of shoes walked by. I looked up, and those shoes were attached to a beautiful young couple who had just stepped out of a green and white Mercury sedan, the likes of which I had never seen. I wondered if I would be lucky enough to ever know such exciting and sophisticated people. Within weeks, that green and white Mercury sedan was parked out in front of my house, Susan and Mother had become great friends, and lucky me got to tag along everywhere with them. Susan was from New Orleans, which added to her glamor, and I loved to listen to her talk. She had a little Cajun dog called Nipper, a name that came out of her mouth as "Nippah."

QUITMAN DIDN'T HAVE too much of anything, but it had everything we needed. There was a bank and a grocery store, a hardware store, two pharmacies, a doctor and a dentist, three or four churches, and two cafes: Busby's and the Westerner Cafe. On Sunday afternoons, it got pretty busy at those cafes, and there was a bit of a rivalry between the different denominations in town over who got the best seats after services ended. Our Methodist church was practically across the street from the Baptist church, and they always seemed to let out about ten minutes ahead of us. We'd still be listening to the end of the sermon when we'd hear the car doors slamming down the block, and everybody would start squirming in the pews, knowing that once again the Baptists were going to get the best tables for lunch. The rivalry hardly affected our family, because Mother would usually have a roast slow-cooking in the oven while we were in church, or else she would fry a chicken as soon as we got home.

WHEN WE NEEDED TO SHOP for good clothes, our whole family would drive to Mineola, eleven miles south of Quitman. The place with the best shoes was Hirsch's store. The Hirsches were small, round people whose voices sounded different than most of the people we knew. Theirs were raspy and high, like they'd smoked a lot of cigarettes or had bad laryngitis, and they talked faster than the slow drawl we were used to hearing. It was a big treat to go to Hirsch's store for better clothes and shoes. Mr. Hirsch was a very good shoe fitter. He would press his thumb near the end of our toes and have us wiggle them up and down.

Then we would walk around the store so he could make sure our heels didn't slide up and down and rub blisters.

One year, Mr. Hirsch bought a special new shoe fitting machine. The marvelous wooden box sat in the front of the store, right next to a large green scale that measured weight and told fortunes. We picked out our new shoes, and I stood behind my brothers as we lined up for our turns at the machine. "Girls first," I heard Mr. Hirsch say in his funny voice. With two older brothers, I was not used to going first. I hesitated. Mr. Hirsch took my hand and pulled me in front of the boys. I climbed up on the big wooden box and slid my feet into the machine while I peered through one of the eye portals on the top. Mr. Hirsch flipped a switch and all of a sudden the bones in my feet lit up inside of my shoes. We could see that this new pair fit me perfectly. When I stepped down, my brothers shoved and pushed each other to try to get on next. Mr. Hirsch was a nice man; he let us use that X-ray shoe fitting machine over and over again, as much as we wanted.

If you didn't want to drive to Mineola for clothes, or have them homemade, the only remaining option was McDade's dry goods on the downtown square. It didn't have much variety or any of the newest styles, but we loved it anyway. McDade's always smelled like sharpened pencils and rubber-soled shoes, and all the merchandise was piled up on open tables where even kids could reach it. They sold overalls and work boots, things like that, and maybe a dress or two. The dresses on the manikins in the front window had been there so long that they were faded on the side that the sun hit, while the back looked brand-new.

McDade's was where we bought our blue jeans. I was so small I stood on a cardboard box to try them on. My brothers got jeans with zippers; I got elastic waists. This was when I first realized that life was not always fair.

· · ·

MY BROTHERS AND I were very close growing up, despite the fact that I was a girl. All I wanted was to be
like Ed and Robbie; I idolized them. After he out-
grew it, I inherited Ed's gray felt cowboy hat and
wore it sideways. It ended up so shapeless you couldn't tell what it was, but
I loved it anyway because it was his.

Once, when I was four, we were playing football in the front yard. It
was summertime, and we were all hot and sweaty, so we took our T-shirts
off. My mother came outside and told me to put my shirt back on.

"Why?" I said.

"Because you're a girl."

That double standard did not sit well with me. I did not like wearing frilly dresses. I wasn't even that interested in dolls, I cut the hair off
of the one fancy Madame Alexander doll my mother gave me. We used
another one for target practice. I just wanted to do what my brothers
were doing.

Then one of my uncles told me if I could kiss my elbow, I'd turn
into a boy.

I spent a lot of my childhood trying to kiss my elbow.

For years, until Daddy built an addition to the house, I shared a
bedroom with my brothers. I had a lot of friends, but Ed and Robbie
wouldn't allow girls to come over to play very often, especially if they
were "sissy" girls. You had to be tough to keep up with my brothers. Of
course, sometimes it backfired on me. When I was in grade school, a boy
in my class dropped a rock on my head from the top of the tallest slide. I
was still seeing stars when the teachers came running and I heard one
of them ask the boy, "Now, why in the world would you drop a rock on
Sissy's head?"

"'Cause I like her," he said.

MY BROTHERS AND I were inseparable. I tagged along with Robbie,
and he tagged along with Ed. When Mother asked us what we wanted

for lunch, I'd say, "I don't know. What's Ed having?" "I don't know. What's Robbie having?" And Robbie would say, "I don't know. What's Ed having?" Pretty soon she realized she only needed to ask Ed. Robbie and I weren't always that much fun for our big brother, but he was a patient, sensitive boy and he took good care of us, in spite of the embarrassment of having his little brother and sister around all the time.

Robbie was a beautiful, sunny child with olive skin, light hair, and a wide-open smile. When he was born, my mother said he looked up into her eyes so deeply that it frightened her. There was always something special about him, but his good nature didn't keep us from fighting. We'd have some real knock-down, drag-outs. Once my mother caught him hitting me in the stomach. "Robbie, you can't hit Sissy there!" she said. She pointed to my leg, arm, and backside. "If you want to hit her, hit her here."

Parents in those days didn't think their children were too fragile for a few lumps. One morning my mother looked out the window and saw our neighbor Bev Benton's two-year-old, wearing nothing but diapers and crawling on the roof of their two-story house. Some workers had left a ladder leaning against the siding, and Matt went exploring. Mother was terrified and called her friend right away.

"Bev, Matt's up on the roof!"

"Oh, thanks, Gin," said Bev.

Then Mother watched from across the street as Bev calmly put down the phone, leaned her head out the window, and shouted, "Matt, you come down off that roof right now! You're gonna make it leak!"

I'm sure that story spread all over town before the two women had hung up. In the 1950s, Quitman still had party lines and a central telephone operator named Ganelle Rushing. She was a friendly, portly young woman who worked out of a concrete building next to the dentist's office. She was command central and knew everything that was going on in town. When I was little, I'd pick up the phone and hear her say, "Number please?"

"Ganelle, do you know where my mama is?"

"Well, Sissy, let me think," Ganelle might say. "I believe she's over at Susan's. Let me check." And I'd hear her talking on another line, "Miz Merritt? Is Gin over there? Sissy's looking for her mama . . ."

Quitman didn't need a 911 center; we had Ganelle Rushing. Years later, when I played a WW2-era telephone operator in *Raggedy Man*, Ganelle was my role model, right down to her trilling, "Number please?"

WHEN I WAS GROWING UP, Gaston Cain was the mayor of Quitman, the fire chief, and the owner of the local insurance company and, with his brother, Zack, the funeral home. He was also the undertaker, and the father of two of my best friends, Pam and Debra. I guess you could say the Cains were the tycoons of our little town, because Zack also had the hardware store, and he and his wife Imogene—pronounced *Eyema-jean*—owned and operated the town's only tourist court. It was a one-story, L-shaped motel for the handful of motorist visitors who might be passing through town on the way to somewhere else. All the Cains were hard workers. For years, Imogene cleaned every room of that little motel herself. She also ran a business out back raising chinchillas. Imogene made her own chinchilla collars and jackets and wore them proudly. She was a good friend of my mom's, and her son, Clifford Zack, was my boyfriend on and off since we were toddlers.

They lived in a big pink brick house on the highway next to the motel. I would play with Cliff or his sister Jeanell if they were around, or I would go outside and visit the chinchillas. They looked like large, furry hamsters with big ears. They were nervous animals that would run around their wire cages and hiss if I got too close. I guess the chinchillas knew what was coming and didn't see any point in making friends.

One morning my mother and I stopped by for a quick visit on the way back from the store, where she had picked up a whole bunch of hams to cook for the Methodist church supper that evening. Shortly after we arrived, Mother realized she had locked the hams in the trunk of the Buick and dropped the trunk key in there with them. This was an emergency, because it was summertime and that trunk was heating up fast. Without thinking, she hurried off for the car dealership, where they had a big ring of keys that would unlock the trunk—and left me behind.

I saw her pulling away and chased the car for a little while but couldn't get her attention. I was embarrassed that someone might see me running after my own mother's car, and I was mortified that she had driven off and forgotten me like that. I could hardly believe it! In my child's mind, I had been abandoned. I moped around the tourist court for a while, then mustered the courage to knock on Imogene's door. I called my mother. She was already home.

"Sissy! Where are you?" she cried, as if I was the one who ran off.

"You left me, Mama!"

"Oh, Sissy," she said. "You're so dramatic. You should be an actress."

Maybe we should be careful what we tell our children.

I WAS MY MOTHER'S SHADOW; I went everywhere with her. Well, almost everywhere. I cried inconsolably when I couldn't go with her to the swimming pool during an afternoon reserved for grown-up ladies who wanted to visit and swim in peace. I survived, but I'm certain I ruined all of her fun that day. She was very willing to let me into her adult world, even when her girlfriends stopped by for coffee and a chat. I would sit on my stool in that cozy red kitchen, or find a spot to hide under the table, while I listened to the women talk about their families, church, husbands, or any of the things that were happening around town. I can still hear their fluttering laughter and the clink of cups settling into saucers on the tabletop while I studied their shoes and stockings. I felt welcome and included, until one day one of my mother's good friends, Grace Black, spotted me huddled under the table legs and said, "Sissy, you run on out of here. Your mother and I are talking. I came to see her, not you." I was grateful that my mother stood up for me that day. She said, "Grace, this is Sissy's house, too. So if you have something to say that you can't say in front of her, then maybe it's best you don't say it." (Apparently there were no hard feelings. Years later, Grace Black would be the one heading up the activities at Sissy Spacek Day at the state park in Quitman.)

Mother had lovely manners, which she'd learned from her parents, and she tried her best to pass them on to her own children. But the three of us subscribed to only one table rule—one foot on the floor at all times. Mother would set the table properly for every meal and instruct us on the correct use of silverware, which seemed kind of useless to me. "Why do we have to learn stupid manners?" I'd complain. "It's just gonna slow us down, and we're hungry."

"Because I want you to be able to dine with the President," she'd say.

"Oh, Mother, that's crazy."

But sure enough, an invitation came one day from the White House, and I was ready. Thanks, Mother.

I NEVER HEARD MY MOTHER SAY a harsh word about anyone. "If they knew better, they'd do better," she'd always say. She even had kind words for the town drunk, a poor soul who we'd see staggering around town, looking like a bum with his scraggly hair and dirty clothes. "Now, don't say anything bad about that man," she told us. "He was a talented young boy who wanted to be a concert pianist, but his parents didn't support him. Now he's a drunk and a house painter." I never looked at a drunk or a house painter quite the same way after that.

BOTH OF MY PARENTS were careful with their money, as were most people who grew up during the Depression. My mother could cut up and fry a chicken into so many pieces that you'd think it was a feast for an army. Neither of them wasted money on junk, but they would save up for good-quality things that would last a long time. My dad was a true conservationist, and we were careful not to use more than our share of water and electricity. He did his best to train us to cut off the lights every time we left a room. Years later, the habit landed me in trouble with the director Robert Altman on the set of *3 Women*. We were doing a very long scene and I had to walk from room to room while the camera followed me. I was still relatively new to the acting business, and I kept ruining the shot by hitting the light switch every time I walked through a door. After the third or fourth take, Bob was exasperated and wanted to know why I kept doing that.

"I'm sorry!" I told him. "I do it automatically. My father wanted to save money on the electric bill."

"Well, the next time you see your father, please tell him that he cost me more money in one day of filming than you saved him in a lifetime!"

DADDY EARNED a modest salary but invested wisely, and we lived a comfortable middle-class life. My brothers and I always got nice presents for our birthdays and Christmas, but never anything extravagant. That made each item more precious.

One present Daddy always bought Mother at Christmastime was beautiful silk underwear from McDade's. She would pick out exactly what she wanted, then he'd stop by after work to pay for it and have them wrap it up. My brothers and I preferred to do our Christmas shopping at White's Automotive. Along with the car accessories, White's had a whole window filled with games, toy trucks, and gift items. One year, Ed and Robbie and I pooled our allowance money to buy one big present for Mother from all three of us. We spent days and weeks staring in that window, trying to decide on the perfect purchase. Finally we settled on a pair of decorative ceramic pheasants. We thought she would just love them. Looking back, they verged on being tacky. But we were so excited to have bought such a big-ticket item that Mother's present seemed even more important than our own gifts that year. When she opened the package, a look of delight lit up her face. She hugged us all and put those Christmas pheasants in a place of honor on the mantel, where they stayed for the rest of her life.

· · ·   2   · · ·

E VERY DECEMBER WE WOULD DRIVE DOWN FROM QUIT-
man to spend the holidays with Mother's family in the Rio Grande
Valley, stopping along the way to visit my dad's parents in Granger. It
was a twelve-hundred-mile round-trip in a 1949 Pontiac with no air-
conditioning loaded to bursting with luggage and wrapped presents. It
was quite a production with three boisterous kids. I was always carsick,
so I was usually allowed to sit up front between my parents and fiddle
with the radio dial while the boys rode in the backseat. Whenever my
brothers complained about the arrangement, and I sat with them in the
back, they quickly regretted it.

There were no interstates then, and we couldn't make the whole
drive without stopping at motels along the way. In the beginning, our
parents allowed us to take turns picking out the motels. But one time it
was getting late, and Robbie, Ed, and I saw the most incredible place
beside the highway. It was the biggest, brightest motel we had ever seen,
lit up like a Christmas tree with flashing neon lights. It was so wonderful it might as well have been in Paris, France.

"That one! That one!" we cried.

"I don't know," said Daddy. "This doesn't look like such a good
place."

"No! No! We want that one!"

So in the spirit of fairness and democracy, we checked in. The room was horrible, with threadbare sheets and a dirty bathroom. How could this be? It was *so* beautiful from the outside. We wanted to move out,

but it was too late to find another place to stay. The next morning we walked out into the daylight and saw that the huge motel was just a tiny row of cinder-block rooms; the lights were all fixed to a tall skeleton of scaffolding. From then on, the family rules changed, and our parents got veto power over any motel choice we made.

Our first destination was Granger, a small farming town about fifty miles northeast of Austin, where my father and his brother, Sam, and his sisters, Thelma and Rose, were born and raised. I love the color of yellow wheat against black soil in this part of Texas. The sky is wide and blue, and you can see rain coming from a long way off. The earth is so fertile underfoot that it feels like a living thing. When it's hot and dry, huge cracks form in the ground. And when it's wet, the black mud sticks to your feet as you walk around, and you get so tall you feel like you're wearing stilts.

For outsiders who think that everybody in Texas is a cowboy on a horse named Trigger, towns like Granger would come as a shock. Granger was—and still is—an ethnic oasis, filled with the descendants of Czech and German pioneers who recreated the old country on the blackland prairie. English was rarely spoken in town until the mid-twentieth century. The kids we played with on our visits were named Bartosh, Zelenvitz, Ehlich, Walla, and Mikolencak. Our family came over from Moravia, now part of the Czech Republic, along with Slovakia and Bohemia, and people in Granger still pronounce Spacek the traditional way: *Spot-check*. My dad changed the pronunciation to *Spay-sik* (like *basic*) when he was in college. One of his professors just couldn't get it right and kept calling him *Spay-sik*; Daddy figured it was easier to change it than to keep correcting people. (Years later, when I met the Czech film director Milos Forman, he insisted on calling me Spacekova—the proper feminine title. I said, "Please, just call me Sissy!")

Daddy was proud of his ancestry and was a great storyteller. His people were simple, hardworking farmers and merchants who knew the value of a *zlaty* and felt a strong, almost mystical connection to the land.

The first to arrive in America was my great-grandfather, Frantisek Jan Spacek II, who was thirteen in 1866 when he left his family's farm in Moravia to sail to Texas. It was a miserable nine-week journey from the port of Bremen to Galveston Bay. The ship was tossed around in terrible storms and everyone on board was seasick. Frantisek later described the giant roaches that swarmed below deck and "flew around like swallows," dropping into their bowls of rice soup. Finally they reached the Texas coast, and my great-grandfather spent three more days traveling by rail, wagon, and ferry to the small town of Fayetteville, halfway between Houston and Austin. The town was brimming with German and Czech immigrants, who took the boy in and gave him work as a farm laborer. After Frantisek's mother died two years later, his father and four younger siblings followed him to America.

In 1875, Frantisek married Julia Gloeckner, whom he had met on the long passage from Moravia to Texas. Frantisek flourished in the new world. He opened a grocery store and saloon in Fayetteville, and at one point he had a six-hundred-acre farm, rental properties, a livery stable, and a beer agency. He and his wife had two daughters, Julia and Albina, and three sons, Frank Joseph, Rudolph, and my grandfather, Arnold Adolph, known as AA.

All the Spacek children grew up speaking Czech, German, and English and worked hard to get ahead in the world. AA started out laboring in his father's grocery store and other businesses, then he went away to an English grammar school to master the language he would need to improve his prospects. In 1905, my grandfather opened a tailor shop in the Czech outpost of Granger, where he met his future bride, Mary Cervenka. He bought a grocery store, traded it for some land in West Texas, and expanded his tailoring business to include the first off-the-rack suits sold in Central Texas. He bought and sold farms and businesses all over the state and helped organize the Granger National Bank in 1920, where his picture hangs to this day.

They still tell the story of how he saved the bank from ruin during the Great Depression. At one time there were three banks in town, but after the stock market crashed in 1929, people lost confidence in the banking system and started pulling out their money. This was before FDIC insurance, and if a bank went bust, you could lose everything. Two Granger banks were wiped out after the farmers demanded to withdraw their savings in cash, on the spot. When AA heard a rumor that there would be a similar run on the National Bank, he decided to take matters into his own hands. The story goes that he rode the train to the federal bank in Houston to withdraw his bank's cash reserves, returning overnight with armed guards and a carload of money.

The next morning, the bank managers set a long table behind the teller windows and piled it high with stacks of bills. As the townspeople came in to withdraw their money they could see that the bank had plenty of cash. The run was averted, and the bank was saved.

My grandfather was an unusual banker. When farmers couldn't qualify for credit, AA would often loan them the money from his own funds. After his death, papers were found in his personal effects showing that he had forgiven the loans of those who couldn't pay, saving farms all over the county from foreclosure. AA was elected mayor of Granger, served as postmaster, was active in the Granger fire department and the Odd Fellows. My grandfather became a big wheel in the Texas Democratic Party, as did his brother, Rudolph, who was elected to the state legislature. AA used to take my dad to all kinds of political events. I still have two tiny lead donkeys Daddy passed down to me— souvenirs from the 1928 Democratic national convention in Houston.

AA was a friend of the future president Lyndon Baines Johnson, who gave him the nickname "Double A." Whenever Johnson was campaigning around Granger, he would spend the night at my grandparents' home. LBJ would call and say, "Double A, I want to put my shoes under your bed." He was a colorful houseguest. My grandmother surprised him one night while he was walking around the house wearing only boxer shorts—white with red polka dots. Johnson was a tireless campaigner who used to fly all over Texas in a helicopter while he was running for the Senate in the forties and fifties. Even towns like Granger and Quitman weren't too small for Johnson. In Quitman he would land in the square, right downtown. The whole city would come out, mainly to gawk at the helicopter. Everywhere he flew, LBJ would throw his Stetson out the door of the helicopter, sailing it into the waiting crowd. Usually some small boy would end up with it, and during his stump speech, LBJ would ask, "Has anybody seen my hat?" The boy would run up to hand it to him, and Johnson would give him a silver dollar. I'm told my brother Robbie caught the hat one time, but I was too little to remember.

IN 1921, MY GRANDPARENTS built a Craftsman-style bungalow in Granger. I loved that house, with its clean lines and breezy hallways; I still visit it in my dreams. There was a deep front porch covered by an arched portico, perfect for sipping Dr Peppers in the shade on hot afternoons. The front door opened into a spacious sitting room and a winding staircase with a wooden bannister rising up to the second floor. All through the house I could hear the clock ticking away from the stairwell. My brothers and I would slide down that bannister, or play school on the stairs with our cousins, blocking anyone trying to make it up to the second floor. The house was near the train tracks— everything in Granger was—and I would fall asleep in an upstairs bedroom, listening to the freight trains loaded with cotton rumble through town, blowing their horns.

The farm where I live in Virginia is near a set of tracks, and in the cool months when we open the windows and listen to the sound of the trains rolling by, it triggers those wonderful dreams of my grandparents' house.

We called our grandfather "Pops" and our grandmother "Momsy." She was a petite, hardworking, old-fashioned woman, who wore her hair pulled back and favored high-collared shirtwaist dresses. She was a homebody who rarely wanted to leave her house and garden. Pops adored her, and always called her *schatzi*—German for "darling." When Pops was offered a position with the federal bank in Houston, Momsy couldn't bear to leave Granger, so Pops turned down the job.

Pops was a fun-loving, stylish man who always dressed in a blue suit and a white shirt and tie, with a fresh rose in his lapel every day. Despite his old-world ways, he was always smiling and laughing. Pops was only sixty-six when he died—probably from meningitis contracted from a horsefly that bit him while he was inspecting one of his cattle farms. I was only three, but I have distinct memories of him. He used to carry me piggyback down from my bedroom; when I picture those stairs, it's from up high, looking down past Pops's ears and the back of his head, with my arms wrapped tightly around his neck.

Momsy lived alone in that house after Pops died, and the family would gather there every few months to visit. Whenever she had company, Momsy worked in her kitchen from sunup to sundown, making bread, biscuits, roasts, and chicken-fried steak, and turning out tray after heavenly tray of feather-light *kolaches,* sweet pastries filled with dollops of fruit or poppyseed paste.

Her only "vice," as she saw it, was a fondness for television. My dad and his brother, Sam, bought her a television set when they first came on the market. She secretly loved it, but pretended not to watch and would switch off the set if she heard someone coming. Daddy would walk into the kitchen and say, "How do like that TV, Momsy?"

"Oh, Eddie. I don't know, I don't watch it much."

But television sets took a long time to shut down in those days, and he would grin when he saw the telltale white dot glowing in the middle of the dark green screen.

· · ·

AA and Mary Spacek raised four children: my dad, Edwin Arnold, born in 1910; his older sister, Thelma; and two younger siblings, Sam and Rose.

Thelma was the beauty of the family. As a young woman, she looked like Vivien Leigh. She was such a knockout that a Hollywood talent agent noticed her at an Interscholastic League competition. The scout, who was recruiting Texas beauties for the movies, offered to take Thelma to Los Angeles for a screen test. Pops didn't trust the man and wouldn't let her go with him. She always wondered what might have happened if she had gone to Hollywood—she might have become the first film star in the family. Instead, Thelma attended college, then met and married her husband, Elmore Ruel Torn, an agricultural economist.

By luck or fate, their handsome dark-haired son, Rip, took the trip to Hollywood that Thelma missed out on. Rip Torn turned out to be an incredibly talented actor. We were so excited to have a movie star in the family. He was particularly close to my dad, who loved him like a little brother and took him hunting and fishing when Rip's father was away in the army. I was in awe when Rip brought his first wife, Ann Wedgeworth, to a family holiday in Granger. Ann, who looked like a red-haired Marilyn Monroe, was the most glamorous human being I had ever laid eyes on. Rip seemed so dashing as he tossed a football with my brothers out in the yard. Momsy loved to watch Rip in those classic *Playhouse 90* productions. Years later Rip married the stage actress Geraldine Page. And it was with their help, more than a decade later, that I would get my first taste of the acting life during a starstruck summer in New York.

While his sister Thelma was starting her family, my dad, the first-born son, went off to college at Texas Tech University in Lubbock. He was a history buff, but he loved the land and the soil even more, so he studied for a degree in agriculture. Pops paid his way for the first couple of years, but by then the Great Depression was setting in and times were hard all over Texas. Sam had just graduated from high school, and it was his turn to go to college. My dad was concerned that it might be a strain on his father to put two sons through college, so he came home one weekend and told his father not to send him any more money; he would work the rest of his way through school. He took a job mucking stalls in a horse barn in the mornings before class. Then, after he finished studying at night, he'd put on a tuxedo and play in a dance band. He was an ace on the four-string banjo and the baritone guitar, and that's how he earned his way through college. After my dad graduated, he toured with his band for a while and I think he seriously considered becoming a professional musician. But his more practical nature trumped his artistic side, and he decided to pursue his career in agriculture.

There must be an artistic gene in the Spacek family because Thelma was a talented painter, and so was their baby sister, Rose, who also acted in local theater productions. Rose loved hats and was always wonderfully dramatic. When I started acting, I would often send her hats that I'd worn in films. I used to get calls from her whenever my movies ran on television. "Sissy!" Rose would trill. "Guess what? I just saw my hat on TV!" She rarely mentioned that the hat she saw had been on my head.

Daddy's younger brother, Sam, graduated from Texas Tech and became a cotton farmer in Ralls, Texas, near Lubbock. He married Maurine Alexander, a beautiful porcelain-skinned redhead who must have kept busy looking for shade on the treeless plains. Sam had a grain elevator business for a while and made a good living. I remember him as a charming man and a real character. He would never let go of a car once he owned it, always thinking he was being cheated out of the trade-in price, so he kept their chassis around his property, like monuments to his good sense. He was also an amateur photographer and something of a storm chaser, for which there was plenty of opportunity on the plains of West Texas. He was known to hustle the family into the storm cellar when a tornado was approaching, then tie himself to the door and take pictures. The one time he didn't have his camera with him he was driving around in his old pickup when a twister took him by surprise. The way he told the story, the tornado lifted up the truck, tore off the driver's side door, then set the rig back down in a pasture with the engine still running. Sam didn't have a scratch on him, and he proceeded on his way.

Sam and Maurine liked to travel, and they used to load the family into their Airstream trailer and visit us back in East Texas. We loved to play with our cousins, Jan Kathryn and Sam Pat, who were about our ages. Eventually they all moved to Quitman to be near the rest of us, drawn by the powerful bonds of family that have held the Spaceks together for generations.

AFTER VISITING MY GRANDPARENTS in Granger, we'd pack up the car again and head south. It might be chilly, even snowing, in East Texas when we left home. But the air grew warmer and the land greener with every mile of the journey, and by the time we reached the Rio Grande Valley, it was like being in the tropics. We could throw off our jackets and run barefoot in the winter sun (if, of course, Daddy said it was okay). It was exciting and exotic to spend Christmas on the Mexican border with our maternal grandparents, Thomas Holliday and Elizabeth Holliday Spilman, who we called Papa and Big Mama.

Thomas Holliday Spilman, known to his friends as T. Holl, descended from a family of wealthy merchants in Ottumwa, Iowa, but his heart was in the South. His father, Thomas Percival Spilman, had been a major in the Union Army during the Civil War and was stationed in Mississippi. At the end of the fighting he bought a large plantation near the city of Canton, where he befriended Isaac Newton Holliday, a Confederate veteran. A year or so later, Major Spilman leased out the plantation and returned to his family in Iowa. His first child, my grandfather, was born in 1867 and given the middle name Holliday in honor of his Mississippi friend.

T. Holl was raised in Ottumwa and grew prosperous running his father's hardware store and tinning business. He married a local girl named Nettie, with whom he had four children, but Nettie's health was precarious. So he moved the family down to his father's Mississippi plantation to take advantage of the warmer weather. Sadly, Nettie didn't survive, and he was left a widower with young children to raise.

Two years later, he saw my grandmother, Elizabeth Holliday, sitting across the aisle from him at a Methodist prayer meeting in Canton. "She was the most beautiful woman I had ever seen," he said. She was also the granddaughter of his father's Confederate friend, Isaac Newton Holliday, T-Holl's namesake. Elizabeth was fifteen years younger than her new admirer. She had just returned home after being away for a few years teaching school and then attending business college in Jackson. She wore her long, strawberry blond hair rolled up in a bun, just like I do now. (I am her namesake; I inherited her coloring, and was always told I favored her. I treasured this comparison because my grandmother was so loving and kind.) T. Holl fell for Elizabeth instantly. She was taken with him, too, describing him as "the cutest gray-haired man." She also liked to say he was the second Yankee she had met in her life—"and the first one was crazy."

In a way, Elizabeth and T. Holl's marriage was born out of the deep and unusual friendship of two men—his father and her grandfather—who had fought on different sides in a terrible war. The spirit of civility and grace followed them all their lives. Their first child, born in 1907, was named after Elizabeth's father, Joseph. They nicknamed him Bud.

But all was not civil in Mississippi. According to family legend, T. Holl was despised as a Yankee carpetbagger by a lot of the white folks around Canton, and he had to carry a pistol in his belt for protection. He eventually persuaded his young wife to move back to Ottumwa with him. Once again, he prospered in the hardware and tin business, and Elizabeth bore him a daughter named Elizabeth, whom they called Sis, or Spilly. But after four years of cold northern winters, T. Holl's health began to suffer, and his doctor advised him to move to a warmer climate. He chose the rustic lower valley of the Rio Grande, where, in

1912, he bought his first section of land seven miles outside of the small town of Mission, near McAllen. When the family arrived, Mission was little more than a railroad stop surrounded by mesquite and huisache brush.

In those days Pancho Villa was roaming the Mexican border, terrorizing Texas settlers. Although Villa never quite reached Mission, he came close enough. Once Papa was showing some property in his Model T, and a bullet went right through his hat, missing his head by a hair. It was a wild time in the valley. Gangs of thieves would break into homes while the owners were off at church. The outlaws would pile the valuables on the bed and make bundles out of the blankets and sheets to carry off the loot.

It was a hardship for Elizabeth, living on the remote, primitive ranch while she was pregnant with their third child. Papa installed, at great expense, a telephone line from town, so that she could call the doctor when her time came to deliver. But when she went into labor, the doctor couldn't be found anyway. She gave birth to my uncle Newton right on the ranch, with help from her visiting brother-in-law, who happened to be a physician.

As soon as the infant was old enough to travel, she took baby Newton and the older children on the train back home to Mississippi. From there she sent her husband a letter, refusing to return until she had a place to live in town. T-Holl found a house in Mission the next day. After his family returned, Papa moved on from ranching to land trading.

My mother, Virginia, was born in 1917, followed six years later by Wade, the baby of the family. My mom was a beautiful young girl with thick, dark hair, dimples, and a set of slightly crooked front teeth that protruded a bit beneath her upper lip. She begged not to have to wear braces because she had heard that they could rot all her teeth and make them fall out (a realistic fear back in those days). And so all her life Mother had a tiny flaw in her smile that became part of her charm. She was a good student and loved music, but for some reason she hated piano lessons so much that she would hide behind the piano when the teacher arrived. She idolized her siblings and her parents, particularly her father. She told us that when she was a little girl she got God, Santa Claus, and her daddy all mixed up.

The Spilmans were a gracious, happy family even though their lives were complicated and sometimes tragic. When Mother was a toddler, both of her grandfathers decided to ride the train down to Mission to visit the family. As soon as they arrived, T. Holl offered to take everybody out for a spin in the Model T. The story goes that T. Holl was standing in front of the Ford, cranking the engine, when it suddenly caught, and the car lurched forward. Joseph Holliday tried to stop the car and was crushed under its wheels. He died from his injuries a few weeks later. My grandfather broke his leg in the accident and walked with a cane for the rest of his life.

From the stories our mother told us about growing up in that large family, it's a wonder any of them survived to adulthood. One afternoon Big Mama invited a group of women over for a special tea. Her four young children were instructed to go outside and play, and under no circumstances were they to interrupt while she had company. The kids started playing out in the field where they kept a little mule, and somehow young Newt got on the wrong side of him and was knocked out cold. The other children debated for a while what to do; they had been told not to go into the house under any circumstance. Finally they got up their courage and knocked on the door. "We're sorry to disturb you, Mama, but Newt's been knocked unconscious for a long time," they told Big Mama, who screamed and came running. Somehow Newt survived and lived to a ripe old age.

Wade, the youngest, also had more than his share of close calls. When Mother was about eight years old, she was left to babysit Wade, who was still a toddler. She was trying to get him to sleep, but he kept fussing and fussing, getting out of his crib and asking for a glass of water. Finally she told him, "All right, Wade. I'll get you a glass of water, but if I do you'll have to drink every drop of it and then go to bed." On her way to the kitchen, she saw a glass of water on the mantel, grabbed it, and made him drink it down. But the glass on the mantel wasn't filled with water like she thought, it was filled with clear coal oil. She shuddered telling us how sick it made that baby, and how he nearly died from the poison. But Wade bounced back and grew up tall and athletic, and never seemed to hold the coal-oil incident against her.

AFTER THEY MOVED to Texas, the Spilmans never had much money, but they loved one another, and by all accounts had a wonderful life. T. Holl adored his wife; always gave her a kiss when he left the house and when he returned. They were never known to argue, even about politics, although their views were diametrically opposed. She was a yellow dog Democrat, and he was a Republican. Every Election Day, my grandfather would link his arm in hers and say, "Come, Elizabeth. Let's go to the polls and cancel each other's votes." And that's just what they did. Even after they lost almost everything, they lived out their lives in threadbare gentility.

T. Holl had invested in land all over the Rio Grande Valley, but he was a notoriously bad businessman. What land he kept was leased out to tenant farmers. He was a generous landlord—some say to a fault. He lent his farm equipment to anyone who needed it. You could see it parked in fields all over the valley. And he didn't have the heart to kick families off his property for nonpayment. So when the Depression hit, the banks foreclosed on most of his holdings. He ran for justice of the peace in Mission, and his only income during those years was his civil servant's salary and the small fees he'd charge for marrying couples, usually right in his own living room. They called him "The Marrying Judge."

MY PARENTS MET on a blind double date in Mission, Texas, in 1938. My dad was a dashing employee with the South Texas Chamber of Commerce; my mom was a darling, spirited young woman finishing business college. Mother wasn't even my dad's date—she had been set up with his friend. Daddy was driving and it was dark, so he only occasionally caught a glimpse of her tucked into the backseat of the car. But once he heard her soft, musical voice, he was smitten. "That's the girl I'm going to marry," he told himself. But he was working under a slight disadvantage. It was hot in the valley, and on a dare from a buddy, probably after a drink or two, he'd shaved his head. And he was being transferred to another job, in another town outside of the valley, in two short weeks, so he had to move fast. Fortunately for him, my mother thought his bald head was cute. After a brief courtship, they were married in the Methodist Church in Mission, on a sweltering hot August afternoon. Just as the pastor was asking, "...if any of you know just cause why these two should not be joined in holy matrimony, speak now or forever hold your peace," the bride and groom were startled to hear one loud crash after another, as the candles arranged behind the pulpit slumped over in the heat and tumbled to the floor.

The newlyweds moved to Abilene, but didn't stay long. Daddy kept transferring to new positions all over Texas until World War II broke out and he joined the army air corps. While Daddy was in the army, Mother moved back home with her parents in Mission, where my brother Ed was born in 1944. When Ed started talking, he couldn't understand why his mother was always calling his grandmother "Mama." So to keep things straight, he called his mother Little Mama and his grandmother Big Mama. Before long, everybody was calling our grandmother "Big Mama." It must have started sounding like a Tennessee Williams play inside those white clapboard walls.

MOTHER'S YOUNGER BROTHER, Wade, inherited his family's gentle spirit, good looks, and easy way with people. She was as close to him as I was to Robbie and Ed. Wade was a champion tennis player and a junior at the University of Texas when he volunteered for the infantry. He was sent to the European theater, where he quickly worked his way up the ranks to sergeant. Mother wrote him several times a week, and even got some letters back. Then suddenly his letters stopped coming, and the army sent a telegram declaring him "missing in action." Big Mama retreated to her bedroom and barely came out for the next five months. Nobody in the family told her when all of their letters were returned in bundles stamped "Deceased" and a telegram confirmed his death. My mother never gave up hope that Wade might be a prisoner, and she would sneak over to a neighbor's house to listen to ham radio reports of American prisoners being liberated across Germany. Then, in the late spring of 1945, the phone rang and it was Wade, calling from a hospital in France. He was gravely ill but alive. As Mother had hoped, Wade had been rescued from a German POW camp.

After he was shipped home, Wade married his sweetheart, Arlette Fowler, a vivacious, whip-smart girl from Austin. He went on to law school at UT and became an influential member of the Texas State Legislature.

SHORTLY AFTER HE LEFT the service, my dad was offered the job in Quitman as a county agriculture agent with the Texas A&M Extension Service, advising farmers on the best crops to plant and how to eradicate weeds and pests. Quitman was so far north in Texas that Mother's family teased her about living way up in "Yankeeland." Our family was a long way from the Mexican border, but every year at Christmas, we would join the whole Spilman family at my grandparents' home in Mission.

Papa and Big Mama still lived in the rambling old wood frame bungalow where Mother was born. It had been added to piecemeal over the years. When they first moved there, the roads were still dirt. But by the time I arrived on the scene, there were sidewalks and fat palm trees lining the paved street. During our weeklong visits, the whole family slept in a guest room at the front of the house. In the morning we'd wait until we saw the light under the kitchen door that meant Big Mama was already up cooking breakfast. Then we'd creep through the sleeping house, across the breezeway, and into the kitchen.

"Would you all like some orange juice?" she would ask.

We'd all three nod our heads in unison.

"Well then, climb on up in the tree and pick some."

"Okay, Big Mama," we'd say, and we'd tear out of the kitchen as fast as we could go.

There were huge orange and grapefruit trees in the yard right by the kitchen door. The best orange tree had low branches that you could climb up like a monkey. We'd each bring back an armful of fruit and watch Big Mama squeeze it right in front of us. Sometimes she'd slice up some grapefruit that we'd scoop out with the silver spoons she kept in a special glass in the middle of the table. Now I have that glass of spoons in my kitchen in Virginia. It was the thing I wanted most to remind me of Big Mama.

The kitchen table was enormous—to us kids it seemed as long as an aircraft carrier. All the family could fit around it, and we'd gather there for every meal.

I loved my aunt Arlette dearly—and still do—but there was a time when we locked horns over a tray of Christmas cookies. Every year Big Mama slaved in the kitchen making her Southern delicacies for the family to enjoy—biscuits, fried chicken, roasts, and pies. Every afternoon after the family dinner Big Mama set out trays of homemade sweets. As Arlette tells the story, I would come by, pick up a cookie or piece of cake, take one bite, and put it back. One day, after I had ruined four or five cookies and was coming back for more, Arlette decided to put a stop to it.

"Sissy," she said, "Big Mama has worked her fingers to the bone to make those for us. Eat as many as you want, but if you taste one, you have to finish it."

I looked at her sideways, then picked up a piece of fruitcake.

"I'm telling you, if you bite that, we're gonna sit here until you're done eating it."

We were eye to eye. I nibbled a small piece, then put it down, never taking my eyes off of her.

"Okay, Sissy. You and I are going to sit here until that's eaten."

I sat down. The rest of the family cleared out, but Arlette and I sat there, the piece of fruitcake between us. It was like the Old West and we were gunslingers. An hour went by. Finally Arlette gave up in defeat. Little did she know that if it had been a sugar cookie, she would have worn me down in seconds. But I hate fruitcake and always have.

BIG MAMA LOVED all children and drew them to her like a magnet. She saved us bowls of trinkets that she'd collect from cereal boxes and would have them waiting for us by the front door as soon as we walked in. My brothers and I would fight for position next to her when she read us stories from *Boys' Life* magazine. I was so little, I used to just lay on top of her while we all snuggled on the couch.

Papa was fifteen years older than Big Mama, and was going blind from glaucoma toward the end of his life. What I remember best about him were his hands, which danced lightly over my face and ponytail whenever I ran up to greet him. It was his way of seeing me. Because Papa was so much older than Big Mama, he never expected to outlive her. And nobody could believe it when she died after a short illness at age sixty-one. I traveled with my mother down to Mission to see her before she died. Big Mama always had beautiful long hair, but when she took to her sickbed she cut it off into a blunt bob. It looked so strange to me. That's probably why I never want to cut my own hair. I remember her looking up from her bed and smiling at me, and that was the last time I saw her. Papa died a year and a half later.

I WAS TOO YOUNG to really understand what death was when I lost three of my grandparents, all within a couple of years. I just knew that for a while I had them, and then they were gone. During this time, my mother also lost two babies. Yet I never remember her complaining, or even being cross with us. She had a strong faith, but not a completely conventional one. Even though we attended church every Sunday, my mother never bought into the traditional view that God was an external deity who ruled his kingdom from above. She always told me, "The kingdom of heaven is within," and "God is love," not restricted to any religion. A thumb-worn copy of Norman Vincent Peale's *The Power of Positive Thinking* was always nearby. She believed that what happens to you in this world isn't as important as how you respond to it. She could find God in the daily routines of life, and I must have absorbed those lessons from her, because it's what I believe. I find the divine in the ordinary, a miracle in every breath. And like her, I try to keep things simple.

Mother told me that when she went through Big Mama's things after she died, she found lacey handkerchiefs and other precious gifts that she'd saved but never used. My mother encouraged me to enjoy the beautiful things that surround me, not just put them up on a shelf to admire or hide them away in a drawer. And that's just what I do. I use things up, wear my favorite clothes until they have holes, put the good rugs on the floor in the hallway, and stir my coffee with Big Mama's silver spoons.

Sometimes I hear myself repeating my mother's favorite sayings. She seemed to have something to fit every occasion. Some were rather pointed ("Pretty is as pretty does," and when she caught me chomping my chewing gum: "That's cute now, Sissy, but pretty soon it won't be very cute . . ."). Whenever I wished I was taller or didn't have freckles, I was likely to hear "If wishes were horses, beggars would ride." But my favorite was: "Don't kick against the pricks." Anyone who has grown up in cactus country will instantly understand the meaning of this advice. But I have found myself repeating it often in New York and Hollywood, and it seems wiser all the time.

And now I know that everything we tell our children probably doesn't go in one ear and out the other; it really does stick somewhere inside those little heads of theirs. If you ask me to list all the wonderful things my mother told me, I couldn't. But they always seem to come to me when I need them most.

$$\cdots\ \ 3\ \ \cdots$$

M Y MOTHER WAS NOT A STAY-AT-HOME HOUSEWIFE; SHE took a part-time job typing up documents for Don Roberts's abstract company. Those were the days before Xerox machines, and all the property deeds and liens had to be copied by hand. Her office was in the county courthouse, and she was proud to be one of the fastest typists around. I loved visiting her at work. She was a modern woman and very stylish. She often had her clothes made from Vogue patterns and wore high-heeled shoes that would click on the marble floors when she carried those heavy, leather-bound deed books across the hallway to her desk. Then I'd watch her red-painted fingernails fly across the keys.

Her office was located on the south side of the first floor, across from the little booth where Jewel Thomas—we all called her Sister—operated a snack concession. Sister had some sort of affliction, probably cerebral palsy, that twisted her up and made it hard for her to get around. But she was sharp as a tack, and everyone loved her. I used to save my nickels to buy a Coca-Cola from her, sometimes with a bag of peanuts. I'd drop as many of the peanuts as I could into the thick glass bottle and let it fizz up a little, then suck down the salty soda and the deliciously soggy peanuts. I thought I'd invented something new until I learned that kids all over the South were doing the same thing in their small towns in the 1950s.

Mother worked with five others in the typing pool, but the most memorable was Claude Bruce. He was a little different, a nervous man who wore his shirts buttoned at the neck and wrists and who jumped back whenever he was spoken to. He was so terrified of dirt and germs that he scrubbed his hands raw. This was a problem for a typist, because the ribbon ink would get all over his fingers and Claude would have to run to the sink every few minutes.

"Claude, don't wash your hands again," my mother would call after him. "Just do like this!" she'd say, licking her fingertips to wipe off the smudges. But somehow that didn't work with Claude. Luckily he was a good typist, and he had other amazing skills. He remembered the name of everybody he ever met, along with each person's birthday. And if you told Claude what day you were born and which year, he could tell you what day of the week it was in the blink of an eye. I've heard it told that when he was in the service, he could recite the dog tag numbers of every man in his battalion. I guess today we'd call him a savant. But to us he was just a real good guy with chapped hands and a great memory.

Their boss, Don Roberts, was also unusual. He walked with a wooden leg and wore a patch over one eye, just like Long John Silver. He had a big voice that echoed up and down the corridors when he was visiting the courthouse. He'd had lockjaw when he was younger, and that caused all of his physical problems. "That's what can happen if you don't get a tetanus shot," my parents warned us.

One day my mother showed me a broken office chair that she had been trying to fix and asked me if I could give it a try. I was just a little bit of a girl then, probably about six, but I was famous in our family for fixing things. Toys, roller skates, oscillating fans, alarm clocks—I somehow knew how to put them all back together again. So I had gotten down on the floor and started fiddling with the wheels when I heard a booming male voice—it may have been Don Roberts himself.

"Sissy, you get away from that chair!"

I left the room long enough for everyone to go back to typing, then crawled back through the door and slunk along the floor underneath the desks until I reached that old chair and fixed it. I was good at sneaking around, too. In fact, my dad gave me a nickname, Snooter, which was some sort of variation on "snooper."

Nobody ever found out, but when I was five or six years old I used to slip into our neighbor Edna Lipscomb's house when she wasn't home. I'd watch until her car pulled out of the driveway, then look all around and let myself in the front door, which was always unlocked. Once I was inside I would walk quietly through the darkened rooms, just looking at things. I was curious to see how she lived. The only time I touched anything was when I took one piece of candy from her candy dish. I figured that was for visitors anyway. Although probably invited ones.

But my favorite place to explore was the courthouse. With the summer days long and the adults all focused on their grown-up jobs, a clever enough child could become almost invisible in its nooks and crannies. I would sneak into the courtroom and sit in the judge's swivel chair when nobody was looking. There was a balcony overlooking the main chamber, and I would take the side stairway up there and root around in the boxes of odds and ends that were stored up behind the highest seats. I'm sure the county records have never been the same. My favorite of all was the spiral staircase behind a heavy door next to the judge's bench. That was where deputies would take the prisoners up and down from the holding cell on the top floor of the courthouse. Most days there were no trials and no prisoners, so I could play on the metal steps in that spooky old stairwell.

My dad's office was in the courthouse basement, so I could go down there and visit him when I got tired of snooping around the building. His main job was advising farmers about which varieties of seeds to plant, how to get the best yields, and how to control weeds and pests. In those days, that meant massive applications of fertilizers, DDT, and dioxin-based herbicides. Years later Daddy agonized about the environmental damage and the health risks caused by all those chemicals. But then it was standard practice, and nobody questioned the chemical companies or the recommendations of Texas A&M. My dad told me about an herbicide that the state and county suggested for lawns, to make them beautiful and weed-free. People would spray their yards, and then before long a school bus might come by and let off a group of children who would run through the sprayed lawn and then track it into their own homes, where their little brothers and sisters crawled around on the floor putting things in their mouths. The chemical was called 2,4,5 T—better known as Agent Orange. Sometimes when my dad went out to the field to work with farmers and ranchers, he noticed that an awful lot of them seemed to be getting sick, and he wondered if there might be some connection. But nobody was keeping those kinds of records back then.

And nobody thought twice when a city truck rolled through the streets of Quitman at dusk, exhaling a cloud of DDT that was supposed to keep down the mosquitoes. My brothers would run or ride their bikes behind the fogger with the other neighborhood kids, all of them dancing and squealing in the sweet, acrid mist that was so thick they could hardly see their hands in front of their faces.

A COUNTY AGENT was responsible for a lot of things, including handing out bounties on coyotes. The old-timers called them "wolves," even though the last big lobos had been exterminated decades before. To them it was all the same. If it had four legs and a bushy tail and it preyed on livestock, it was a wolf. The county paid $10 per animal, so the farmers and ranchers went out of their way to kill them. Everybody knew where Daddy lived, so sometimes they'd ring the doorbell, or sometimes we'd just open the front door in the morning and find Mason jars stuffed with "wolf" ears. Later, the rules changed and the bounty hunters had to bring the whole carcass to collect the money. That was exciting, because there'd be pickups filled with dead coyotes in the open beds, and my brothers and I would run outside to see them. Eventually the county ran out of money—and "wolves"—and the program ended.

Sometimes we'd find less gruesome offerings at our door. Farmers were grateful for all the help and advice my dad would give them, and they showed their appreciation at harvest time. There'd be bushel baskets of fresh vegetables on the front steps, jugs of honey or tubs of pecans. Daddy could have done a lot of other things, taken a big job with the state or gone to Washington, but he loved our little town and the life we made there together.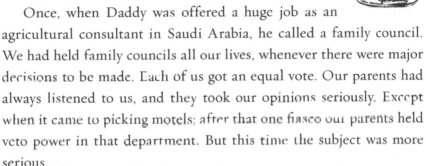

Once, when Daddy was offered a huge job as an agricultural consultant in Saudi Arabia, he called a family council. We had held family councils all our lives, whenever there were major decisions to be made. Each of us got an equal vote. Our parents had always listened to us, and they took our opinions seriously. Except when it came to picking motels; after that one fiasco our parents held veto power in that department. But this time the subject was more serious.

"It will mean a lot more money than working for the county, and it would be an adventure," Daddy told us. "But we'd have to leave Quitman and move to Saudi Arabia."

At first we were excited. Daddy was asked to be the king's county agent! We'd go to a new school. Saudi Arabia had camels! And sand dunes! We all wanted to go.

Then we went to bed. I spent the night tossing and turning, and so did everybody else. The next morning we filed into the kitchen one by one and changed our votes. By the end of breakfast it was unanimous. We would stay in Texas.

MOST DAYS, DADDY WORKED behind his desk in his office in the courthouse basement. The city library was in a large room just down the hall, and when I was finished visiting him, I could while away the hours looking at picture books. When I got a little older, I devoured all the biographies, particularly of strong women: Clara Barton, Florence Nightingale, Helen Keller, Joan of Arc. I may have picked up my reading habits from my dad, a history buff who loved books. In fact, he was the one who saved the Quitman library.

One day when he was leaving work for his lunch break he saw the courthouse janitors throwing books into the hallway. The county apparently needed the space and was evicting the city library. The books were going to be tossed on the burn pile because there was no place to store them. My dad couldn't stand to see perfectly good books wasted like that, so he got together with some friends in town and rented a house up on Billy Goat Hill to start a new library. Eventually the city moved the library into the old bank building, where it still is today.

Daddy loved everything about history, and he was responsible for having historical markers placed all over East Texas. He also helped save the Stinson House, family home of the great Texas philanthropist Ima Hogg and one of the most important buildings in Wood County. It was built in 1859 out of virgin pine and oak, with clapboard siding, wide porches, and bay windows, but by the 1960s, it had been abandoned and was targeted by vandals. My dad arranged to have it moved to the state park in Quitman, where it could be protected. The house was cut into three sections and jacked up onto huge dollies, while crews took down power lines along the route. Onlookers lined up for miles to watch as heavy trucks slowly pulled each piece along the two-lane highway into town. It was the biggest parade the county had ever seen, and even more entertaining than when the circus elephants walked through town. My dad spent years restoring that house, piece by piece, and it became a museum and a place for the community to hold functions. Although he never asked for any recognition, the Stinson House stands as a monument to his love for the community and its history.

· · ·

IN SECOND GRADE my whole class got to visit the local salt mine in Grand Saline. It was an annual class trip for second graders. Everybody lined up to take the rickety old elevator down hundreds of feet into the earth. We clutched our paper lunch bags while the elevator bounced back and forth from side to side as it scraped its way down the shaft. Occasionally the lights would flicker as we descended, and we'd be in total darkness for a few moments. Some kids got scared and cried, but I loved the thrill. Down below was a huge translucent white cave of solid salt, like Carlsbad Caverns, but without stalagmites and stalactites. And it was slippery and cold. My little cotton sweater was not warm enough. There were big pieces of machinery scooping up buckets of salt while we were sliding and falling all over the place. They finally got us settled down and gave us a lecture about mining while we ate our sandwiches. Then we filled our empty bags with chunks of rock salt for souvenirs before the return trip to the surface. We carried that salt around like a badge of honor and would suck on big pieces of it for days, proof that we were big enough to go down in the salt mine and come up alive again. Eventually the school district realized that sending little kids down into a slimy old mine wasn't a great idea, and the class trips were canceled. It was a sad day.

There were no government safety rules back then. No seat belts or bike helmets for kids. The world was a precarious place, but somehow more fun. My brother Ed tells a story I vaguely remember about a little boat trip our family took on Lake Lydia. It was a small private lake about five miles from town, very beautiful and peaceful, with tiny wooden cabins all along the shore. Our father's friend John Morse had a place out there and had been building a boat in his garage for months. It was a small thing, more like a large rowboat with a motor. When he was finished, he offered to take both of our families for a ride. Daddy stayed near the shore, fishing in his waders, while Ed, Robbie, and I piled on board. I was just a toddler. Mother, who was pregnant with one of the babies she later lost, was also in the boat, along with John's wife Emily, daughter Elaine, and son, Tom. None of us was wearing a life vest. It reminded Ed of a life raft from the *Titanic*.

It was getting to be dusk and everyone was having a big time. Daddy was casting a fishing line nearby, and John was speeding along at a nice clip over by the dam when suddenly the boat hit a submerged stump that tore a gaping hole in the bottom. "This cannot be good," Ed remembers thinking as the overloaded boat started taking on water. By some miracle, John was able to gun the engine and reach the shallows just as the boat sank. Nobody made a big deal out of it, but the adults seemed pretty quiet after that. John Morse patched the hole and was back on the water by the next weekend.

MY DAD WAS AN AVID FISHERMAN, and Lake Lydia was where he could escape for a little peace and quiet. But sometimes he brought the whole family to share this most tranquil place, and we proceeded to shatter the silence. Before there was a public pool in town, the lake was the only good place to swim, and the best place to go was the spillway. Daddy would point our 1949 Pontiac sedan down a steep hill to a place where the lake drained into a creek, then parked the car on two raised concrete strips. On one side, the water flowed from the lake and ran underneath the car. On the other side, the water rolled down a steep embankment covered with moss. When Daddy opened the doors and we got out, water rushed around my legs. We waded and squealed and splashed, sliding on our bottoms down the spillway and into the creek.

Mother brought a picnic, peanut-butter-and-jelly and bologna sandwiches. We sat at a picnic table next to the creek with a gallon of milk and ate our sandwiches. When we were finished playing and picnicking, we loaded up the Pontiac and the next phase of the adventure commenced: Would we make it up the hill? The incline seemed much steeper driving out than it did driving in. The car chugged and coughed. Sometimes it chugged and coughed and rolled right back into the middle of the spillway. For me, that was the best part.

THE ONLY THING our parents really seemed to fear was polio. The disease had always been around, but by the early 1950s the epidemic was at its peak, and its victims were usually young children. It could cause paralysis and even death, and there was no known cure. To add to the panic, nobody knew how polio was spread. The worst waves of it seemed to come in the summer months. Mothers who thought heat might spread the disease kept their children inside in the afternoons. People were afraid to use public swimming pools. The fear didn't end until the mid-1950s, when scientists finally developed a vaccine to prevent polio. The medicine was administered through a hypodermic needle that opened up like a shotgun, the vaccine loaded in like ammunition. The needles were long and dull. I could see the hole in the point of the needle from where I was standing halfway across the room. It made me feel queasy. I shifted my weight from one foot to the other and waited my turn. It was like waiting to be executed. We lined up in the cafeteria in front of the nurses. Nobody talked much and I wondered who would cry. Not me. I looked away, stuck out my arm, and suddenly it was over. After that the summer was nothing but fun again.

THERE WAS ALWAYS PLENTY TO DO in Quitman, even when school was out. We didn't need to go to camp; we made our own fun and had our own adventures. It could be as simple as playing a game of jacks on the kitchen floor, or walking along the road chewing on stalks of sour grass that we called goatweed. We also chewed on chunks of tar we'd find in a heap behind the Gem Theater. It wasn't nearly as bad as it sounds—kind of like smoked taffy. We did a lot of interesting things in the alley

45

behind the picture show. We lit grapevines like cigars; they were hollow, and we breathed in the sharp smoke until we doubled over coughing. It hurt, but it hurt good. Once some tough boys came down the alley and threatened to beat us up, then changed their minds when they saw my ponytail. I think this was the first time that being a girl seemed like it might be a good thing. After that, my brothers didn't mind as much when I tagged along.

I would get right in with them when they had dirt clod wars or played baseball in the back lot. They made me catcher until a fast ball hit me right between the eyes. I saw some serious stars that afternoon, but it didn't stop me. I would have been home plate if they had asked me, just to be a part of their world.

Sometimes our schemes were more elaborate, like the time Ed and Robbie fashioned giant wings out of cardboard boxes and tape. The wings were not just for dramatic effect; they were for flying. My brothers would climb up the rose trellis and sail off the roof like Superman. The challenge was to land in the grass and not end up dead on the sidewalk. I would stand and watch in shock and awe, like any good little sister. I really expected them to fly. Probably one of the reasons they kept me around was that I believed.

We spent hours just running barefoot along the network of trails that crisscrossed through the fields and woods that connected all the different neighborhoods. We memorized every rock and stump so that we could sail along without even looking, jumping high over prickly bull nettle, missing rocks that could stub a toe, and avoiding yards that we knew were full of sticker burrs. It was common knowledge that the best time to play was after supper in the summertime, that magic hour when the sun was going down and all the kids were out in their yards or in the street, playing hide-and-seek or "Piggy Wants a Signal." One by one we'd hear parents start to call their children in for the night, but we'd keep on playing, as if we were racing for something, the last rays of daylight, the last little bit of fun, trying to make the magic last just a few minutes longer. But when we heard our dad's familiar whistle cutting through the trees, we would drop everything and run down the trail to home.

SOMETIMES ON WARM NIGHTS, Mother and Daddy would spread a quilt on the grass in the backyard, where all of us could stretch out and spend hours looking up at the stars. Daddy pointed out the Big Dipper and the Little Dipper, and we'd watch for shooting stars blazing through the endless dark. I would always make the same three wishes when I saw one: to be beautiful, to be loved, and (always thinking ahead) to have a million more wishes. My brothers and I had long conversations about the meaning of "infinity." Like, where does the sky end? And what's beyond that? We contemplated "infinity" until our little brains were throbbing.

Sometimes we asked our parents big questions, such as "How big is the universe?" and "Why are we here?" Mother had the best answer to that one. "You're here," she said, "to make the world a better place because you've lived."

IT'S HARD TO IMAGINE NOW, but in those days people threw all their trash out of their cars onto the side of the road. It was like leaving your empty popcorn bag on the floor of the movie theater; nobody thought anything of it. It was out the window, out of sight and out of mind. One of the hidden benefits of this awful practice was that people would toss their returnable soda bottles out with the rest of the trash. My brothers and I became great scavengers of Coke bottles, which we would collect all over town and cash in for 2 cents apiece at Mr. Butler's convenience store. It was just down the street from us, a little wood frame building with big rocks instead of steps. Mr. Butler was always kind to us, and he had the best selection of candy in town. Robbie, Ed, and I would load up on grape bubble gum and Red Hots and Slo Pokes and saltwater taffy, the kind that was flat and had stripes and was covered in wax paper.

After we cashed in our bottles, my brothers would spend everything all at once and eat the candy on the spot. I would usually save a little of my share of the money and stash most of the candy in the top drawer of my dresser. Every once in a while I would reach up and pull that drawer out—I was too short to see inside—and I'd listen to the candy slide back and forth over the wooden boards. It was like money in the bank. Of course, eventually I'd lose my self-control and gorge on the candy until I made myself sick. But then I'd go back out and pick up some more bottles to bring to Mr. Butler's store.

I can still hear my mother whispering on the phone to one of her friends, "Oh, my goodness . . . it knocked him right out of his shoes?" It was a terrible blow to the whole town when Mr. Butler was hit by a truck and killed while crossing the road right in front of his store. After that, we would buy our candy and gum at the filling station owned by the family of our friend Joe Doyle (that's pronounced Jo'dall) Reynolds. It was a neighborhood place, just a few blocks in the other direction from Mr. Butler's store. But it didn't feel the same.

Before long our bottle collection business grew big enough to warrant some capital investment. Robbie, Ed, and I pooled our allowance money and bought a shiny red American Flyer wagon. It cost $12.95. Actually, I put in almost ten dollars, Robbie contributed maybe two and Ed, who was older and had plenty of places to spend his money, put in the rest. So I was the major investor. Which didn't amount to much in their eyes. Before we took the wagon out on our inaugural bottle run, Ed and Robbie decided to take it for a trip down Billy Goat Hill.

Billy Goat Hill held special fascination for daredevils of all ages. It was the steepest hill around and a favorite destination for local boys who loved to race one another to the bottom on anything with wheels—cars, bicycles, wagons, go-carts, even homemade skateboards. A narrow road wound up through a leafy little neighborhood and then dropped down suddenly through the woods, dipping and then curving abruptly to the left. That turn, which you couldn't see from the top, caused real problems for novice racers. The steep incline provided speed and the dip launched the rider into the air. And if the dip didn't send you flying off into the wooded marsh on ei- ther side of the road, the sharp turn at the bottom probably would. Legend had it that more than a few had met their fate on Billy Goat Hill.

I was still too little to go to such a dangerous place, so Ed and Rob- bie tested the new red wagon by themselves. They limped home a few hours later; both the boys and the red wagon were scraped up and cov- ered in mud. The boys healed quickly, but the wagon was never the same. Its axle was bent, and even though we used it for bottle collec- tions, it always lurched around when we pulled it along the road.

Robbie was almost a year and a half older than me, so he started rid- ing a bike first. It took him a while to build up his courage to tackle Billy Goat Hill on two wheels, but he was ecstatic when he finally did it. He was changed after that. He seemed older, wiser, taller . . . well maybe not taller, but certainly more sure of himself. It was a rite of pas- sage for boys in this little town, and Robbie joined the ranks of those who lived to tell. After this initial victory Robbie looked for bigger challenges. He climbed up the water tower a few blocks from our house. It was huge! He had the first skateboard in town; he made it himself out of a pair of old skates. He learned to water ski on one ski, then he mastered shoe skis. Before long he could ski barefoot. But he'd always walked on water as far as I was concerned.

THE HIGH SCHOOL STADIUM was just a few blocks behind our house, and my brothers and I had grown up in the shadows of those outdoor bleachers. We could see the lights of the football games from our backyard and hear the beat of the drums and the sound of the band practicing almost every day. We would pedal our bicycles there on Saturday mornings, then crawl through the underbrush to find the hole under the fence to get onto the football field. Once inside we could pick through whatever had fallen out of people's pockets when they stood up to cheer the Bulldogs. If we were hungry, we'd eat from bags of stale popcorn while we were scavenging.

One of the only drawbacks of living right on the highway was that it was too hard to keep our dogs safe. My first dog was named Tippy, a sweet collie who was already part of the family when I was born. She managed to stay out of the road and lived a long and happy life. My brothers and I loved animals, and there were always shoe boxes, jars, and bowls around the house filled with frogs, lizards, goldfish, and tadpoles that Robbie was always bringing home. We even had pet bees that would walk all over our arms. But I preferred the june bugs that we kept in cigar boxes and played with like toy cars. For extra entertainment, we'd tie a string to their legs and let them fly around in little circles.

For a while we had a pet crow that flew into our backyard one day and started to talk. My brothers were tossing around a football when the bird landed on the clothesline and squawked, "Play ball!" It was straight out of a Disney movie. We fed it, and the bird just hung around. When word spread that we had a talking crow, we got a call from Carson Seago, a warden with the fish and game department who lived down the street.

"Eddie, I hear you've got a tame crow living in your yard," said the warden.

"That's right, Carson," said Daddy.

"Well you can keep it," he said. It turned out that his sons Don and David had trained the bird to talk, but now they had gone off to college. "Our kids have grown up," said Carson. "Let yours enjoy the crow." We did keep it for a while, until one day it just took off again.

Along with the dump, the courthouse square was a great place to find pets. Every Saturday morning, people would park their trucks in the shade of the big old sycamore trees and hold an informal swap meet right in the parking lot. One Saturday morning we noticed some commotion around a pickup truck. A farmer had caught a full-grown alligator out at Lake Lydia and wanted to show it off. The man had taken its nest, too, so there were a bunch of eggs in the truck bed that were starting to hatch. Robbie and I, who were about ten and nine years old, hoisted ourselves up onto the side of the pickup and watched, dropjawed, as the tiny heads poked out into the sunlight. The man was letting people take the hatchlings, and of course Robbie just had to have a baby alligator. He rode his bike home with one stuffed inside of his shirt and named it Allie. The alligator lived in a tin washtub in the boys' bedroom until it started getting too big. One day Robbie came in for breakfast, holding up one of his fingers and wincing. "Allie bit me!" he said, astonished at the sudden turn of events. His pet alligator had hurt his feelings. We all pitched in to feed it worms and flies and spiders if we could catch them. Allie lasted about six months before she died mysteriously.

THERE WAS ALWAYS SOMETHING interesting going on around the courthouse and the town square. The Spit and Whittle Club congregated there every morning; that's what we called the old men in overalls who sat on benches and traded stories. The courthouse square was like the beating heart of Quitman, where all the parades ended up. Santa Claus arrived there every year on a fire truck; there were Easter egg hunts and political rallies. Competitions were judged on the grassy lawn in front of the courthouse, including a hula hoop contest that taught me one of my first life lessons. I was a wizard with a hula hoop. I could spin it around my knees and ankles and even my neck. If I put my arms up in the air and held my hands together, I could spin that hula hoop up over my head and around my wrists. I could keep it going for hours if I wanted, and none of my friends could outlast me. So when I marched up those steps and started swinging that hoop around my hips, I was already planning my victory speech and wondering where to put my trophy. All my short life, I had played to win.

When I was a toddler, my parents took me along to an Easter egg hunt out in the country. They gave me an enormous basket and lined me up with kids of all sizes at the edge of a lawn covered with colored eggs. Before the man who organized the hunt could say "Ready, set, go!" I was out in front of everybody, scooping up eggs. They couldn't hold me back. I had tunnel vision in a world of eggs and I wanted them.

One time we were visiting some family friends out in West Texas, where we'd swim all day in the pool on their big ranch. Our host would throw silver dollars into the deep end and challenge me, my brothers, and cousins to dive in after them. I was one of the youngest, but I could hold my breath the longest and swim the deepest, so I got them every time. I would let my eyeballs explode and pop out of my head before I would risk losing one of those silver dollars. I was the champion.

So I couldn't imagine not taking first place in the hula hoop contest in front of the county courthouse. I watched in horror as the hoop started to wobble and then dropped around my feet. I could hardly believe it. I had lost. My mother would have said, "Never count your chickens before they've hatched, Sissy." I'd say: "Never celebrate before the trophy's in your hands!"

THE EVENT WE MOST LOOKED forward to was the Old Settlers' Reunion, held in Jim Hogg Park every August since 1900. Part carnival, part county fair, it was set up on the sandy ground amid tall oak trees. The same company would come every year, and they knew exactly where to put the midway and the rides and the Ferris wheel, the colored lights draped throughout the leafy canopy and rising up above the branches, transforming the park into a magical landscape. People came streaming in from everywhere in Wood County and beyond.

I'd load up on Cokes and hot dogs, frozen custards, cotton candy, and my personal favorite, candy apples, before getting on the rides. The scarier the better. Somehow I never got sick, which is kind of amazing for someone who couldn't even sit in the backseat of the car without turning green. My favorite was "The Tubs"—a diabolical contraption where you were strapped into big metal buckets that spun around on huge mechanical arms, which were also whirling and dipping crazily. I'd ride the Tubs over and over, then move on to the Ferris wheel, which spun at a leisurely pace and lifted you up for a bird's-eye view of the fair. If you were lucky, or cute enough, the carnies would let you stay on for an extra turn while they let everyone else off, and then make sure you stopped for a long time at the very apex of the wheel, rocking in your cart, breathing in the tree-cooled air, taking in the lights below and the stars above.

THE OLD SETTLERS' REUNION lasted for almost a whole week. But the traveling circus that came each summer would only stop in Quitman for one enchanted day and night. The circus would arrive in Mineola by train, and the keepers would walk the elephants, trunks holding tails, along eleven miles of hot dusty asphalt to Quitman. My brothers and I would pedal our bikes to the great big field near the courthouse square to watch the spectacle. First we'd ride out to the field and marvel at the tall green grass swaying in the breeze and the quiet empty space— where we knew there would soon be a circus! Then we'd watch as the wagons arrived and the workers set up the big canvas tent. In the daylight, everything was a bit shabby and tattered, both the animals and the circus workers looked flea-bitten and malnourished, like they had really hard lives. Finally the elephants lumbered into town, shimmering in the heat like a mirage from the African plains. While the keepers watered the animals, and the performers put on their costumes, my brothers and I would rush home for supper. Then we'd rush back with the whole family for the evening show.

But once the lights came up, it was all magic. The lions and tigers seemed sleek and supple, jumping through flaming hoops while the ringmaster cracked his whip. The clowns and trapeze artists dazzled us as we stuffed ourselves with popcorn and cotton candy and cheered from the benches. Then it would be over. The next day my brothers and I would pedal back to the green field and find it empty and wonder: Had we imagined it? Had the circus really come to town? Then we would see the trampled grass where the big top had been, and elephant poop where the pens had stood, and some trash blowing around: proof that it wasn't a dream, the circus had really come to town.

4

Quitman was luckier than a lot of small towns; it had its very own picture show called the Gem Theater. It belonged to an older couple named Mildred and Theo Miller who were friends of my parents. The entrance was in a boxy storefront on Main Street, and the only thing fancy about the theater was the art deco sign out front that said GEM in neon letters and stuck out from the brick facade like a single feather in a headdress. Theo always manned the front booth, where we paid 15 or 25 cents to get in. It was tiny inside, with a black-and-white checked linoleum floor that rose up as it funneled you to the popcorn counter and the theater itself. My favorite thing was to buy a big dill pickle for 5 cents before the movie started.

At first I would go with my parents, and sometimes I'd end up in the "cry room," a place set aside for mothers to take their babies and young children when they acted up. As I grew older, I was allowed to tag along with my brothers to matinees. We'd watch old Tom Mix cowboy movies, or ones with scary dinosaurs chasing people, or Zorro, which I loved. What was going on up on the screen seemed so real to me that I believed that stuntmen who died in the movies were actually condemned prisoners who had volunteered for the job. I could lose all track of time and forget everything else for an hour or so, sunk down in the dark seats and pulled into the flickering magic world on the screen.

I sometimes had a hard time focusing my attention on any one thing for a long time, but at the Gem I was completely absorbed.

When Mildred and Theo retired and shut down the Gem, we'd have to drive to Mineola to watch movies in the Select, a bigger, more modern theater. Once I was a teenager, my date would pick me up at six-thirty in the evening, and we'd drive to Mineola to go to the picture show. We never thought to find out what time the movie started and would stumble down the aisle trying to find two empty seats in the dark. We would watch the end of the movie, then stay for the beginning of the next showing, leaving when we'd gotten to the part where we'd first come in. The challenge was to figure out what the movie was about. It was like solving a puzzle. Years later, when I got to New York, I learned how real film lovers watched movies, from beginning to end, and I thought, *Gee, this is easy!*

The Select is where I saw some of the most influential films of my life: *The Night of the Hunter*, a noir classic with Robert Mitchum. *The Miracle Worker*, with Anne Bancroft—with whom I was thrilled to work once I became an actor myself. My favorite of all time, though, was *To Kill a Mockingbird*.

There are so many reasons why I love that film, and the book on which it's based, but what really pulled me in, I think, was the depiction of small town life in the South, a time and place where "somehow it was hotter then.... And people moved slowly.... A day was twenty-four hours long, but seemed longer." The fictional town of Maycomb reminds me so much of the Quitman I knew in the 1950s and '60s. And the way the story is observed through the eyes of a young girl resonates to my bones. I was a tomboy, like Scout, who climbed trees and spoke her mind and hated wearing dresses; who kept a box filled with private treasures stashed under her bed. Like her, I had a wise and capable father who loved me unconditionally and never tried to break my wild spirit. My dad was my Atticus Finch. But I was much luckier than Scout, because I had a mother.

There were other similarities. While Quitman had never gone through a racially charged trial like the legal lynching of Tom Robinson, a black man falsely accused of raping a white woman—a scenario that drives the narrative of *To Kill a Mockingbird*—my hometown was just as much a part of the Jim Crow South as the fictional Maycomb. I'd heard whispers of a lynching by an angry mob on the courthouse square sometime back in the nineteenth century and rumors of a dark side to my otherwise sweet little town.

The first time I noticed the segregation of races was at the Gem Theater, where African-Americans had to line up outside a separate side entrance and then sit in the balcony. I didn't understand it. Pretty soon it dawned on me that whites and blacks had separate just about everything. The Wood County courthouse had separate bathrooms: I'll never forget the signs, one for WHITE LADIES and the other for COLORED WOMEN. Even as a child, I knew that had to hurt someone's feelings. During my days of snooping around the courthouse, I couldn't resist walking into the colored restroom to see what it looked like. An African-American woman whirled around from the sink when she saw me. "You'd better get yourself on out of here, young lady," she scolded. "You don't belong in here." Wide-eyed, I backed out the door. The courthouse also had separate drinking fountains labeled WHITE and COLORED. (My husband, Jack, grew up in Illinois, and the first time he saw a "colored" drinking fountain he thought that rainbow-colored water was supposed to come out of it.) The Jim Crow rules were perplexing, but segregation was all we ever knew. To white children, it was an abstract concept. So many white folks say, "There was never any trouble in our town," but that's only because it wasn't trouble at all for them. So I don't really know what race relations were like in Quitman, because it really didn't touch my world. Except for one time.

Like just about everywhere throughout the South, whites and blacks in Quitman had their own schools and lived in separate neighborhoods. Sometimes we'd be driving through the "colored" part of town, and my brothers and I would stare out of the car windows at families sitting on their front porches enjoying the evening; the kids would look back at us with similar fascination. We might as well have lived on different planets.

But if their mothers or fathers did housekeeping or sewing or yard work, they would often bring their young children along and we would play together. Churches and schools might be separated, but commerce was different, and trading for services was the way people got to know one another back then. And all children are color-blind unless they're taught otherwise.

We had some favorite friends, Sevitra and Brusker Fannin, whose mother, Martene, was a schoolteacher who also had an upholstering and sewing business at home. Mother often drove out to her house to drop off fabrics or pick up finished pieces. Robbie and I always went along to play. The Fannins lived on rolling farmland a few miles north of town, and they had the softest, sandiest soil in their yard, like a sandy beach or flour that had been carefully sifted, so that it felt wonderful on bare feet. We loved playing with Sevitra and Brusker, just running around like crazy while our mothers visited inside.

It was hot and dusty in the summertime, and playing hard made us thirsty. There was a covered well beside the house, and one afternoon we all climbed up there for a drink of water. Brusker lifted aside the wooden lid and dropped a bucket deep into the well, while we gathered around in a circle, staring down into the hole. After Brusker hoisted the bucket up with a rope, he filled a metal dipper and started passing it around. Everybody took a sip, and then it was my turn. This was the time of polio, and I'd been raised never to drink after anybody. I didn't even drink after my brothers. Now the prospect of sharing seemed even more illicit, and thrilling. *I'm doing something I'm not supposed to be doing*, I thought, as I held the dipper to my lips and drank long and deeply. It was the coolest, sweetest drink of water I'd had in my life. In that moment I had an epiphany. From then on I would trust my own instincts about people and their rules. If I always did what was expected, I might miss out on the most wonderful things in life.

I STARTED RIDING COWS at a young age. My parents thought I was too little for a pony, so I decided the old milk cow that grazed in the fields across from our house would have to do. My girlfriend Vickie Johns would run the cow down in the gully and I'd jump on its back. Then I'd run it down in the gully and she'd jump on its back. We'd ride that cow until we got pitched off, then we'd start all over again. One day a lady called my mother and said, "Mrs. Spacek, do you know your daughter and her little friend are out back riding a cow?" When I got home my mother said, "Honey, you shouldn't be riding that cow. You might sour its milk."

Vickie Johns and I were always having adventures together. Sometimes in the summer months, when Vickie was sleeping over with me, we'd wait until everybody was asleep in the house and then slip out for midnight walks around town. In our pajamas. We couldn't have been more than nine or ten years old, and I can't tell you why we did it other than for the thrill of doing something forbidden. Of course we would take Vickie's old dog, Queenie, along with us for protection, as we walked the back streets toward town, past the empty brick school buildings, past the church, through the cemetery with the moon throwing scary shadows between the rows of stones (we hurried a little through this part), and then looped back into the center of town with its quiet shuttered stores. We weren't afraid of anything except getting caught by the night watchman, Shorty Horton. There was no crime to speak of in Quitman back then, and we didn't have much of a police department. The county sheriffs and Shorty were the only protectors of public order while the city slept.

Shorty's nickname was not ironic; he was a very, very small man who wore a large cowboy hat and cowboy boots and patrolled the night streets in a very large pickup. We knew he would turn us in to our parents if he found us wandering around in pajamas. So we kept our eyes and ears open for that white truck; it added to the danger of our walks. One night he nearly caught us. We were rounding the corner of a three-sided parking shed, just past the graveyard, when suddenly there was Shorty, coming the other way. We ran around the other side, but he'd already spotted Queenie standing next to the building so he decided to stop and investigate. He was a nice man and he leaned down to pet Queenie.

"What are you doing out this time of night, girl?" he asked the dog. "Shouldn't you be at home asleep on the rug?"

He pointed his flashlight beam in our direction just as we made the corner. With our little hearts pounding—and trying not to giggle—we stayed just ahead of him as he circled the building. He finally gave up and drove off into the night. We ran the whole way home with Queenie as our sentinel.

I WAS ALWAYS A GOOD STUDENT, but I wasn't the smartest in my class. That was Hill Goldsmith, my sometime boyfriend. We sat next to each other in first grade while we were taking achievement tests. It was multiple choice so we had to color in a little circle with our pencils next to the right answer. I happened to glance at Hill's paper and saw that one of his answers was different than mine. So of course I changed my answer. But when I got my paper back, the answer I'd copied from Hill's paper was wrong. You would think that experience would have taught me a lesson, but I had one more ill-fated brush with cheating.

Vickie Johns was my childhood partner in crime. We were both in Mrs. Frost's fourth grade class when we came up with another brilliant idea: I liked to do math, which was simple for me, but hated writing out all the spelling sentences. Vickie loved to write but hated math. So we decided to join forces and do each other's homework. We figured it was stupid to have to suffer through work we didn't like, when the solution was so obvious. For about a month we had a real production line going. The last thing I'd always say when I handed Vickie my assignment was "Remember! Write like me!" Apparently, she was a pretty good counterfeiter. But we made the fatal mistake of bragging about our system to some friends.

One day Vickie and I convinced our mothers that we were both sick and that we should be allowed to stay home from school and convalesce together at my house. We had a big time lounging in our pajamas. When we got tired of reading comic books, we decided to do an art project in the bathtub. First we melted down dozens of wax candies that we had been hoarding—those miniature soda bottles filled with horrible, sweet, colored liquid. Then we sculpted a magnificent horse out of the wax. Vickie and I were congratulating ourselves on our creation when the phone rang. It was a friend warning us that we were in deep trouble. Another one of our classmates, emboldened by our absence from school, told Mrs. Frost what we had been up to. First we panicked. Then we came up with a plan: We'd apologize and give Mrs. Frost the wax horse as a peace offering, hoping we could bribe her into forgetting about the whole thing.

The next morning Vickie and I slunk into Mrs. Frost's class a few minutes early and presented her with our great gift. She put it on her shelf without saying a word and then told us she'd like to talk to us at recess. We sat through the class wringing our hands, worried sick. Not only was Bonnie Frost our teacher, but she and her husband—yes, Jack Frost!—belonged to the same church and knew our parents. Disaster loomed. But much to our relief, Mrs. Frost didn't turn us in to the elementary school principal, Mr. Goolsby. She talked to us about the importance of doing our own homework, that it was about learning, not just grades. We promised her we would never do it again, and didn't. But every Sunday, Vickie and I would see her talking to our parents at church, and the sweat would drip off of us. She never told on us in all those years.

Sometimes I got in trouble in school without even knowing it. Pop

Pearce, who taught science, took points off my grade for every day I was chewing gum in class. Except he never warned me, and I only found out when I got a low grade on my report card.

I couldn't be mad at him, though, because his wife, Peggy, was one of Mother's best friends. Peggy was a dear, sweet woman who was frightened of many things. When Pop, who was also the football coach, was with the team on away games, Peggy could only sleep with the radio on and a baseball bat under her bed. When I was about nine years old, Mother would send me over there to stay with her so she wouldn't be so afraid. She had two children, Mike and Andy, who weren't that much younger than me, but I babysat for them sometimes. I've been friends with Mike and Andy all my life.

I'VE KNOWN for a long time that some of the best things in life you just have to wait for, like going barefoot and riding your own horse. I must have driven my father crazy begging him for a pony of my own. When I was eleven or twelve, he finally gave in. Daddy had a conversation with Granville Benton, the president of the bank and the town's premier horseman, and asked for help in picking the right horse for me.

"I don't know much about horses," my dad told Granville. "Do you think you can find one for Sissy that won't kill her?"

A few weeks later, Granville pulled up in front of our house with a horse trailer. He'd found me a twelve-year-old buckskin roping horse, well behaved and small, somewhere between fourteen and fifteen hands. I couldn't believe my luck. He was so beautiful, with a dark mane and tail and a tawny coat, the color of the quarry rocks they use to build houses in Central Texas. I named him Buck, and he turned out to be as smart as he was gentle. I learned to ride him bareback. I cried when I finally put a saddle on him and lost that physical connection, the heat of his coat and the feel of his spine and his muscles working as he moved.

About the same time Vickie got a pinto she named Rebel Joe. He was very young and athletic and was quite a character. She would give him a pop on the rump with a little wire switch to get him to go, but it would also make him buck. We thought it was fun to ride bucking horses, and I got good at hanging on. Pretty soon I started fancying myself a real cowboy. When we watched *Bonanza* on television on Sunday nights, I'd imagine myself as the fifth Cartwright, rounding the corner right after Little Joe.

Vickie and I rode our horses all over the county, sometimes as far as Lake Quitman. We'd lope along the highway in the summer heat, stopping at the filling station about halfway to drink a Coke and water our horses. I'd give Buck a coffee can filled with water; he'd hold it between his teeth and tip his head back to drink.

One time I was riding Buck out to the lake when a guy drove by in his pickup and slowed down alongside us.

"How much you take for that horse?" he shouted.

"A million dollars!" I said, throwing my chin in the air. I meant it, too.

As much as I loved that horse, I had a lot to learn about taking care of him. I gave him pneumonia by swimming him in the cold lake after the long, hot afternoon rides. Vickie and I would take off our saddles and ride the horses bareback, then swim around with them all afternoon. One day Buck started coughing. "Why are you doing that? Stop it!" I told him. Luckily a course of antibiotics fixed him right up.

After that I joined the 4-H club out in Coke to learn more about horsemanship. Mother would drive me out to the dusty rink in her Buick with a homemade trailer hitched to the back. Around the same time, Robbie got a bay quarter horse named Gunsmoke that never wanted to be separated from Buck. Gunsmoke would follow the horse trailer when we loaded up Buck, so we'd load him up, too, and off we'd go, me and Buck, Robbie and Gunsmoke. It was fun learning to ride in formation and doing square dances and quadrilles on horseback. Before long, Robbie and I were competing in rodeos.

One of my favorite events was barrel racing, where you ride your horse at top speed, circling around an obstacle course of three upright barrels in a cloverleaf formation. It was a perfect event for Buck, who had only two speeds: on and flat out. Buck was a roping horse; he was trained to stop when you get off. He didn't understand "whoa." So I'd have to throw off one leg to get him to stop, which was challenging to say the least.

Robbie and I competed as a team in the Rescue Race. He would ride Gunsmoke as fast as he could to the end of the ring, circling around me as he threw his arm out to pick me up. It was supposed to go like this: I would grab his arm, jump on the back of the horse, and then race to the finish line triumphantly. The only problem was that I couldn't seem to figure out how to throw my leg all the way over Gunsmoke's rump after Robbie reached down to pull me up. One time I never even got mounted, and Robbie just held on to my arm as we galloped to the finish line. Mother was watching the race and told me I looked like a little flag, flapping in the wind.

AT FIRST WE BOARDED Buck and Gunsmoke with our aunt and uncle Sam and Maurine, who had some pasture around their house on the outskirts of Quitman. Later we rented the fenced field across the highway from our house to keep the horses. As soon as I'd get home from school, I'd run over there with my saddle, and off we'd go. One day after a particularly long ride, I thought I'd bring Buck back to the house and put him in the backyard for a while. I thought it would be nice to let him graze on the cool, thick grass. I couldn't tie him to the cherry laurel tree because it was poisonous for horses. So I took his saddle off and tied him on a long rope to the clothesline out back, which was two T-poles sunk in cement, with three wires strung between them. I figured Buck could move up and down the line like a dog, and eat grass wherever he wanted. Another bad idea. As soon as I had him situated, he got all tangled up in the long rope, which is something I quickly learned horses don't handle very well. Before I knew it, he'd taken off running, pulled down the clothesline, and stretched the wires so tightly, the sound they made when they snapped behind him was like ricocheting rifle shots. Buck tore through the side yard and across Edna Lip-scomb's beautiful front lawn, tearing up her Saint Augustine, and headed for the highway.

I was running after him when I saw a huge tractor trailer bearing down on my horse. I closed my eyes and all I could hear was the driver leaning on his horn. When I opened my eyes again, the truck was gone and Buck was standing across the street in a neighbor's yard, shaking like a sweetgum leaf. I don't know who was trembling more, me or Buck. There were skid marks in the asphalt from his metal horseshoes. I still don't know how he survived.

ONE THING I WAS GOOD at was fishing. My dad and I would spend hours together out on the lakes around Quitman, although once I did hear him mention to my mother that my chattering scared away most of the fish. My crowning achievement was when I was six and the whole family spent the summer in Colorado, where Daddy was taking some post-graduate courses. We drove out to a big river to fish for trout. He and the boys had fly rods, but nobody thought I would catch anything, so all I had was a pole with a string and a hook. I didn't even have a worm on my hook, but something that looked like a worm that had fallen from a flowering tree.

I was standing upstream from my brothers holding my pole when all of a sudden I saw a huge fish splashing on the far side of the water. I was so transfixed, I couldn't move as I watched that fish jump and twist in the air. I heard someone yelling, "Pull it in, pull it in!" but it wasn't until Robbie and Ed came running and grabbed my fishing pole that I realized that the big fish was attached to the end of my line. I got all the glory, but they saved the fish. And they were so proud of me. For years they told the story of how Sissy caught the biggest fish. I even have a picture to prove it.

My brothers were great sportsmen, but both were too sensitive to get much pleasure out of hunting. Ed sometimes tells the story of how upset he was the first time he killed anything. He was eight or nine years old and home alone with Robbie. He figured our mom had probably stepped out for a quick errand and taken me with her, because the boys were rarely left by themselves. Ed had just gotten his first BB gun, a Daisy Red Ryder, and he was itching to try it out. He looked out the window and saw a bird splashing in the birdbath. *Look at that bird*, he thought. And his next thought was *I can shoot that bird.* So he loaded his little BB gun, went outside, and crept up on it. He took aim, then shot. The bird flopped to the ground, dead.

Ed's mouth dropped open. And then the reality of what he had just done hit him—he had murdered a living thing for no reason—and he began to cry. He dropped the gun and ran into the house, hysterical. Ed knew he wasn't supposed to bother his father at work, but Mother wasn't home and he was panicked. So he called Daddy's office and got him on the phone. By now he was so upset all he could do was sob, "I've killed him! I've shot him, I've killed him!" And of course, Daddy thought he was talking about Robbie.

Daddy jumped into his car and raced home, probably about to have a heart attack thinking Ed had shot his brother. He ran into the house and saw that the boys were both okay, and quickly figured out what had happened. He hugged them both for a long time.

As they grew older, Daddy didn't take the boys hunting as often. When Robbie was in his early teens, he still hadn't shot his first deer and he wanted one so badly. He kept asking Daddy to take him deer hunting, and finally he did. They spotted a three-point buck in a thicket, and Robbie brought him down with one clean shot. At first he was excited, but when he walked closer, he looked the deer in the eye and watched the light drain from it as it died. Then he sat down, put his head in his hands, and wept. I still have that mounted deer head somewhere in our garage. I can't bear to put it up on the wall, but I can't bear to part with it.

... 5 ...

WHEN I WAS SIX, MY PARENTS TOOK MY BROTHERS AND me to the tiny brick schoolhouse in Coke, Texas (pop. 25) for a picnic and a performance by the Coquettes. It was the day I decided to go into show business.

Coke sat about five miles outside of Quitman, surrounded by rolling plains and oil fields. The whole town consisted of the school, the riding arena where I later rode my horse as a member of the 4-H club, and one country store. The store was constructed like it should have been part of a city block. But the rest of the town was never built, and the store stood alone against the sky, with nothing around it as far as the eye could see.

About forty kids from all over the county attended the little public school, which ranged from first to eighth grade. One magical evening my parents took the family to an open house out at the school. It started with a picnic on the lawn, and then we moved inside for a tour.

There were two classrooms and an auditorium with a painted mural behind the stage. Inside the front door were glass-fronted cupboards, like the dining room furniture from somebody's grandmother's house, but they held a cornucopia of wonder. I pressed my nose against the glass for a better look at the displays of rabbit skulls, giant bugs, rattlesnake rattles, and all kinds of bird nests. There was more than the cabinets could hold, so tables were set up and laden with jars and jars of baby alligators, horned toads and frogs suspended in formaldehyde, and living things, too: tadpoles, real frogs you could play with, rabbits, and even a few mice and rats. It was the most amazing place. And it got even better when we took our seats in the auditorium. The music started up, and out marched the Coquettes. As soon as I saw them on that stage, boys and girls twirling their batons, dressed up in shimmery silver cowboy outfits, hats, and white majorette boots, I knew show business was for me. *I could do that*, I thought. *I should be up there.*

I STARTED TAKING TWIRLING and tap dancing lessons to prepare for my career. By the time I was six or seven, I had formed an act with my friend Pam Cain, who had debuted on the Coke schoolhouse stage, and started performing at school and civic events around town. We wore leotards and tap shoes, and our mothers sewed us little white vests with tails and tiny jingle bells. We went to the hardware store and bought wooden dowels and rubber tips, the kind that keep chair legs from scratching the floor. We painted them gold and sprinkled them with glitter. We were ready and we were awesome. My dad was president of the Rotary Club for many years, so those poor Rotarians had to sit through "On the Sunny Side of the Street" and "Charley, My Boy" about a million times.

When I was a bit older, Robbie and I started an act together. Mother signed us up for dance lessons, but when it was time for us to go, Robbie would wrap his arms around a tree, and she couldn't pry his fingers from the bark. So I went on my own. Later, after much cajoling, he ended up pantomiming playing banjo while I sang and danced the Charleston. I wore a flapper dress and Robbie had on a straw boater and suspenders. He was a natural performer, so handsome and bright— you couldn't take your eyes off of him. We performed at local talent shows, and all kinds of community, church, and school functions. These events drew huge crowds in Quitman, where entertainment was scarce, usually filling the school auditorium. Daddy was in charge of the dance music, placing LPs on the record player we'd brought from home. But somebody had borrowed it before one big performance and left the setting on 45. So when the curtain opened, Robbie and I, about eleven and twelve years old, stood center stage, waiting to start the act, but the music that filled the hall was racing and squealing at crazy lightning speed. From the side of the stage I heard my father shout, "Dance, Sissy! Dance!" We stood there for a moment, unsure of what to do, until finally some good Samaritan drew the curtains and put us out of our misery.

I took up guitar shortly after that.

I tried piano lessons, but I decided what I really needed to do was to learn to play guitar. By the time I was twelve, I had saved up $14.95 to buy a Silvertone guitar, ordered out of the Sears and Roebuck catalogue. Nobody knew I'd bought it until a big cardboard box arrived one day. It came with a plastic record of instruction and a booklet of Hy White songs. I spent hours every day practicing "Little Brown Jug" and "What Do You Do with a Drunken Sailor?" I took lessons and progressed pretty quickly. Later I formed a hootenanny group that performed around town.

One day, a girl sat in with us and played a song called "Copper Kettle." She far outclassed us. Instead of just strumming, she was picking the strings with her fingers, and that sound was thrilling. I asked her to slow down and show me, and spent the next couple of months teaching myself to Travis pick—thumb, thumb, finger, thumb; finger, thumb, finger—over and over and over until my fingers bled. Then one day, I could do it without thinking.

Sometimes I'd be practicing in my room and my dad would walk by, poke his head in the door, and say something like "That E-string's a little flat, Sissy."

By now I had graduated to a real guitar, a twelve-string Vox that sounded amazing when I finger-picked. I began writing my own songs and started searching for my own style. Although there were great country musicians in

East Texas, I grew up listening to what my parents listened to: show tunes, big bands, Perry Como. Fortunately, all through elementary school, I had a wonderful music teacher named Mary Margaret Pepper, who was responsible for most of my early musical training. She recognized that I had talent and she gave me great confidence. She also did not encourage us to watch *The Lawrence Welk Show*. In fact she forbade us to watch it.

When I got to be a teenager, one of my friends who had older sisters came to school singing and dancing to a pop song I didn't recognize.

"Where'd you learn that?" I asked.

"Why, on the radio," she said, like it was the most natural thing in the world.

"Radio? You mean there's something on the radio besides the farm reports?" That's all my dad ever listened to. So I asked for a box radio for Christmas, just so I could find out what this radio thing was all about. I 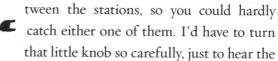 would lie across my bed at night, trying to catch WNOE in New Orleans or KLIF in Dallas. We were right in between the stations, so you could hardly catch either one of them. I'd have to turn that little knob so carefully, just to hear the scratchy distant sounds of the Everly Brothers, Buddy Holly, or Little Eva doing the Loco-Motion. Elvis was all over the airwaves, but I wasn't such a big fan then and I think I know why. One day Mickey Scott, a friend of ours, about Ed's age, stood in the middle of the highway in front of our house, rocking and singing "You ain't nothing but a hound dog . . ." We were worried Mickey might get hit by a truck. Thank goodness he didn't. But he did kill the song. That was my introduction to Elvis, and I was not impressed.

I never really fell hard for any pop act until I was thirteen and the Beatles crossed the Atlantic. I had the first Beatle book in town. John was my favorite. My mother was the Methodist Youth Fellowship counselor for our church at the time, and she always encouraged us to listen to music. Whenever the MYF met, the church fellowship hall would be packed with kids; we even got the Baptists to come, because we danced, and they couldn't. We were wild. We drank Cokes and popped popcorn and played lots of Ping-Pong. On the Sunday night that the Beatles were playing for the first time on *The Ed Sullivan Show*, Mother invited the whole group back to our house to watch it. She was the coolest mom ever.

I'm still so grateful to her for taking us all home to watch what turned out to be history being made. Afterward, we went back to church feeling very special—like we had a fabulous secret.

I LEARNED TO DRIVE a car when I was still a little kid, seven or eight years old. When Mother took Ed out in the Buick to teach him to drive when he was twelve, I pestered them to come along. I would fret until they gave me a turn, sitting on my mother's lap, steering down the country road barely able to reach the pedals, and I had to stand up to get the clutch in right. By the time I was thirteen, I was driving all over town with an older licensed driver: Jackie Rushing, who was thirteen and a half and one of my best friends. (Her sister, Ganelle, was the telephone switchboard operator.) It was common for young teens to drive in rural areas. They were needed to help on the farms and ranches; they drove tractors and all kinds of farm equipment. And a licensed driver, regardless of age, could take anyone along (they have wisely changed this rule).

Jackie and I were talking and laughing and listening to music when the woman in front of me slowed down to turn, and I plowed right into the back of her car. Thank goodness nobody was hurt badly; I just banged my chin. It was bad enough, causing $365 in damage to the Buick, which was a lot back then. My father, once he knew I was all right, didn't come down to the accident. He was so put out with me, he sent my mother. When the police officer turned on the ignition, the radio came on, blaring pop music loud enough to be heard in the next county. Funny thing, I don't remember being punished for the accident, but I certainly didn't drive for a long time after that.

What I remember most vividly after all these years is that the woman I hit got the traffic ticket, not me. It may have been because my parents worked in the courthouse, who knows? But it was so wrong and unfair that it's bothered me all these years. If you're reading this book right now and you were driving the car I hit from behind at Goode and College Street (now known as Sissy Spacek Drive!) in the early 1960s, I am so sorry. I should have gotten the ticket and paid for the damage to your car.

IN JUNIOR HIGH I was a cheerleader, and as a freshman in high school, I marched with the band as a drummer. But I developed a nasty staph infection on my knee from wearing a brace for the snare drum and decided to rethink my choice: The next year, I was a twirler with the marching band.

Becoming a cheerleader or a majorette was the ultimate social achievement for a high school girl in Texas. Majorettes wore short shorts and boots with jingle taps, and worked up fabulous routines, marching while twirling a baton in each hand, much like the Coquettes. We marched with the school band in all the parades, but our biggest performances were, of course, halftime shows at the football games. High school football comes right after Jesus and family in Texas, as anyone who has ever seen *Friday Night Lights* can tell you. So the pressure was on for the band and the majorettes. The biggest game of the year was homecoming, when the Quitman Bulldogs played our arch-rivals, the Mineola Yellowjackets.

One homecoming, we prepared a spectacular routine for the end of the halftime show: We had made special batons with asbestos-wrapped tips soaked in kerosene. At the designated moment, each of us twirlers lit the batons and gave the signal for all the stadium lights to be shut off. The band played a drumroll as we marched into the dark center-field, twirling and throwing our double-fire batons high up into the air.

The crowd oohed and ahhed as the flames cut figure eights and spun in the black night. We were giddy; it was a triumph. Meanwhile, back in the locker room, our coach was revving up the team with an inspirational speech and a lot of shouting and chest-thumping. The plan was for the Bulldogs to run out on the field, all pumped and ready to play the second half, as soon as our finale was over and the lights snapped back on.

It all went perfectly as we tossed our fire batons in the air for the last time and gave the signal to flip the switch. The revved-up team burst out of the locker room, into the darkness . . . and straight into a chain-link fence. Nobody had realized how long it takes for halogen lights to fire up again. And so for the next ten to fifteen minutes, our previously pumped-up team milled around aim-lessly in the sputtering half-light, while the coach chewed out our band director in no uncertain terms. I can't remember whether the team won or lost that night, but we didn't get to walk the boys off the field. And I don't think we got to march or play the next few games. We were in the doghouse for a long, long, time.

WHEN I WAS A TEENAGER, my life revolved around school, music, horses, and boys. I had a lot of boyfriends when I was in grade school, but Clifford Zack Cain was the first one to break my heart. Cliff's mother, Imogene, who raised chinchillas behind the tourist court, was one of my mother's close friends, so he and I had known each other since before we could walk. By the time we were in fourth grade, Cliff had been my boyfriend on and off for years. (I thought it was funny that I had one friend named Hill and another named Cliff.) One day Imogene called Mother. "Gin, Clifford Zack wants to give Sissy a little ring." They measured my finger, and before long he gave me a beautiful sterling silver ring with his initials engraved on it. CC. I wore it to school the next day, happily showing it off to everybody.

A few weeks later a new girl moved to town, about four houses down from me. She was really cute, and mature. In fact, she already had breasts. All the boys, including Cliff, started buzzing around her like bees. I was a tomboy and couldn't compete, but I was still surprised when Cliff asked for his ring back. I reluctantly handed it over. I was devastated when he gave it to her! It was humiliating, because everybody knew that ring was for me. My first broken heart didn't last long though, and neither did Cliff's romance with the new girl. I suspect she only wanted the ring in the first place, so she soon got bored and broke up with him. But the ring that had been made especially for me was too small for her and got stuck on her finger. Her father had to get out the tin snips to cut it off. Clifford got the ring back sure enough, in two pieces. Me, I would have sliced my finger off before I clipped that ring.

I WENT ON MY FIRST REAL DATE when I was thirteen, while my parents were away on a road trip with some friends. It was their first vacation without us kids. Ed was about eighteen and home from college, so he was keeping an eye on Robbie and me for a few weeks that summer. Mother and Daddy were visiting Washington, DC, and Monticello in Charlottesville, Virginia. In those days, long-distance calls were expensive, and when our parents phoned home to check in with us, the conversations were generally loud and fast.

When they called one evening, Ed and Robbie got on the line, and after the hellos, Mother said, "Okay, let us talk to Sissy!"

"Um, she's not here," said Ed.

"Well where is she?"

"Oh, she's on a date."

"She's what!? She's never been on a date before! Who let her go on a date?"

"It's okay," said Ed. It was a harmless date, he explained. The boy's mother had picked me up and we'd gone to the movies together. "We held a family council and decided it was time she was allowed to go out with boys."

WHEN WE WERE LITTLE KIDS, the big place to go was Mrs. Huckabee's Sno-Kone stand. It was just a little wooden shed, the size of a guardhouse, set up off the oil road in front of where she lived. It was only big enough to fit Mrs. Huckabee, a cooler of ice, and a Sno-Kone machine attached by a long extension cord to her house. She did a good business on hot school days. When I was in first and second grade, I stopped at Mrs. Huckabee's Sno-Kone stand almost every day on my way to the Wood County courthouse to see my mom and dad. If I had a nickel for a Sno-Kone, the walk downtown seemed much shorter and a whole lot cooler.

There was also a drive-in called the Dairy Bar where you could buy a hamburger, French fries, and a Coke for 26 cents. Then, when I was a young teenager, a Dairy Queen opened on South Main Street, and suddenly the entertainment possibilities in Quitman doubled. We could now get into a car with our dates and slowly cruise between the two drive-ins until we got tired of it and went home. There were dances during the school year, but in summer it was either the drive-ins or Shell Camp a few miles outside of town. That was where the oil company built a pavilion for the community to throw big parties. It was where I had my first kiss, in sixth grade, playing spin the bottle then walking around the building with whomever the bottle had landed on.

My second kiss was on Halloween when I was thirteen. I was dressed up as a flapper; my date, Barry, was a pirate. Barry was the boy who took me to the movies for my first real date. He rode all over town on his turquoise motor scooter. Even though I wasn't allowed to ride on it, I couldn't resist sitting on it in the driveway. Barry and his whole family had strawberry blond hair, like mine. When I cut off my ponytail, that was the end of our romance; he broke up with me. When I was in tenth grade, I started dating Paul Low, a senior and the quarterback of the football team. He was a sweet guy. Paul would call me every night, and the conversations would go something like this:

"Watchoo doin'?"

"Nothing. Watchoo doin'?"

"Nothing."

He would drive by in his gray Ford, a four-on-the-floor he called Old Gray, and we'd spend the evening cruising between the Dairy Queen and the Dairy Bar, or head down to Mineola to walk into movies halfway through and stay until we'd seen the whole thing. Sometimes we'd park by the oil derricks way out in the county. One night after a football game we drove to the derricks in his parents' new Bonneville. My curfew was 10:30 sharp, so at about 10:15 when Paul turned the key in the ignition . . . and nothing happened, I had to be resourceful. I got out of the car, dressed in my majorette uniform and jingle tap boots, and pushed that Bonneville down the hill and through the dust till Paul could pop the clutch and get it started. I had some explaining to do when I finally got home that night.

We dated for a while after he graduated, but our lives drifted in different directions. Paul went on to college, then volunteered for Vietnam. When I was in high school, a lot of boys from Wood County were shipping out to Southeast Asia, and some of them weren't coming back. (Fortunately, Paul did.) All through the mid-to-late sixties, the war was like a faint rumbling in the distance, a reminder that a more precarious world existed beyond the safe cocoon of family and friends and the tranquil streets of Quitman.

LIKE MANY TEXANS MY AGE, I got my first dose of the real world in November 1963, when John F. Kennedy was shot in Dallas. I was in eighth grade, and our big tough junior high principal, Mr. Browning, was crying as he came around to each classroom to tell us that the President was dead and classes were dismissed for the day. My mother drove to school in Ed's red Corvair to pick up Robbie and me. She was crying, too. We were too stunned to speak. It was like the world was coming to an end.

With the rest of the country, my whole family sat transfixed in front of the television set watching the awful events unfold. We saw Lee Harvey Oswald gunned down on live TV, and watched as the President's funeral procession rolled through Washington. I remember feeling so ashamed that the assassination had happened in Texas, and only ninety miles from our front door. I was shocked because I loved Texas so much and couldn't have imagined something so ugly springing from such a wonderful place. But I had read the papers, and I'd seen the inflammatory full-page ad denouncing Kennedy—paid for by the business tycoons Bunker Hunt and Bum Bright—in the *Dallas Morning News* on the day the President was shot. It made me so angry that I wrote a letter to the editor. It was never published, but it was my first political act.

Kennedy was hated by segregationists in Texas and across the South for his support of the Civil Rights Movement. Although the *Brown v. Board of Education* Supreme Court ruling had outlawed separate schools and other public facilities since the mid-1950s, integration came slowly to many parts of the country, including Wood County, Texas. Quitman schools were finally, quietly integrated in 1965. It took a few years before the black and white students started sitting together at the lunch table, but there was no serious trouble. And everybody danced to the same music at the prom.

I think it was because blacks and whites all knew each other so well that we were spared the turmoil that beset so many communities, North and South. Having everybody in the same school seemed as natural as breathing to me. And it was a relief that the last, degrading symbols of Jim Crow were finally gone from my hometown.

Beverly Waddleton, who was two years younger than me, was the first African-American elected to the student council. She was a brilliant girl, the daughter of Joe Waddleton, my father's favorite mechanic, so I had known her all my life. After integration, Beverly rose to the top of her class at Quitman High School. She gave the salutatorian speech two years after I graduated. Beverly went on to college and medical school, and then returned to our hometown as a family practitioner. Since then she's been Quitman's most beloved doctor and runs the East Texas Medical Center.

Dr. Waddleton remembers how my father went out of his way to support her and her friends as they navigated the new, integrated Quitman. Daddy used to pick up Beverly and drive everybody to and from the 4-H camp. Beverly thought that was completely wonderful, except for one thing: The kids just wanted to get home at the end of the day, but Daddy insisted on stopping at every historical marker between the camp and Quitman.

··· NEW YORK ···

··· 6 ···

ROBBIE WAS REALLY THE ACTOR IN THE FAMILY. HE WAS handsome, talented, and relaxed; he got roles in all the school plays. I never did. After I won the Oscar for Best Actress for *Coal Miner's Daughter*, my mother ran into our high school drama teacher in the grocery store. She must have been feeling a little sensitive, because she pushed her cart right up to Mother's and said, "Well, I guess you wonder why Sissy never got into any of the school plays."

"No, actually, I never really gave it any thought," said Mother.

"Well, she didn't learn her lines!" she said, as she moved on down the aisle.

Because a career in high school theater was obviously out of the question, I poured my efforts into music. I carried my guitar with me wherever I went, singing for anybody who would listen. I performed for seniors at the old folks' home, kids at their grade school assemblies, church functions, parties, Rotary Club meetings, between acts at school plays. Late at night, I would sit cross-legged on my bed, hugging that guitar and plucking out tunes, then writing lyrics in a spiral notebook, on napkins, paper bags—whatever was available. I wrote songs like "Tiny People," about young people wanting to be older, older people wanting to be younger, and nobody being satisfied to be who they are; and "Sweet Cheeks," about laughing so hard that your cheeks hurt. We had a lot to laugh about in our house, most of it instigated by Robbie.

· · ·

As MY BROTHERS and I became teenagers, Mother and Daddy would always say, "If you want to drink and smoke, do it at home. Don't go off drinking and driving in a car somewhere." So one evening when Robbie was about fifteen, he walked into the den while we were all watching TV and plopped himself down in a chair. He was holding a beer in one hand and a cigar in the other. We all stared at him while he casually lit the cigar. Finally my father said, "Robbie, what do you think you're doing? Have you lost your mind?"

Robbie just grinned and took a puff.

"Well, you said if I wanted to smoke or drink, to do it at home," he said. "So here I am!"

My parents could hardly get angry; after all, it was their idea. Ed never tried to pull anything like that. He was perfect. I was the sneaky one, but just never got caught—even the time I was playing with matches and set the backyard on fire. But Robbie was an open book. He was always up to something, most of it funny.

EVEN THOUGH ROBBIE and I fought like cats and dogs sometimes, we were best friends, even as teenagers. I used to pick out his clothes for him. I didn't let him pick out mine, but he would stop me from going out of the house if he thought my skirt was too short.

"You're not wearing that, Sissy," he'd say.

"Why? What's wrong with it?"

"Trust me."

We did everything together, and we had a lot of the same friends. Most of my girlfriends had crushes on him. He went out on dates, but most of the time he was busy with sports, or hunting and fishing, or just keeping up with his studies.

School was always easy for me, but not for Robbie. He was dyslexic, although we didn't know the term back then. All we knew was that he had a hard time learning to read and write, even though he was very smart. If he had to write things down on a test, he struggled. But if you asked him the questions out loud, he got every one right. So he had to work twice as hard as everyone else on his class work to keep from falling behind.

When we were little, Mother would spend hours with Robbie, helping him with his homework. Before too long, I'd be tugging at her sleeve and making a lot of noise that it was my turn. I needed to read a story out loud to her. "Sissy," she would say, "why don't you take your book into my bedroom and read out loud to yourself?" I thought that was a wonderful idea. My parents had a full-length mirror on their closet door, and I loved to sit in front of it and read aloud to myself. I would give all the characters different voices and imagine how they would behave in the stories. I might not have known it then, but this could have been the dawn of my acting career.

Robbie made it through elementary school with a combination of charm and determination. When he was in seventh grade, he took up track and football and met a coach who changed his life.

My brother could run like a deer. Even when he was a tiny boy, my dad had a hard time keeping up with him. If he got into trouble and knew my dad was looking for him, he would race around the house as fast as he could to avoid a spanking. Daddy knew there was no possible way to catch Robbie. He would have to outsmart him. One day he waited for Robbie to circle the house, and when he came around the corner, Daddy stepped out in front of him. It frightened Robbie so, he shot straight up in the air. Daddy fell over laughing and gave up any idea of punishing him. Robbie was such a fetching child, you just couldn't stay mad at him. When Robbie and I were still in diapers, Mother would put us down for naps in the same room. He hated naps and always managed to escape from his crib. Often he made it clear out of the house. Somehow he was able to unlatch the screen and crawl out. My mother happened to look out the kitchen window one afternoon and saw Robbie out on the back road, wearing only his diaper, marching up and down through a puddle with one of Daddy's hunting rifles over his shoulder while the other neighborhood mothers grabbed their own children and pulled them inside to safety.

Another afternoon, when Robbie was eight or nine, the whole family was driving back from picking blackberries in the country when a jackrabbit ran down the road. Robbie shouted, "Daddy, let me out! Let me out! I want to catch that rabbit!"

"Oh, Robbie, you can't catch a rabbit," my dad said. "It's too fast."

"No, Daddy! Let me out! I can catch him!"

So Daddy pulled the car over and opened the door. He was chuckling to himself, figuring this would teach his son a lesson. Robbie took off down the road and disappeared into the thicket. A few minutes later, Robbie reappeared holding the rabbit.

When Robbie joined the track team, his coach, Fred Billings, started working with him to channel his energy into running and help him focus on his schoolwork. Before long, Robbie was making better grades than I was because he worked so hard at it. And once he started competing on the sports field, nobody could beat him. By the time he was in high school, he was a bona fide star in the relay race and hurdles. The whole family would go out to watch him run at all of his track meets. Daddy took reel after reel of 8mm home movies that captured Robbie's grace as he flew over the hurdles and his long strides as he sprinted across the finish line.

IN MAY OF 1966, when he was a high school junior and I was a sixteen-year-old sophomore, Robbie started to feel run down. He was still running and winning, but he was tired all the time and achy at night; he just didn't feel right. At first we thought it might be a cold or flu that he couldn't shake, or maybe he was training too hard.

One night I was arguing with Robbie about something, and Mother pulled me into another room for a private talk.

"Please be patient with Robbie," she said. "I'm worried about him.

He could be really sick." She paused for a moment, then said, "He might even have leukemia."

"Oh, Mother," I snapped. "He's fine!" He was my brother; nothing could happen to him.

My parents took Robbie to see Ben Merritt, our family doctor who had known us kids just about all our lives. He examined him and did some blood tests. When they came back from the lab, Ben just couldn't bring himself to tell us. So he sent Robbie to a hematologist in Tyler, who finally made the diagnosis. Mother had been right.

It was surreal. We'd gotten a diagnosis, but we really didn't know what it meant. We didn't know how afraid to be. I guess mostly we felt kind of numb.

After the initial shock, our family rallied together and approached Robbie's illness as a problem that could be confronted, like any other. My uncle Wade Spilman, who had been in the Texas legislature and knew everybody important in the state, arranged for Robbie to be admitted to one of the best hospitals in the country for the treatment of leukemia and other cancers: MD Anderson in Houston. My mother called our friend and high school principal, W. T. Black, to let him know that Robbie would be missing the rest of the semester, while Robbie told his coach and his teammates the bad news. He had to start chemotherapy right away. But he had one last thing to do before going into the hospital.

Robbie had been training hard all year to qualify for the state track finals in Austin the next weekend. Our plan had been to drive down, meet up with Ed, attend the meet together, and watch Robbie win. But now, of course, all that would change.

First Robbie called the boy that he had beaten to make it to the finals and said, "I'm not gonna be able to run, and I wanted you to know that you're up." Then we drove on to Austin as planned. I know Robbie wanted to be there to cheer on his teammates, but also, I think, to help steel himself for the unknown that he was facing. When we got to the stadium, Robbie went down to the track to see the runner who had taken his place. He shook his hand, wished him good luck, and helped him set his blocks.

One of the officials saw Robbie in his street clothes and yelled for him to get off the field. But the young man stepped between them and said, "No, no, no. You don't understand. He should be the one running. He beat me."

My brother was in and out of MD Anderson for the next sixteen months.

Robbie's illness turned our ordinary, orderly lives upside down. Mother was no longer working at the courthouse, and Daddy took a leave of absence from his job as the county agriculture agent. We rented an apartment in Houston to be near the hospital during Robbie's treatments. Ed commuted back and forth from college in Austin, and I did the same from Quitman. I missed a lot of school, but my teachers let me make up the work. Sometimes my grandmother would come up from Granger to stay with me. Sometimes I lived with the other Spaceks, my aunt and uncle Sam and Maurine, and my cousins Jan and Sam. Sometimes it was just me and the dog. I had to grow up fast in those months, but everyone in Quitman looked out for me.

When I was in Houston, I spent all my time with Robbie on the hospital's sixth-floor pediatric cancer wing. I made friends with the other leukemia patients, who were all young teenage boys, like Robbie. We got to know their families. In fact, we became like one extended family, all facing the same challenge.

The treatment for leukemia wipes out the good blood cells along with the cancer cells, so after chemotherapy, the patients are extremely susceptible to infections. Robbie and the other boys often couldn't leave the hospital, and it got boring for them pretty quickly. It was always a cause for celebration when someone's blood counts went up and they could go out and be teenagers for a little while. When Robbie's counts were high enough, we'd go out for lunch or to a movie, or even to the Astrodome for a ball game. If any of his friends had good enough counts, we'd take them along with us to join in the fun.

Every Wednesday there was a big party on the sixth floor. We'd decorate the lounge and serve refreshments. I'd bring my guitar and put on a concert. Sometimes football players or astronauts from the Houston Space Center came by to visit. Robbie had his picture taken with an astronaut and thought it was pretty cool. It made the boys feel like they mattered; that they hadn't been forgotten just because they were ill.

Robbie had been so healthy and strong before he developed leukemia, and he just couldn't get used to being sick. He refused to give in to the disease, and rarely lost his sense of humor. In his mind, he was still in training. And so every day, when Freddie, everyone's favorite orderly, would pull the big trash cans out of the rooms and into the hall to be picked up and emptied, Robbie would run down the hallway and hurdle them. Often there would be a huge cheer.

WHEN ROBBIE'S COUNTS WERE GOOD, he could stay with us in the apartment we rented in Houston. Robbie's friends from home would take turns coming down to visit. One time Daddy took some Super 8 footage of Robbie and me and a few girlfriends from Quitman lounging around the pool at our apartment complex. In the film, Robbie looks relaxed and handsome, in a white shirt and chinos over a long, lean runner's body. When he puts his arm around my shoulders, I barely come up to his neck. Later, Daddy filmed Robbie sitting quietly in a lawn chair, occasionally looking over and smiling. My father, who usually liked to move the camera around, held the shot on his son for a long time, as if he were trying to memorize him.

It was difficult when one by one, our friends on the sixth floor would die, and the boys who were left would wonder if their number was up next. When a patient died, it affected all of us: the other patients, the families, the nurses, the orderlies, and the doctors. The staff was so caring and emotionally involved with the patients that I wondered how they could carry on in the face of such constant loss. Of all the boys on the sixth floor, I only knew of one who was cured and sent home. He was a beacon of hope for all of us.

There were times of brief remission between treatments when Robbie was well enough to come home to Quitman for short visits. One time I found him waiting for me in the driveway when I got home from school. He was sitting in the sun on the back of our big old 1956 Buick, grinning from ear to ear, holding up the *Dallas Morning News*. The headline said, CURE FOUND FOR LEUKEMIA. There were so many times like that, when we would all get our hopes up, only to have them dashed.

Robbie had always wanted a sports car, and my dad decided to buy him one. They walked into a foreign car showroom in Houston to look at a Triumph, which was the car Robbie had always wanted, but right next to it was an Austin Healey 3000 Mark III convertible in British racing green. It was love at first sight. Daddy bought that Austin Healey for Robbie on the spot. He could drive around town with the top down, when the chemo wasn't making him sick as a dog. That fall he was well enough to drive the car back home for a visit. He even drove the Healey in the high school homecoming parade, with some of his teammates perched on the back. Robbie's hair was growing back in thin patches and his face was swollen from steroids, but he had that old familiar smile as he cruised slowly up Main Street. I was right in front of him, marching with the band in my white Keds and short shorts, twirling my baton for all it was worth.

Robbie kept up his schoolwork while he was in Houston, and that spring he was able to graduate with his senior class. When he walked to the podium to receive his diploma, the crowd gave him a standing ovation. It was like the whole town of Quitman was up there with him.

ROBBIE TOOK ME FOR A DRIVE one night in the Austin Healey. When we reached the farmland outside of town, where the road was flat and straight, Robbie opened up the engine. The little sports car growled happily, like a captive animal that was finally set free. With the top down and the wind lashing my hair around my face, Robbie kept going faster and faster until we were flying along that two-lane road at one hundred miles an hour. To me, it was exhilarating, even better than riding the Tubs at the Old Settlers' Reunion. But after a few minutes, Robbie eased off the gas pedal and coasted down to a modest speed, then turned toward home.

"I shouldn't have done that," he said, not looking at me.

"Why? It was fun!"

"No, I shouldn't have done that with you in the car. I've got nothing to lose, but you do."

OUR MOTHER WAS STEADY as a rock through Robbie's illness. She never once left his side when he was sick from chemo, and spent every night with him in the hospital, sleeping in a chair or on a cot. Something deep within her kept her going. My dad put on a brave face, but it was a struggle. He had always been our protector. If he said it was going to rain, it did. If he said it was warm enough to go barefoot, it was. But this was something different, something so big, even he couldn't protect us from it.

With his scientist's mind, he researched everything he could about leukemia, trying to find any connection between the disease and the chemicals that were used to kill weeds and pests. He wondered if the radiation treatments Robbie had taken to clear up his skin might have been the trigger, or being downwind from the nuclear testing at Los Alamos, or even the benign-looking shoe-measuring machine in Hirsch's store that bombarded our feet with gamma rays. There was never a definitive answer, of course, and never would be.

I was cheerful as always, at least on the outside, tackling the world with a confident smile. But the weight of my brother's illness had landed square on my shoulders. I felt helpless. I would wake up in the morning, fresh, my worries washed away with sleep. And then I would remember:

89

It wasn't a bad dream. Robbie was still sick. The fear and grief would come in waves, and sometimes a lump rose in my throat that I couldn't swallow.

Now, when I sat in my room to write songs, often in an empty house, the melodies came out in a minor key, and the lyrics were different. My parents were concerned about me. And so, when the opportunity came along for me to get away from Texas for a couple of months, they decided to let me go.

DESPITE MY FREQUENT ABSENCES, I had managed to keep up my school activities during junior year. I dated; I went to twirling practice and attended my junior prom. That spring I even entered the Dogwood Queen beauty pageant. I had talent, but I didn't have much height. At five feet, two and a half inches, I had been the tallest girl in sixth grade, and then I stopped short. My mom took me to see Ben Merritt and asked him if I would grow any more. The doctor looked at me and shook his head. "Oh sure, she'll grow, just not north or south," he said. The other girls in the pageant were more beauty queen material, but I won second place and the talent competition, playing my guitar and singing my songs. My performance caught the attention of one of the judges, a writer from the style section of the newspaper in Longview, a city in the oil fields east of Quitman. She hired me to sing and play at parties, where I was a big hit. That summer, she invited me to go along with her to New York, where she was covering a week of fashion shows. She thought it would be a fun distraction for me. My plan was to fly up with her and then stay with my cousin Rip and his family in Manhattan.

At first my parents were reluctant to send a seventeen-year-old who had rarely been out of Texas on her own to New York City. And I was torn between wanting to go, and worrying about leaving Robbie. His remissions were getting shorter, and he was growing weaker. But he encouraged me to go and have a good time. We even talked about him coming up there if his blood counts got better.

My whole family went with me to the airport, Love Field in Dallas, where I was supposed to meet up with the woman from Longview. She had a regular ticket to New York; I was flying student standby on the Fourth of July weekend. She got on the plane, but I was stuck in the airport for the next two days as every flight to New York filled up with soldiers before I could get on. I never saw that fashion writer again. Rip rented a car to pick me up at Kennedy Airport and was waiting for me there for nearly twenty-four hours, meeting every flight from Dallas—there were no cell phones in 1967, so we weren't able to reach him. He eventually gave up and went home.

It was my first time flying, but when I finally got on an airplane, I was so exhausted that most of my excitement had drained away. But at the end of the flight, when I saw those New York skyscrapers stretched out below me, filling the whole window from one end to the other, I felt a thrill race through my body. And I knew, with all the conviction of my seventeen years, that I would never be quite the same again.

I stepped into the sweltering terminal wearing patent leather shoes, a suit, and carrying my two guitars. I may even have been wearing gloves. I had bleached my hair blond and rolled it into a straight pageboy with bangs, like Mary from Peter, Paul and Mary. I was so young, people would have thought I was a runaway, except that I was so appropriately dressed. My dad had instructed me to take a taxi to Rip's address in Chelsea. "And act like you've been there before," he said. So I got into the front seat with the cabdriver. On the ride into Manhattan I nearly wrenched my neck gaping up at all the tall buildings, just like the kid from Texas I so obviously was.

The sign above the doorbell on the Chelsea brownstone said: TORN PAGE. I thought that was so clever and romantic, just like the wonderful couple who lived in that house with their three young children.

Rip had met the brilliant actor Geraldine Page in 1959, when they were both performing in the Broadway production of Tennessee Williams's *Sweet Bird of Youth*. My handsome cousin from Taylor, Texas, had hitchhiked to Hollywood when he was in his early twenties, hoping to be a movie star. But he ended up moving to New York City in the late fifties to hone his skills as an actor, studying with Lee Strasberg at the Actors Studio. When she married Rip in 1963, Geraldine Page had been a force on Broadway for more than a decade. Around that time she starred in a couple of film versions of Williams's plays, and the Hollywood press declared her an "overnight success." "That's the longest night I've ever seen," she said. She was funny and elegant, with a soft, lovely voice and the most beautiful hands.

When I arrived at their doorstep, the poor country cousin, Rip and Gerry were the toast of the New York theater and art scene. Gerry was starring in the Broadway production of *Black Comedy/White Lies*, doing eight performances a week. Yet they opened a space in their busy lives and made me feel safe and welcome.

Rip had an office on the second floor, with a piano, a rehearsal space, a bathroom, and a fold-out couch. He turned it into a room for me. When I opened my eyes on my first morning in New York, Rip and Gerry's three babies—Angelica and the twin boys, Tony and John, who were still in diapers—were quietly staring at me, inches from my face, waiting for me to wake up. I had big curlers in my hair and must have looked like an alien life form to them.

Gerry couldn't have been kinder to me. I had only met her briefly, at a family gathering in Texas, but this time we bonded instantly. She wanted to hear me play my guitar, and she seemed to love the songs I had written. From the moment I arrived, she took me under her wing and brought me everywhere with her.

That evening I wrote my first postcard from the city.

Hi Robbie,

    I got here fine. John and Tony and Angelica are just darling. We took a ride all over New York today. Took about four hours. I just love Gerry, she's great, just like a plain person. Will write again soon.

    Love, Sissy

92

It was a wonderful, child-centered household. Because both Rip and Gerry were working so much, the children had a live-in nanny. And yet there was a cozy, homey atmosphere. The children's artwork was everywhere. Rip loved to cook, and on most days he would make dinner for the whole family. Sometimes his eldest daughter, Danae, would visit. The kitchen was always piled with boxes of fan mail, which they would just push up to the table and throw a tablecloth over when they needed to set an extra place. Occasionally other actors, artists, and writers would stop in to see them.

Rip kept his motorcycle chained out front. Sometimes I'd watch from my window as Gerry would hop on it sidesaddle and wrap her arms around him. Then Rip would tie the big chain around his waist, secure it with a padlock, and off they would ride. I was thoroughly dazzled.

Dear Mother, Daddy, and Robbie,

Last night I went to my first two Broadway shows. Gerry stars in both. She's just great! I got to stay in her dressing room between plays and watch her put on makeup. Also got a front row seat. I really felt like a big shot, cause every day everybody was saying, "Miss Page this and Miss Page that," and introducing me to everybody. I just love her to death. Well, I'll write you again tonight. Having a great time!

Love, Sissy

Black Comedy/White Lies was an evening of two one-act plays, performed back-to-back. In the first, Gerry played a very sexy woman who entered the stage wearing nothing but a man's pajama top; then she transformed herself into an old fortune-teller in the next play. I went to the theater with her every night and I was in awe of her acting. Anne Jackson, another great actor and a friend of Gerry's, once described her genius: "She used a stage like no one else I'd ever seen. It was like playing tennis with someone who had twenty-six arms." I ended up watching the show from nearly every seat in the Ethel Barrymore Theatre.

One of the great perks of having a close relative star on Broadway was that I literally had the run of the place. I made friends with the stagehands and prop people. I played pinochle with the guys down in the basement who were running the lights. The theater became like the courthouse in Quitman, a place for me to snoop around and explore. We practically lived at the theater during Gerry's run. For Wednesday matinees, Rip would bring the children there between the afternoon and evening performances, and order spaghetti and meatballs from Sardi's, which we'd eat in the dressing room. Waiters in starched linen jackets served the dinner from large silver platters with silver domed lids. It was a far cry from El Chico's in Tyler, Texas.

Another wonderful Broadway tradition is that many nights just before curtain, the stage managers of all the plays walk the stars' children to different stage doors so they can watch other shows. I got to see everything. Judy Garland was on Broadway that summer, and I crossed paths with her daughter, Liza Minnelli.

I fell in love with the theater, but I still wasn't interested in acting. For starters, I'd had that unfortunate high school theater experience, and I didn't want to embarrass Rip and Gerry if I turned out to be as terrible as my teacher had suggested. Music was what I knew, and that's where I probably had the best chance of succeeding. Making it as a singer/songwriter was a dream. Both Gerry and Rip were supportive. I'd bring my guitar to Gerry's dressing room and play for her while she dressed for the show. She was sensitive and sweet, and sometimes my songs would make her cry. There was one she liked so much, she had me play it over and over, and she would weep every time.

Today, for the life of me, I can't remember a word or a note of it.

ONCE I GOT ACCUSTOMED to the city, I started to venture off on my own. I was warned to stay away from the subways, which could be dangerous, but the buses were fine, so I would take the bus to explore different neighborhoods. New York was so different and exciting that

94

sometimes it overwhelmed my senses. One day I stepped out of a city bus into the middle of a summer downpour. I can still smell the rain on hot concrete, and the exhaust of the bus, and the musky smell of wet clothes and perfume as everybody tried to huddle under one awning until the storm passed. I looked over and right beside me was the most beautiful girl. She wore gads of makeup and had Twiggy eyelashes painted on her lids, like little black starbursts. I thought, *If I could be just like her . . .* I ran straight to the nearest drugstore and bought eyeliner and false eyelashes.

There were so many things I could be. And I had all the time in the world.

Dear Robbie,

In Greenwich Village one can have their picture drawn in ten minutes! It's really amazing. . . . The Village is great. I've met all sorts of people there—hippies, thousands of them! They gather at Washington Square on Sundays and play their guitars.

Love, Sissy

Dear Mom and Dad and Robbie,

I get in free to all the Broadway shows. Neat! Anyway I was in Gerry's dressing room playing my guitar when in walked Jordan Christopher. He's the guy from England who married Sybil Burton. He's so cute! Anyway. He and two friends—Bobby somebody and Billy something—have just formed a record company and he wants me to make the first record. He said that the whole group could get together this Monday and they'd try to write a song that I would like and we'd record in a couple of weeks. But in the meantime I have another audition Tuesday with another outfit, and since I know so little about this, Gerry called Rip in California to see whether I should get an agent, but he said to wait on that, so that I could be sure to get the best deal. All of this is not for sure yet. But things look good. Jordan is really a go-getter with lots of money and very cute. He was really excited over me and said that

my name and the Texas bit would go over big. He also owns and operates
a very swanky nightclub in New York.

Also I'm happy to report that I have approximately $188 left.

Love,

Sissy

Jordan Christopher, whom I've learned was actually from Ohio, was a very glamorous figure in New York. He was an actor in the cast of Gerry's play, but he was even better known as the young husband of Sybil Burton, who had been married to Richard Burton until he left her for Elizabeth Taylor on the set of *Cleopatra*. Sybil had moved to New York and opened Arthur, an incredibly hip club on West 54th Street. (It was named for George Harrison's famous line: When a reporter sarcastically asked the mop-topped Beatle what he called "that haircut" he wore, George replied, "I call it Arthur.") Jordan met Sybil when his band, the Wild Ones, played in her nightclub. I'm glad to say that Jordan and Sybil remained happily married for the rest of their lives together.

I must have had kind of a crush on him. I don't think we ever tried to write any songs together, but my encounter with him was typical of the sort of life I was leading that summer. Rip and Gerry took me everywhere with them, to restaurants and discotheques all over New York City. I couldn't tell you who I met that summer because I didn't know enough to even realize who I was meeting. It was a bit like casting pearls before swine! Mostly I just sat there and listened to them talk, wishing and hoping that one day I might be part of the conversation. That's all I ever wanted—not fame or glory, just a seat at the table and something worthwhile to say.

One night in the private back room at some fabulous club where Rip and Gerry had taken me, Gerry asked me to play my guitar for a group of their friends. I sang a song I had written about Robbie, with the lyric "I feel a soft touch while I'm sleeping, I hear his voice everywhere." When I was finished, a disheveled older man with thick glasses named Terry came over and asked me if I was a virgin. When I got over the shock of being asked such a question, I sputtered, "I don't think that's any of your business." I didn't know at the time that Terry Southern was a famous novelist and screenwriter, who had cowritten *Candy*, about a naive eighteen-year-old girl's sexual misadventures. At the time he was researching another book and would soon write the screenplay for *Easy Rider*. He kept asking me all these questions about my sexual experiences. He was convinced that the words to my song proved that I was sexually active. Gerry was reclining on a chaise lounge, listening to all of this with her eyes closed, when calmly, and without ever opening her eyes, she said, "Terry, darling. You don't have to stomp grapes to know how wine tastes!" She was so brilliant.

BECAUSE PEOPLE WERE TAKING an interest in my songs, Rip decided I should talk to an agent, and he arranged an audition at the William Morris Agency. It was so exciting that I made a long-distance call to Texas to tell my parents. Daddy picked up the phone, and I heard him shout the news to my mother.

"Gin! Sissy's gonna sing for William Morris!"

"Oh, isn't that grand," I heard her say. "Who's William Morris?"

When it came time for the audition, I was ushered into a conference room in a very tall building. Five men in suits walked in and sat down. After I sang my songs, they stood up and filed back out. A short time later, one of them popped his head back into the room and said, "We think you should go home to Texas, lose the accent, and come back when you're older."

My brother Ed, who had just graduated from college and was working for Decca Records in Dallas, set up an audition for me at their New York offices. *This time*, I thought, *I'll wear my lucky socks and sing every song I know.* But it turned out to be a lot like the William Morris meeting. Men wearing dark suits filed in, listened, then filed back out. The A&R guy said he liked my music, but Decca already had somebody on their roster who sounded very much like me. She was a country singer named Loretta Lynn. I said, "Loretta *who?*" I had never heard of her, and I was sure that whoever she was, I didn't sound like her.

I WASN'T GOING to let a few rejections get me down. I knew now that I wanted to be a musician, and I was so in love with New York that I didn't even want to go back to finish high school. I could have stayed forever. But I also knew that this was only for the summer, and the news from home was not good. Robbie was not improving. His letters to me from Houston were usually upbeat and newsy, telling me about the Austin Healey that always seemed to be in the shop for repairs, or needling me for not writing more often ("Sissy, thanks for all the letters I haven't got yet!"). But one letter just about killed me.

> *Dear Sissy,*
>
> *How is my little sister doing?*
>
> *My temperature is still not just right, it goes up and down every day so we don't know what's happening, The treatment still hasn't worked, so they are just waiting to see what is happening on that problem too. They will have to give me another treatment and I am kind of scared because it hasn't worked, and I want to get out of the hospital and come see you Sissy. I really miss you and I am worried about my counts and if I can get out, but the way it looks now I will probably be here a month or so because of the treatment not working. I am really worried, Sissy, because I haven't seen anybody, just hospital people since you left and that has been a long time. I want to get out of this place and I can't stand being in this place not seeing any kids or friends its terrible. You and Ed are doing just great probably both have what you want for the rest of your life, but I was the black sheep getting sick and everything, I feel like I will never get to do anything like you are doing—just stay with Mother and Dad probably for the rest of my life, how long that is probably not long.*

I just hope you and Ed don't get anything wrong like me, and have to ruin your whole life. I don't know what I am going to do Sissy—I can't be with Mother and Dad all my life. I am so much of a problem now that I have Leukemia and I just hope that I will be cured some day that's all I want in life is to be healthy nothing else.

Love, Rob

(Write me every day. Really Sissy, please.)

And I did.

Then one day late in August, Rip came into my room and said, "Your parents called, Sissy, and they want you to come home. They need you there." I flew back to Texas the next day.

By the time I arrived in Houston, Robbie's condition was much worse. He had developed an infection that the doctors were trying to fight with massive antibiotics. My parents and I sat with him every day as he faded in and out of consciousness.

While I was in New York, I'd been in suspended animation. Robbie wasn't sick anymore, and none of this was happening. Things were good. We made plans for the future. We'd share a place in Manhattan, we'd ride the subways, we'd go dancing and laugh off bad auditions. But I was back home now, in Texas, sitting in my brother's hospital room. Robbie was gravely ill. I couldn't pretend anymore or wish it away. It was real.

We never gave up hope that he might somehow pull through this crisis, even after he developed septicemia. The school year had already begun, so I had to make a decision. My parents and I agreed that I should attend school in Houston so that we could all be there together. Moments after I'd gotten back from enrolling in the school, Mother called. Robbie was gone. I looked at the date: September 19, 1967.

It was strange, but we'd fought so long and so hard to hang on to Robbie, that I'd never even considered how life would be without him. I felt a huge void. I was lost.

· · · 7 · · ·

THE NEXT FEW DAYS WERE SURREAL. I MET MY PARENTS at the hospital, and then we went back to the apartment to pack our bags. Within hours, I was driving my brother's Austin Healey back to Quitman, while Mother and Daddy followed in their car. Ed was coming from Dallas to meet us at home. I had the strangest, haunting feeling as I rolled down the highway, like we'd forgotten something. But of course, it was Robbie we had left behind.

I recall almost nothing of the three-hundred-mile trip home; it evaporated like a dream. But I remember arriving in Quitman, and seeing cars parked up and down the highway in front of our house. My first thought was *Oh my God, something terrible has happened!* Then I remembered. I felt like I was floating.

News had spread quickly, and dozens and dozens of friends and relatives were waiting for us at the house. Flowers, covered dishes, and trays of cold cuts arrived with them. I've never seen so many casseroles in my life, or had so many hugs. We felt cradled by our little town, like babies—they held us and fed us, cared for us and loved us. I was so happy to see everybody after being gone all summer that I was crying and laughing at the same time, bursting with news between bouts of grief.

It was a comfort to know that our good friend Gaston Cain, the undertaker, the mayor, the fire chief, and the father of two of my closest friends, Pam and Debra, had driven to Houston and brought Robbie's body back to Quitman. Once he arrived, I felt better somehow. He was back home now, among people who loved him.

I had grown up playing in that funeral home. When I was little, I'd spend the night with Pam and Debra, and we'd play in the garage where they kept all the caskets for sale. We'd poke around in them, looking into their beautiful velvet interiors and at their shiny polished wood. And we'd play in the large wooden crates that they were shipped in and make forts and playhouses.

It felt strange to think that Robbie was gone. I kept waiting for him to walk in the door. They laid him out in a casket, but it wasn't Robbie who was there. Once someone's spirit has left their body, it isn't them anymore. It's like the figures in a wax museum or after a cicada crawls out of its shell.

The whole town came to Robbie's funeral. It was the first time I ever saw my father wear sunglasses in church. Then we all gathered back home after the service. Everyone told stories about Robbie, laughing and crying about the time he caught the jackrabbit, about the time he lit the cigar in the family room. Robbie was still very much alive in our household. His photographs were everywhere, and his track trophies and medals still had their place of honor.

He hasn't been forgotten, and rarely a day goes by that I don't think about him. Whenever our family gets together, we still talk about him. Not too long ago, my nephew, Stephen, asked, "Did I know Robbie? I knew Robbie, didn't I?"

"No, he died before you were born," I said. "But yes, you knew him."

I owe it to my mother for pulling us all through such a catastrophe, and for keeping Robbie so present in our lives. She never lost sight of her positive approach to life. Norman Vincent Peale served us well. "It's not what happens to you in life," she'd say, "but how you respond to it." Now we witnessed how true she was to those words. My mother was determined that something good would come from Robbie's death, if only that his loss would strengthen us as a family and make us appreciate the time that we were given here on earth. She wanted his life to inspire us to lead full and rich ones, and it has. I try to live with no re-grets. I want to know that if I get hit by a truck tomorrow, I will have returned my neighbor's cake pan. And I'll have told the people close to me that I love them.

Rather than making my parents overprotective, I think Robbie's death made them more willing to let me go. For me, the grief was almost like rocket fuel. It made me fearless. And I lost interest in trivial things.

I STARTED MY SENIOR YEAR at Quitman High School weeks after the semester had begun. When I returned to classes, everything seemed different. Even the corridors of the high school looked smaller than I remembered. I had been a model student, but now I stopped caring much about school. Luckily my high school principal, W. T. Black, ran interference for me with my teachers. He'd tell them, hey, she's been a straight-A student, she missed six weeks of classes, give her a pass. Most teachers were wonderful; Mr. Black took care of the ones who weren't.

W. T. Black was an unusual principal. You could hear him laughing all the way down the hall, and when he laughed, he'd lift up his knee and slap his thigh. And that would make him laugh even more. I lived two blocks from school, but I couldn't seem to manage to get there on time. I was usually only a minute or two late, but I'd have to drive by his office in Robbie's Austin Healey to get to the parking lot. The muffler was so loud, I would push the clutch in as I rounded the corner by Mr. Black's office so he wouldn't hear my car and know I was going to be late. Most times it worked, but occasionally I would be sent to his office and he would sigh and say, "Now, Sissy. I don't want to have to call your mother. What am I going to say to Gin? Huh? So please . . . just get up ten minutes earlier. Won't you?" He was such a nice man.

Senior year is supposed to be so cool, but I had lost interest in being a majorette or going out for any of the other school activities that used to mean so much to me. I'd lost my brother, and I'd been to New York. That's where my head was; New York was my light at the end of the tunnel. If I could make it through senior year, I could go back next summer. So I went through the motions of being a high school student. I attended the homecoming dance that fall, and I was elected homecoming queen. It was a gesture of kindness from my classmates, to let me know how much they cared. They wanted to do something for me, to try and make me feel better—and they did.

The only thing that I still felt passion for was my music. My brother Ed was a promotion man with Decca Records, someone who carried the label's latest singles to radio stations and convinced the DJs to play them on the air. Ed would bring some of those records home when he visited, and it opened up a whole new world of music for me, from Jackie Wilson to the Doors and the Rolling Stones. I was listening to folk singers like Judy Collins and, soon, Joni Mitchell, and the Byrds, who later morphed into Crosby, Stills & Nash and other folk rock groups. I kept writing songs, mostly with sober themes, but gradually the lyrics became playful again. After sleepwalking through the first semester of senior year, I gradually returned to life. I kept the experiences of the past two years locked safely away, like the treasures in my old cigar box, and no one outside my closest family could tell the difference in me.

I DON'T KNOW WHY I could never master the Spanish language. I had been hearing it all my life down in the Rio Grande Valley, and when I was very young I could even speak a little Tex-Mex. But once I sat down in Spanish class, everything I knew drained out of my head and never came back. I managed to get high Bs, but it was a struggle. This annoyed my teacher, Sarah McIntosh, to no end. Miss Mac just couldn't understand why I had trouble with something that was so easy for her. She must have thought I wasn't trying. Or maybe she knew my friends and I were the ones who had wrapped her house with toilet paper one Halloween night. She also didn't like the way I wore my hair, with bangs down below my eyebrows. "Why don't you cut those bangs so you can see!" she told me in front of the other students. "And take off those glasses!" I had recently gotten glasses to correct my nearsightedness and astigmatism. Miss Mac wouldn't let me wear them in her class. They were very fashion-forward, round tortoiseshell glasses—today we'd call them Harry Potter glasses—and for some reason she disliked them. (Really, I think it was me she didn't like.) The only thing I liked about her class was that I was elected fire marshal by the other students. I may not have been Spanish Club president, but if the school caught on fire, I was the one who would lead them out of the building to safety— although not in Spanish.

During my senior year, the elected officers in Miss Mac's class had the chance to attend the Spanish Club convention at the University Interscholastic League conference in Austin. I was getting excited about the four-day trip until Miss Mac broke the news that I was not going— being elected fire marshal didn't seem to count. I was devastated, but I saw a way around her decision. There was a contest to win one slot at the convention by writing an essay—in English, thank God—about why you wanted to attend. The entries were submitted without names, just numbers. I can't remember what I wrote, but it must have been convincing because my paper was picked. Miss Mac's face fell when the winning number was announced and I raised my hand. She was so upset that she changed the rules to keep me from going. Still undaunted, I heard that the Interscholastic League was having a big talent show during the convention. I entered the contest and won a place in the competition. Now she couldn't stop me from going. Miss Mac was peeved because I had defied her and beaten the system. That's probably another reason she didn't like me: I would never give up. So when six or seven deserving Spanish students, Miss Mac, and a couple of chaperones piled into a van for the ride to Austin, my guitar and I rode along with them.

The talent contest was in a huge auditorium at the University of Texas that held about three thousand people. Kids and teachers from all over the state were there. I was chosen to go on last in the talent lineup, and I was ready. One time when I visited Ed in Dallas, he took me to a showcase performance by a girl group called the Cake that Decca had just signed. One of them was wearing the coolest outfit—like a Little Lord Fauntleroy suit, with velvet shorts, a velvet jacket, and a satin and lace blouse. I came right home and had Mother's seamstress—by now it was Jeannie Derr, one of our neighbors—make me a copy of the design. That's what I wore as I stepped up to the microphone with my twelve-string guitar. I played "Copper Kettle" and a couple of other songs. After I finished my repertoire, the crowd kept asking for more. I think I sang every song I knew that night. And I won first prize.

Suddenly Miss Mac loved me. And when the young man who had emceed the show invited our group back to an off-campus party at his fraternity, she not only allowed us to go, but she stayed up late to chaperone us. I've always appreciated that she did that for us. After the Austin trip, she was always friendly. I think my music made her see me in a new light—but it didn't improve my Spanish grades.

THERE WAS NEVER A QUESTION in anyone's mind that I would go to college. My mother and my aunts on both sides of the family were fortunate to go to college back in the day when most American women were lucky to finish high school. My grades were good enough to get me into the University of Texas, where many of my friends were going. But I never would have made it that far without the help of family and friends, like Susan Merritt and my aunt Arlette Spilman, who helped me prepare the application forms and get my recommendations while my parents were with Robbie in Houston.

I was grateful when I got my acceptance letter from UT, but not particularly elated. And high school graduation was anticlimactic. All I could think about was going back to New York City for the summer. I was going to give my singing career one more try before college. While my friends were enjoying their last days of high school and writing in each other's yearbook, I was thinking about where I would stay in New

York, and trying to find clothes that wouldn't feel too out-of-date the minute I got to the city. Since I wouldn't be living with Rip and Geraldine this time—I could only impose for so long—my mother decided to come along. We packed our bags to spend the summer together and sublet a place on Riverside Drive from a vacationing Barnard college professor.

We had a wonderful time exploring the Upper West Side. Mother was so sweet that she would start a conversation with anybody on the street, and if she saw someone lying on the sidewalk, she'd stop to help them. I found myself saying, "Mother, you've got to stop talking to strangers! Look straight ahead and don't say a word." But she just couldn't seem to do that. One day when we were walking together along the sidewalk, I noticed she wasn't holding up her end of the conversation. I wheeled around and saw that a man had reached out from a phone booth and grabbed her. He was pulling her inside when I ran back and dragged her away from him, yelling, "Let go of my mother!" I think she had nodded and said hello, and he'd gotten the wrong idea.

I spent a lot of time in Greenwich Village that summer. I would take the bus all the way downtown to wander around Washington Square Park in my moccasins and play my guitar with all the hippies. Sometimes I would play in coffeehouses and clubs, like the Bitter End, during open mike nights.

I also made some new friends. One of them, a songwriter named Jack Carone, was a college student from Montclair, New Jersey, who'd already had one of his songs recorded by Cass Elliot of the Mamas and the Papas. We hit it off right away, even though we seemed so different. He was tall, with a mass of curly black hair and a distinct New Jersey accent. Because he lived in Montclair, he always had to leave in time to make the last bus out of Manhattan at the Port Authority. But one night he missed the bus, so I insisted on taking him home to the apartment to spend the night on our sofa. Mother was as sweet as she could be to him. When he woke up the next morning, he was amazed to find his shirt ironed and draped over a chair. And breakfast was on the table.

Jack Carone took me along to some recording sessions at the legendary Brill Building and the studios at 1650 Broadway, where I sang background vocals or clapped along with the beat. I was meeting such great musicians and having so much fun that I could hardly believe it when my six weeks were up and it was time for me to go back home.

EVERYTHING WAS ALL SET for college. My parents had paid for my first year's tuition at the University of Texas, and I was going to be rooming with Jane McKnight, one of my best friends. Jane's grandparents were a prominent couple in Quitman who had struck it rich in the oil and gas business. They had mentored my parents when they first moved to town, and the families became good friends. The McKnights were like rock stars to me. They had a plane and an exciting life hobnobbing with celebrities, but they were still down-to-earth, nice people. Jane lived with her parents in Tyler but was always coming up to Quitman. Everyone knew when she was visiting me because she pulled into town in her burgundy red Cadillac, towing a matching trailer full of fancy cutting horses. Jane was an expert on horseback and could perform amazing tricks. She could literally ride circles around me, but she wasn't above mucking out stalls or cleaning tack. We were going to be roommates at UT, and in the same sorority, and we made all kinds of plans to have fun together in college. And face it, Austin is pretty much close to heaven. I should have been thrilled.

BUT WHEN I ARRIVED on campus for rush week, the thought of spending the next four years in school was making me queasy. I put on my sweet, college-girl dresses and pumps. I went to a few of the parties, but none of it felt right to me. I'd just spent the summer wearing moccasins and bell-bottoms. I'd played the Bitter End! I felt like if I was going to make it in the music business, I needed to be in New York, not here. I was only eighteen, but there were a lot of younger singers out there, getting deals, like Janis Ian, who wrote "Society's Child." The way I saw it, my life was passing me by.

I never made it to the dorm.

"HAS SISSY GONE and lost her *mind?*" It was my aunt Arlette on the phone, talking to my mother, a week after I left Austin without telling anybody. "She's ruining her life!" Arlette said. "She had such a great opportunity, and now she's throwing it away."

Actually, I wasn't throwing away the chance to go to college, just postponing it. The deal I made with my parents was this: Daddy was willing to support me in New York for four years, just as if I were going to the university. If I didn't make it in show business by then, I'd go back to school and get a degree. And this time, I would be living in the city on my own.

My parents never got angry with me or tried to talk me into going back to Austin. But I doubt they would have agreed to let me go to New York alone if Robbie hadn't gotten sick. I think my parents realized that even when you do everything right to keep your children safe, sometimes you just can't protect them. So you have to let them live their lives and hope for the best. When Mother asked Daddy why he was willing to let me go, he said with a grin, "She'll learn to drink and smoke just as well in New York as in college."

MY FIRST APARTMENT was a studio on East 44th Street, between First and Second Avenue. The building had a doorman, which was my parents' only request. I wrote a check for the deposit and two months' rent—the biggest I had ever written—and moved in with two guitars and a trunk full of clothes. I bought a little black-and-white TV on 42nd Street and hauled it back on the crosstown bus. I felt like a real New Yorker.

There was a steakhouse in the same building, frequented by the former prizefighter Rocky Graziano. I went down and told the manager, "You know, I think you need me to play music here." I took out my guitar and sang him a couple of songs and he hired me for $10 a night, plus tips. It was the "plus tips" that got me by. I loved it. I performed six nights a week, going from table to table playing for the customers. It was my first real job in show business. And since they gave me dinner at the restaurant, I didn't starve.

Rocky Graziano would come into the restaurant every week or two, sometimes more often. My dad loved to watch boxing on TV, so I had seen him fight. He was a nice guy, but really punch-drunk after so many years in the boxing ring. He was still a big celebrity who made regular appearances on the Johnny Carson show, always making fun of himself.

A few months after I started working there, Mother flew up from Texas to see how I was doing. She was having dinner with me at the restaurant when Rocky came in. I introduced them and he sat down at the table with us. We were having a lovely time making small talk, laughing, and visiting, when after a few minutes, Rocky got very quiet and began slowly listing to the left. Suddenly he pitched right out of his chair and fell to the floor sound asleep. Or, as Mother would say, "He was out like Lottie's eye." It must have happened a lot, because he picked himself up, brushed himself off, and apologized like it was nothing unusual.

During her visit, Mother sat in the restaurant's bar most nights to listen to me sing. Sometimes Rocky would come in and sit next to her and make conversation. He was a great raconteur, but every other word out of his mouth was some kind of profanity. My mother listened politely and then said, "Mr. Graziano, you seem like such a nice man. Why do you have to use words like that to express yourself?" He never uttered another cuss word around her again.

IN THE DAYTIME, I worked at a little dress shop. It was fun, because even though I didn't have money to buy new clothes, I could dress everybody else. And when I wasn't on the clock, I was writing songs and recording jingles with new friends, like the young songwriter and producer Kenny Laguna and the talented troupe of musicians and writers in his orbit. Kenny worked as a sideman with groups like Ohio Express and the Shondells and ran what he called a "bubblegum shop" that churned out ready-made songs for the teen market.

He seemed to know everybody in the music business and could compose just about any style of music. In early 1969, Andy Warhol asked Kenny to produce the soundtrack album for one of his avant-garde films, *Lonesome Cowboys*. I sang on a few songs, including the title track. Too bad the record label folded and the album was never released. But it was an intriguing introduction to New York's underground art scene and led to my first work in film, as an extra in the Andy Warhol feature *Trash*. Fortunately, I ended up on the cutting room floor.

Later I teamed up with Kenny Laguna and some other musicians to create a group called Moose and the Pelicans. We practiced a cappella harmonies in the subway stations and recorded a few songs, including a wonderfully silly takeoff on the Davey Crockett theme. One song, "We Rockin'," made the Top 100, but the hit record we all were hoping for eluded us.

I was briefly signed with a small label called Tomorrow's Productions, run by Artie Wayne, a songwriter and singer who recorded under the name Shadow Mann. Like Kenny Laguna, Artie packaged songs and matched them with performers. He had bought one called "John, You've Gone Too Far This Time," a novelty tune about the naked photo of John Lennon and Yoko Ono that appeared on their album *Two Virgins*. They needed a girl singer to record it, so I was hired and given the name "Rainbo." The single got some attention, mainly as a footnote to the controversy about John and Yoko. But thankfully, Rainbo never recorded again. Artie later went on to head the publishing division of A&M Records, and I went back to the drawing board, trying to find my niche in the music business.

·   ·   ·

EVEN THOUGH RAINBO WAS NO MORE, I was thinking about taking another stage name, or at least dropping "Sissy." My parents thought I should call myself Holliday, since it was a family name, but I couldn't come up with anything that seemed to fit. So I asked Rip and Gerry if they could think of something. I often consulted them when I had big decisions to make, because I had such respect for the way they lived and worked as artists. Mostly I learned from them by example. And when I did ask their opinion, Rip in particular was very careful not to try and influence me, but to encourage me to think for myself. He would often ask me questions rather than giving me an answer. In this case he said, "How will people know who you are, Sissy, if you change your name? How will they know who your family is and where you come from?" Of course, Rip Torn was born with the best name ever, so that was easy for him to say. But he planted a seed in my head, one that grew over the years: Nothing I accomplished would be worth salt if I lost track of who I really was.

· · · 8 · · ·

ALTHOUGH MY DAD WAS SUPPORTING ME, NEW YORK WAS expensive, and to help make ends meet, I took a roommate in the studio apartment. Then Barbara Blalock, an old friend from Texas, moved in with us, so for a while we had three people crammed into one room.

Barbara had five beautiful sisters back in Texas, all popular girls and all honor students. I visited that family often when we were kids. The Blalocks lived out in the country, and we would take walks together and play for hours in a field we called "The Boneyard," littered with the bleached bones of long-deceased cows. The Blalock house was much livelier. All six girls slept in two rooms in double bunk beds. There were always boys from town hanging around, clamoring to be invited in for the yummy cakes and pies that were forever being baked and for the beautiful sisters who baked them.

Barbara was a great roommate. We only had one disagreement in the short time she stayed with us. She thought that the fruit in the bottom of Dannon yogurt was the prize you got to after finally eating all that icky plain, unsweetened yogurt. I thought it should be stirred up. Turns out I was right, Barbara, but other than that one thing, you were perfect.

The other roommate? Not so perfect.

This girl, whom I'll call Club Girl, worked in an office by day and went out to nightclubs every night. Club Girl was strange. She would borrow my clothes without asking and return them dirty. I put a lock on my closet to keep her out, but when she asked me for the key, I didn't have the guts to tell her that she was the reason I put the lock on in the first place. Maybe she thought I was protecting my clothes from intruders. Despite her faults, I still agreed to move with her to a larger apartment on the Upper East Side after Barbara decided to return to Texas.

By then I had quit my job singing in the steakhouse, and I needed some extra cash. When Club Girl told me I could fill in at her office for a receptionist who was on leave, I jumped at the chance. After I had worked there for a few weeks, the regular receptionist returned and I went on my way. I never gave it another thought until a few weeks later, when my roommate came home from work, wide-eyed.

"We're in trouble, Sissy," Club Girl said. "They caught us."

"What are you talking about? Caught us doing what?"

She explained that the corporate office didn't stop sending my paycheck after I left the receptionist job. Club Girl was the office manager and she was taking those checks, signing my name, and cashing them at the bank. She kept the money and never told me a thing.

"You did what?!" I said, sputtering mad. "No, *we're* not in trouble. *You're* in trouble!"

I went straight into the office the next morning and told them what had happened, that I hadn't been getting the checks. When I got back to the apartment, she had changed the locks on the door and thrown my clothes—except the ones she wanted—into the hallway. She also left my guitars out there. I guess she knew I would have busted down the door for them. But she did keep all the furniture.

I had no place to go, so I stayed with friends for a few nights. Kenny Laguna had a girlfriend named Meryl Feldman who was thinking about moving to the city, so she and I decided to rent an apartment together.

We found a beautiful second-floor walk-up on East 19th Street, near Gramercy Park. Meryl's mother was a decorator on Long Island, and she turned our little apartment into a showplace, with bentwood chairs and a couch made from a sleigh bed. I brought up a little antique table that I found in an abandoned house during one of my trips home to Texas. It reminded me of my roots.

In the summer of 1969, Meryl and Kenny went to the Woodstock Festival in upstate New York. I could have gone with them, but the weather report said rain, so I said no thanks. I wasn't the kind of girl who liked to camp or use Porta-Potties. And I loved the idea of having the apartment all to myself for a whole weekend just to write songs and play music. I wasn't all that much of a counterculture person anyway. And even though I was strongly opposed to the Vietnam War, I wasn't much of an activist. I went to a few demonstrations in New York and I joined some friends in Washington for a march on the Pentagon, but I wasn't politically committed, like some people I knew. My parents were alarmed when they found out I was going to protest in Washington, even though I assured them that for me it was nothing more than a long weekend trip with good friends. But there were other things that I never told them about that would have given them plenty of sleepless nights.

MANHATTAN IN THE LATE 1960s was not the same tourist destination that it is today. Instead of the Disney Store and the Hard Rock Cafe, Times Square was lined with peep shows and crawling with addicts and hookers. The crime rate in New York was through the roof. Once when I was waiting for a bus in Times Square, a thief grabbed my guitar case and took off down the sidewalk. Without thinking, I ran him down and wrestled the case out of his hands. He would have had to kill me before I would give up that guitar. I didn't think for a minute how dangerous that might have been.

Another time when I had just arrived in New York, I got locked out on a balcony while escaping from a record producer who gave me the creeps and was trying to get me to do drugs. I had on a little white dress and was carrying a big Martin twelve-string with me. When he turned

my dad

AA Spacek and Mary Cervenka Spacek were first generation Americans who raised their family in the Czech community of Granger, Texas.

AA with his sister Albina and his fiancée, Mary Cervenka (left).

The Spacek family: Sam, Thelma, Momsy, Pops, Eddie (my dad), and Rose.

AA Spacek and frequent houseguest, Lyndon Johnson, who nicknamed him "Double A."

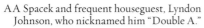

AA ("Pops") and Mary Spacek ("Momsy") outside their Granger home in a rare snowstorm.

My dad checking the cotton crop in his white linen pants and two-toned shoes.

My dad at eighteen in Granger, contemplating his future at Texas Tech.

In college, my father, Edwin A. Spacek (above) played the banjo in a dance band. When he met my mother they were on a double date, and he was with the other girl. But when he heard my mother's voice he thought, *That's the girl I'm going to marry!* Two weeks later they were engaged.

— my dad

I inherited my strawberry blond hair from my grandmother. After T. Holl moved the family to the wild Rio Grande Valley, where bandits roamed the border, Elizabeth insisted they get a house in town.

My grandfather, Thomas Holliday "T. Holl" Spilman, married Elizabeth Holliday, the granddaughter of his namesake.

That's my mother, Virginia, with my grandfather in front of their "in town" house in Mission, Texas.

T. Holl and Elizabeth with four of their five children (my mother is the baby).

They lived out their lives in threadbare gentility.

My mother in grade school in Mission. I think she looks like Scout in *To Kill a Mockingbird*.

Virginia Spilman, known as "Gin," must have dreamed of the life she helped me live.

Here she is a teenager with *Screenland* magazine.

My aunt Arlette and my mother in the 1940s. When I was very young, Arlette and I had a standoff over a plate of Christmas cookies. I won.

An all-American family in the 1950s. Little did we know then that tragedy would change all of our lives.

Here I'm checking to see if a stick of gum I'd put in Robbie's pocket for safekeeping is still safe.

Mother loved to dress us in sailor suits. Years later I tried out for *Carrie* in a sailor dress she made for me in seventh grade.

Ed, Robbie, and me in front of our house in Quitman, Texas. It must be Sunday because I'm wearing shoes.

Robbie

that's me

Sunday school Christmas party. My mother taught all of our Sunday school classes. Her most important lesson: "God is love." Those are little Bibles hanging on the tree; a circus is painted on the floor.

DEC. 1953 *Studio* E.A.TEX.

My brothers and me after a squirrel hunt with some friends in Granger, Texas. I had to be tough to keep up with the boys. But if I couldn't be rough, at least I had to be quiet.

Me and Robbie just hanging out. When he was a newborn, Robbie looked so deeply into my mother's eyes that it almost frightened her. He was a soulful boy.

My brothers Ed and Robbie right before I came along.

My brothers and I were very close growing up, despite the fact that I was a girl. I tried kissing my elbow for years because my uncle Sam told me that if I did, I'd turn into a boy. That's me and Robbie in 1953.

Ed and Robbie in 1966 at Arlette and Wade's home in Austin, Texas, right before the big race that Robbie couldn't run. The next day Robbie was admitted to MD Anderson Hospital in Houston.

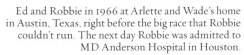

Robbie was a talented athlete and track star who qualified for the Texas State Meet in Austin. As an eight-year-old he begged my dad to let him out of the car so he could catch a jackrabbit he saw running down the side of the road. My dad laughed, but decided to let him try. Robbie caught the rabbit.

his back, I'd taken my guitar and slipped out a door and closed it behind me. I found myself locked out on a fire escape balcony with no way
down. But I didn't dare knock on the window. And it was not in the
kind of neighborhood where you would want to shout for help at night.
So I just sat down on my guitar case and waited. I was covered with soot
and shivering cold when a building watchman found me the next morning. I didn't have a dime on me, so the kind man gave me money to get
a bus back home. I was dirty, but I was okay. And getting out on that
balcony may have been the smartest move I ever made.

I had another close call near Times Square. I was going to a recording session with a hot new group called the Cherry People. But as usual,
I didn't have enough cash to get to the studio. So I opened my piggy
bank—yes, I had an actual piggy bank—and grabbed a handful of
change, enough for a taxi to and from the session. My parents had given
me a full-length rabbit-fur coat for Christmas that year, so I would be
warm and stylish for the New York winter. So when I stepped out of the
cab on Eighth Avenue, one of the neighborhood muggers must have
thought I would be a rich mark. He followed me into the lobby and ran
to get on the elevator with me. I politely held the door for him.

As soon as the door closed, he turned to me and whispered in a
threatening voice, "Give me all your money!" Something in his tone
convinced me I'd better do what he said. He had his hand out, so I
opened my purse and dumped all my change into it. The coins went
everywhere. He cursed and instinctively bent down to try to scoop up
the coins. I used that moment to take off the ring I was wearing, an
heirloom that had belonged to Big Mama, and put it in my mouth.

When he stood up again, he had a better look at me and realized I
had no money and wasn't worth the effort. When the elevator doors
opened at my floor, he ran out and disappeared. I rode that elevator
back down to the lobby and waited for a long time to give him a chance
to escape before heading back up to the recording studio. Mostly I was
shaken up, and embarrassed that my good manners had gotten me into
all of this. I swore I would never, ever hold a door for a mugger again.

There were other strange encounters, like the time a guy invited me and some friends back to his apartment, where he had a butcher's knife attached to a chain hanging from the ceiling. He entertained himself by sailing the knife around the living room, slicing through the air just over our heads. The only time I'd ever seen anything like that was at Kreuz's (pronounced "Kriteses") barbeque place outside of Austin. But they were friendly there, and they used the knife to slice barbeque, not terrorize guests.

MOSTLY, THOUGH, I WAS HAVING wonderful adventures. One of my friends, Jonny Podell, was a song runner—an independent promotion man, like my brother Ed. He would take me along on trips to radio stations all over the Northeast. In the morning I would climb into his tiny sports car, which was filled with stacks of 45s, and end up in Philadelphia or Boston by noon. Then I'd be back in New York for another night at the recording studio.

He introduced me to his girlfriend, Monica Faust, who became one of the best friends of my life. She was beautiful and smart and mischievous—the hippest girl I had ever met. One time we hitchhiked around Manhattan just for fun. We would walk into fancy department stores, like Bergdorf's, and speak to the salesclerks in gibberish, pretending to ask for the ladies' room in a foreign language. They would try to find translators for us, to no avail. Most days Monica worked in an office, but every night when Jonny came home from his job, she would have dinner on the table. When I was really hungry, I would go to their house.

Jonny quickly morphed into one of the most powerful music moguls in the industry, and before long he was managing just about everybody who was anybody. He managed the Allman Brothers Band, and he introduced me to them when they came to New York for their very first show, at the Fillmore East. I think Jonny thought that since I was Southern and they were Southern, we might all get along. He was right.

They were great guys, extremely talented, and so young they seemed fresh off the peach truck. Plus, they had good Southern manners. Gregg and I jammed a little back at my place. And as much as he liked my accent, he loved my twelve-string guitar even more.

The Fillmore was my favorite music venue in New York, and it was within walking distance from our apartment. The other hot spot was Max's Kansas City, which I walked past all the time. Occasionally I would press my face against the glass and try to look inside. (It's hard to look cool with your face smashed up against the glass.) Pretty soon I started hanging out with my friends at Max's. It wasn't too hard to get into the club itself, but it was next to impossible to get into the back room, where all the "it" people were. You either had to know someone or be really, really cute or cool. I made it back there once by accident, but had forgotten my glasses, so I couldn't even see who the "it" people were. I did hear someone say that Mick Jagger walked by, but I missed it.

By now I was starting to feel a long way from Quitman.

I HAD A RECURRING DREAM in the years after my brother's death: Late at night I'd drive the Austin Healey to the cemetery, where Robbie would be waiting for me. I'd climb over to the passenger seat and Robbie would drive us around all night. We'd talk and laugh like we always did. Before dawn, he'd pull back into the cemetery and get out of the car. As he walked away, he'd turn and put his fingers to his lips and smile.

In another dream, Robbie walked into the kitchen at home in Quitman, where the whole family greeted him with surprise.

"Robbie! Where've you been?"

"You forgot me!" he said.

In fact, he was as present in my life as ever. Once I was browsing in a card shop in New York, when I saw a pair of familiar hands sorting through the cards next to me. I knew those hands as well as my own—the olive-colored skin, the long fingers and wide nails. They were Robbie's hands. I stared down at them for the longest time. I never looked up to see the face of the person they belonged to, not even when he walked out of the store.

SO MUCH WAS HAPPENING to me so quickly that I sometimes felt like my life was spinning out of control. I'd sit in my apartment at night, looking out the window at all the lights in the city and thinking about home. It reminded me of being stopped on the top of the Ferris wheel at the Old Settlers' Reunion, suspended motionless in the dark, while the carnival just kept on going down below me, with all of its music and motion and noise. New York City was like that carnival; it never stopped. I was the one who needed to slow down occasionally and take a deep breath to remind myself who I was and what I was doing. Whenever New York started to overwhelm me, I knew it was time to go back home and get my bearings. I would stay for a few weeks, sometimes a few months. And when I felt like myself again, off I would go, back to the carnival.

I was experimenting with the way I looked and dressed, and Mother and Daddy never knew which Sissy would be coming home each time. One day I showed up in a micromini-dress and boots. My mom opened the door and said, "Oh, Sissy! What a nice blouse."

"It's a dress, Mother!"

One time, a vanload of hippie friends stopped by to visit me on their way through Texas. The counterculture hadn't caught up with East Texas yet, and we attracted a lot of attention. My urban friends were fascinated with rural Texas and wanted to photograph everything they saw, especially the bucolic-looking cows grazing beside the road. But someone called the police to report "some strange-looking people" out in the pasture, bothering the cows. That took a little explaining, but luckily I was a local, even though I looked like a hippie, too. It certainly helped that my father, the agriculture agent, was in good standing with the local farmers.

I took my friends swimming at Lake Quitman, and, like a scene out of *Easy Rider*, some burly guys drove up in a hot rod and started yelling, "Hippies, go home!"

It embarrassed me to death that anyone would talk that way to my friends. I had told them how wonderful and friendly Texas was, and now they were being scared to death by a bunch of shirtless teenagers. I was so mad that I marched right up to the car in my bathing suit, determined to straighten things out. As I got closer, I could see that the ringleader was someone I'd gone to school with.

"Oh, for heaven's sakes!" I said. "Why are you being so mean to us? You know better than that!"

"Sissy Spacek?" he said in a little voice. "I'm sorry. . . . I didn't know it was you." He was normally the sweetest guy in the world. I still don't know what came over him.

My parents always gave me plenty of space when I came home to visit, and sometimes gentle doses of good advice. My father would tell me, "Sissy, you'll meet the same people on the way up that you meet on the way down, so act accordingly" My mother would remind me, "We are a product of our choices." It's advice I've never forgotten. But the best part of being at home was to be caught up in the simple rhythms of my parents' lives, how they woke up early and watched the sun come up together while they had their morning coffee, and how they enjoyed every day. After spending time in Texas, I would always come back to New York refreshed, my confidence and strength renewed, ready to tackle the next challenge.

ONE OF OUR FRIENDS was a fashion photographer who took a lot of pictures of me for his portfolio. When he showed one of my head shots to his agency, they sold it to Chanel for an ad campaign. I got $25 for being the face of Chanel No. 5 that season—and since it was the only perfume my mother ever wore, I figured it was a good sign. I developed a lifelong love for that perfume.

It was the beginning and end of a short-lived career in modeling.

Dovima, the former supermodel who ran the modeling department at the agency, wanted to meet me, so I showed up at her office with my guitars in tow. She took one look at my five-foot-two-and-a-half-inch self and let me down gently. "We love your pictures, but you're much too petite," she said. "Perhaps we can set up a meeting with the theatrical side of our agency?" And that was where I met Bill Treusch.

All the times I felt like I was spinning my wheels trying to get ahead in New York, and all the times I would call home tired and discouraged, my mother would say to me, "Sissy, as soon as you meet someone who's smart enough to realize how talented you are, you'll be on your way." Bill Treusch turned out to be the person she was talking about.

The day I met Bill, everything changed. I dragged my two guitars into his office, and we talked for a long time, and then I sang and played a few songs for him. Before I knew it, we were having dinner together and meeting some of his other clients and going to the theater. We just clicked from the first moment we met. He believed in me from the start and right away began sending me up for auditions. I only remember Bill being at Dovima's agency for a short while. He moved into an office in the small yellow house on East 30th Street where Marion Dougherty had her casting agency. Marion was amazingly talented, one of the most highly regarded and successful casting directors in New York. Bill and Marion gave me the professional seal of approval that I needed to get a leg up in the business.

Bill had a warm smile, and he always wore a crisp white shirt. He was an insatiable reader, and he saw every play in New York and every movie. He didn't just *appreciate* film and theater; he was a huge fan, and he loved artists. He made his clients feel like they were special, brilliant, undeniable. I never dreamed I would be invited to join such an exclusive club. Through the years he represented Christopher Walken, Eric Roberts, Carol Kane, Melanie Mayron, Mary Beth Hurt, John Heard, and Diane Keaton.

I used to hang out at the offices on 30th Street. It was like visiting a favorite relative's house. The parlor was warm and cozy and filled with antiques. And wherever Bill was, I always felt welcome.

One afternoon I was visiting with Bill when Marion Dougherty popped her head out of her office and said, "Sissy, come on in and meet Bob."

Bob? I walked in and saw her standing next to Robert Redford. I was so discombobulated that I shook his hand and said, "Hello, Bobert." He laughed out loud.

That old saying "the journey's the thing" is true. When I met Bill Treusch, mine took a positive turn. I finally felt like I was heading in the right direction, my course was set. It was Bill who suggested that I might try acting.

Rip and Gerry had both studied with Lee Strasberg at the Actors Studio, so I decided to take some classes at the Lee Strasberg Theatre and Film Institute near Union Square. The closest I ever got to Lee Strasberg himself was riding up in the elevator with him on my way to class. The technique taught there is known as Method acting, which boils down to using your own life experiences to bring truth to the characters you play. You learn to relax, concentrate, call up specific memories and the emotions they bring, then impose them on the thoughts and actions of your character—a technique called substitution.

I admit that I was more than a little intimidated in class. Everybody seemed so intense and so, well, *urban*. I imagined they had come from broken homes, or had been to reform school, or had some other traumatic personal history to dig into for their exercises. I was a former majorette from a loving, stable family. What kind of angst could I bring to the table?

Of course, I eventually realized that I had my own private stockpile of experiences, that cigar box of secrets (which by now was a trunkful) I could draw on to bring life to my characters. And in mining them for insight, I discovered the beginnings of a simple theory that would guide my work: To be an actor, you have to live a life. If you want your work to be real, you have to be a real person yourself. I began to understand that the art forms that excited me most were those that illuminated the human condition, explored our shared experience, and connected us in some way. What I loved most about performing music was the way the audience was *right there with me*, feeling what I was feeling. It reminded me of the way twilight feels, shimmery and soft, when the day and the night blend together and envelop you. With music, I could conjure up that magic hour whenever I wanted. And now I could see how acting could create that same kind of connection by weaving my own life and experiences into what I was doing.

One of the most intriguing exercises I learned from my short time at the Strasberg Institute is using "sense memory" to create the emotional state of the character. It's a pretty simple technique. If your character is happy, you focus on a sensation that has brought you happiness: the taste of a fresh peach, or the feel of warm sunshine on your skin at the beach. Every actor uses something different to help conjure certain emotions. I've learned a great deal about process from other actors. When I worked with Diane Keaton, she listened to music. Jessica Lange used scents. When I was working with Anne Bancroft on 'Night, Mother, I noticed that she would pull a small, folded-up piece of paper out of her pocket just before an emotional scene. She would quietly read whatever she had written there, then carefully refold the note and tuck it away. I've always been fascinated by the processes of different actors, and I've observed that women are much more willing to share them than men. Male actors tend to keep their process secret, like a favorite fishing hole.

As much as I got out of my time at the Strasberg Institute, I can't claim to be a "trained" Method actor. I didn't even stay long enough to graduate from exercise classes to scene work. And because I had never worked before I studied there, I had no idea how I would use what I learned. When I did start working and was able to apply those simple techniques, I realized just how amazing they are. But, honestly, I think I learned as much about acting on my way to and from the Institute as I did in class. The sketchy characters I saw along 14th Street late at night gave me enough material for a lifetime.

I LIVED WITH MERYL FELDMAN in the 19th Street apartment for almost two years. When she moved out to live with Kenny Laguna, Alice Passman moved in. Alice worked in the fashion district and was going to night school to become a speech therapist until she met me and my friends. She ended up working for Alice Cooper and going to acting school.

Unfortunately, Meryl's wonderful furniture moved out with her. But Alice and I filled the place up with things we would find left out in the trash on Park Avenue, like an old church pew and abandoned table lamps. Ours was the original shabby chic apartment.

Alice was a wonderful girl with a great pair of legs. If you walked into a party with her and she had on her favorite miniskirt, you became suddenly invisible. She was also very smart and funny. One of her dates was a friend of Woody Allen's. They were having dinner one night when Woody joined them. Afterward, they wanted to get some dessert, but everywhere they stopped, people kept bothering Woody for autographs. So Alice offered to take them back to our apartment so they could have some peace.

I was in my pajamas when Alice called to tell me someone was coming over.

"Oh, Alice, I'm already asleep," I moaned.

"It's Woody Allen."

"No problem! Just give me a minute."

I joined them for coffee, expecting to be entertained by the famous comedian. But Woody was quiet and serious, and all he talked about was the recent breakup with his ex-wife. Alice and I looked at each other, wondering: *When is he going to start being funny?*

I couldn't take it any longer, and I began to crack jokes and tell funny stories. I noticed Woody checking his watch. Alice tells me I was charming, but I wonder if I didn't scare Woody off. As it turned out, Alice played a bit part in *Annie Hall* after she turned to acting. And I get to tell the story of the night I was funnier than Woody Allen.

BECAUSE I WAS REPRESENTED by Bill Treusch, I got a lot of auditions. One was for a Broadway musical called *Terre Haute High*, about a space station filled with young people from all parts of the country. It was being produced by the same people who created the hit show *Hair*. I tried out for it, even though the auditions called for singing and dancing. I was not a trained singer, and I'd never taken anything other than tap dancing lessons when I was a kid. But for some reason the director and the producers thought I was the find of the century, and they cast me in the lead. Now all they had to do was finance the show.

Terre Haute High was a very expensive production because it had such a large cast and required elaborate, space-age sets. To try to raise money, the producers would take me along on their rounds to potential investors. I was thrilled to be introduced as "our star" and then perform my signature song, a soaring number about a phone call to home from space. It was a wonderful song, and the show would have been great, but the producers never could mount enough financing. And so my budding Broadway career went down in flames along with the imaginary space station.

But before I had time to dust myself off from the experience, another opportunity came my way. This time it would take me to Hollywood.

··· C A L I F O R N I A ···

··· 9 ···

T HE APPOINTMENT BOOKS I'VE SAVED FROM MY NEW
        York years are filled with hopeful, handwritten entries: a meeting
with John Huston on East 61st Street to discuss his next film, *Fat City*;
an appointment for "Breck shampoo"; a few hours set aside to do "test
shots in the park." I did not get the part in John Huston's film, and I no
longer remember what the test shots were for, or whether the Breck
booking was for a TV commercial or a print ad. Several times I wrote
"THE JOHNNY CARSON SHOW" in capital letters, underlined
and circled, across the top of a page. I had gotten an audition with the
Tonight Show producer, and I was thrilled when they booked me as a musical guest. But each time I was scheduled to go on, I came down with
some sort of ailment—a sore throat, stomachache, swollen glands. Appearing on that show might have been the biggest big break in my musical career, but it never came to be.

By now I had pretty much given up on the idea of becoming the
next Joni Mitchell. Yet I still carried at least one guitar with me to every
audition, even when I was trying out for dramatic roles. It was no different in the spring of 1971, when I met with a young director named
Michael Ritchie to discuss a part in his film *Prime Cut*. During our interview I told him that I was a singer-songwriter, and he asked me if I
could write a song about any topic he named.

"Sure," I said.

127

He looked over at his drink, sitting on the table, with a cherry stem sticking out of the top.

"Okay. How about maraschino cherries?"

"That'll do," I said, pulling out my twelve-string. "Why don't we write it together?"

We worked for the next few hours and came up with a pretty fabulous song. Actually it's one of my favorites, "The Maraschino Red Blues":

> Put one more cherry in my ginger ale,
> Smoke another coffin nail,
> Oh sweet, sweet cherry number four,
> I ain't coming back here no more. . . .

By the time we were finished, Michael wanted me for his film. I was up for the part of Poppy, an orphan waif who is rescued from white slavery by Nick Devlin, a mob enforcer played by Lee Marvin. My character was supposed to be young and scared, and I *was* young and scared, so I guess you could call it typecasting. There was only one more hurdle: The studio wanted to fly me out to Los Angeles for a screen test.

I had only been to LA once before, for a brief visit, and I was still thrilled by how everything seemed so green and shiny and new. At the end of a long New York winter I was astonished by the sunshine and palm trees; even the grass on the freeway median strip looked lush and green. I landed at LAX with one suitcase and two guitars, wearing a flowing skirt and tapestry boots—the cool, funky-girl look I had perfected in New York. But I blew my cover as soon as I arrived in Studio City and started jumping up and down when I saw Mary Tyler Moore strolling across the street.

The screen test at a producer's house in the Hollywood Hills was just a formality, and it went well. I was more intrigued by the tall, young filmmaker operating the camera. Gary Weis would later go on to fame as the creator of short films for *Saturday Night Live* (including one of me twirling my baton in slow motion). But back then he was a cute, wild-haired guy just starting in the business.

Gary and I instantly hit it off. He took me to the beach in Santa Monica—not a great place for a redhead, but I was happy to watch him surf. He also invited me to visit the studio he was sharing with another artist named William Wegman and his soon-to-be-famous Weimaraner, Man Ray. I was fascinated by the work Gary and Bill were doing with photography and the new medium of video, but I felt more like a voyeur than a participant in their world. I still thought of art as something you put on your wall, and I wasn't sure how posing a dog on a big white box fit into the equation. I had a lot to learn.

Shortly after, I was officially offered the part in *Prime Cut*—my first real film! But there was one thing that made me hesitate: The role called for at least one nude scene. It wasn't an unusual requirement in those days; everyone seemed to be running around naked in the movies—and even on Broadway. So I figured if I wanted to be an actor, I'd better get over it. I called my parents and told them the good news. I'd gotten my first part in a movie, and it starred Lee Marvin and Gene Hackman. Then I told them the bad news: I wouldn't always be wearing clothes. After much deliberation, we decided that this was a wonderful opportunity, and the good far outweighed the bad. I packed my bags and never looked back.

Filming started in Calgary, Alberta, in the summer of 1971. I loved working with Lee Marvin, and he was actually very protective of me. But he was a prodigious drinker, and he warned me to avoid him when he was inebriated. When we first met on location, I blurted out, "Lee, you have the greenest eyes!"

"Yeah," said Lee. "And whenever you see them turn blue, stay away from me."

It was true. When he'd had a few too many, his eyes turned ocean blue, and everybody gave him a wide berth. But mostly he was a good guy, and very professional.

Gene Hackman also starred, as a gangster with a sideline in human trafficking. Gene had appeared with Robert Redford in Michael Ritchie's latest film, *Downhill Racer*, and was already well on his way to stardom after two Oscar nominations for Best Supporting Actor. I was surprised that he was such a normal, humble person. A young actress named Janit Baldwin and I had adjoining rooms in one of the production honeywagons (that's what we call trailers with flush toilets). We used to sit in our dressing rooms, playing games and making elaborate collages while we waited for the crew to set up shots. Gene would occasionally tap on the door and say, "Hey, can I come in and help work on the collage?"

"Sure, Gene, just don't drop the glue this time!"

He was such a nice guy and a good artist that we didn't mind.

I WAS SO CAUGHT UP in the filming that I hardly noticed the battles going on behind the scenes. Michael Ritchie was constantly fighting with the powers that be over the tone of *Prime Cut*. Michael wanted it to be more of a camp satire; the studio wanted a straight gangster thriller. Lee Marvin shared the director's vision for the film, and it led to some tense moments on location. One day he had a huge fight with a production executive who was visiting the set. We were in the middle of shooting a scene that called for Lee to rescue me from a slave auction. I was wrapped in a horse blanket, and he was supposed to carry me to a waiting town car and drive off. We had done the scene numerous times and would get to the end of the road, hear "cut," and then turn around and do it all over again. But this time, Lee was so furious with the studio that he threw me in the backseat, got in next to the driver, who was another actor, and barked, "Take me back to the hotel!" The hotel was more than an hour away, but of course, the actor driving the car followed Lee's instructions and took off down the road for Calgary, leaving nothing but a cloud of dust, a very angry studio executive . . . and all of my clothes. I don't remember a word being spoken on the drive back to the hotel. When we got there, I had to waddle through the lobby, still barefoot and rolled up in a rug. It was a rather humiliating experience, and I'm sure tongues were wagging. Janit brought me my clothes at the end of the day, and we all went back to work as if nothing had happened.

I might have been more upset about it if I'd known any better, but I was too busy having a great time on my first film location. Gary Weis had been hired to make a short film about the making of *Prime Cut*, and he asked me to write and record the music to go with it. We were an item for a while, but mostly I remember him as a happy and free-spirited artist who helped open my eyes to the possibilities of the world.

Prime Cut came out in the summer of 1972 to lukewarm reviews. Michael Ritchie had made wonderful films before, and would make wonderful films after—including the classic film *The Candidate*. But because he lost the battle with the studio over who would have final creative control, everybody suffered. Instead of having a funny, edgy film, the studio had outsmarted themselves and ended up with an uninspired movie created by committee, which is never a good thing. For my own purposes, *Prime Cut* served me well. I was now a working actress with footage, who'd been in a film with Lee Marvin and Gene Hackman.

By then, I was already living in LA, and starting work on a film that would change my life forever.

I RETURNED TO MY NEW YORK APARTMENT after we finished filming *Prime Cut*, but the city seemed to have lost some of its luster. The bustling streets just felt crowded, and the noise level was obnoxious. I missed going barefoot; I missed the sun on my face in the morning. Besides, most of my best friends were leaving town to be part of the growing music scene in LA. It felt like time to move on.

I stopped by to visit Rip and Gerry shortly after I got back from Canada. Gerry was immersed in a household project in one of the bathrooms, so I sat on the edge of the tub and entertained her with tales from location while she spackled the ceiling. I can still see the great

Geraldine Page applying the spackle in slow, graceful strokes with her long, beautiful fingers while she listened to me rattle on about acting. I cringe to think of it now, but she was patient with me, and supportive— and, I'm sure, thoroughly amused. But she made me feel like we were two seasoned actors talking.

I felt like a door had opened, and it was time for me to step through. All I wanted was to be a performer. Music was the magic wand that had gotten me this far, but I was tired of banging on doors, asking to be let in. With acting, I seemed to have something that people wanted. It was a whole new feeling.

It also felt good to pay off the landlord who had been threatening to evict me every time the rent was two days late. Mr. DeLorenzo was so impressed that I was in a movie with Lee Marvin that he offered me a whole week's grace period. I handed him a check and walked out that door for the last time.

JANIT BALDWIN OFFERED ME a room in the California bungalow-style house in Beechwood Canyon where she lived with her mother, Dona. It was like having a real home, with regular meals and clean sheets. I helped with the rent while we were trying out for parts and Janit was working as a photographer. Dona ran the local Schick clinic that helped people quit smoking. She was pretty tolerant of us. One day she walked through the living room with her arms full of groceries and found us sitting on the floor. Janit and I had taken the legs off all the tables and chairs in the house. We were giggling, and there was a lingering whiff of smoke in the air. "Well, isn't that an interesting thing to do with the furniture!" Dona said with a smile as she continued into the kitchen.

Like other young actors in town, I tried out for commercials. Once I was cast in a national commercial for some big product (that I can't remember now), but when Janit walked in to pick me up, the director saw her curly auburn hair and said, "No! Wait! Her! We want her!" He saw the puzzled look on my face and said, "Oh, sorry, Sissy." I didn't hold it against her; that was the business. The moral of this story: take your own car to auditions.

NOT LONG AFTER I arrived in LA, I met with a young director named Terrence Malick. He had written an amazing script called *Bad-lands* and was just beginning to interview actors. The plot was based on the story of Charles Starkweather and Caril Ann Fugate, teenage lovers who went on a killing spree through the northern plains in the late 1950s.

Terry held the auditions in a big, half-empty house he'd rented off Doheny Drive, in the hills above Sunset Boulevard. He was an MIT graduate who had studied philosophy at Oxford before deciding to become a filmmaker. Terry had won a fellowship at the American Film Institute, where he produced and directed a short film about two cowboys plotting to rob a Texas bank. *Badlands* would be his first feature. He was only twenty-eight years old, but he was an old soul, with an easy laugh and a gentle way about him. He spoke in a quiet drawl that I immediately recognized as coming from my corner of the world. We shared a love of the Southwest and small-town Texas. We'd both grown up there in the 1950s and were deeply connected to that time and place. From the moment we met, we felt like family. We knew the same things, and could communicate them without speaking. I was thankful that I'd ignored all those New York agents who told me to lose my accent and hide my Southern roots. Terry hired me for the film because of all those things. I hadn't changed. I was still a small-town girl from Texas. That was what he wanted for the role of Holly Sargis, a naive, impressionable high school girl who falls for Kit Carruthers, a charming, sociopathic young garbage man who happens to shoot people.

I was the first actor cast in the film. From the very beginning, Terry included me in his creative process. He asked me all kinds of questions about my life, as if he was mining for gold. When he found out I'd been a majorette, he worked my twirling routine into the script. Before I knew it, we were driving down Hollywood Boulevard to a music store to buy a Starline baton like the one I'd had in high school. Terry would give me little pieces of paper with a few lines of dialogue on them, and when I read the lines out loud to him, he'd fall over laughing. My opinions mattered to him. I felt like a filmmaker.

Terry interviewed just about every up-and-coming young actor in Hollywood for the role of Kit, and I got to read with a lot of them. I didn't really know what Terry was looking for, but I figured he'd recognize Kit when he saw him. So we kept looking. The casting director suggested bringing in Martin Sheen. Terry wasn't very optimistic about him because he thought he might be too old for the role, but since his agent had been so nice, he decided to audition him anyway.

The moment Martin walked into the room, everything changed. The chemistry was immediate. Martin wore his hair slicked back and had a swagger like James Dean, and he looked plenty young. I had done that scene with dozens of actors—wonderful actors—but with Martin, it was completely different. He *was* Kit. And with him, I was Holly. Terry and I could hardly contain ourselves. After Martin left, we were like giddy schoolkids.

I SPENT THE SUMMER and fall of 1972 on location in La Junta, Colorado, a tiny town on the south bank of the Arkansas River, surrounded by endless miles of short-grass prairie and not much else. This part of the state leans more toward the dustbowl of Kansas than the Rocky Mountains to the west, and it was the perfect location to film *Badlands*. Sometimes the sky seemed so blue and limitless that it had a weight of its own, pressing down on us and wiping out all memories of the other world beyond the one we inhabited at that very moment. Out on the edge of nowhere, working with a virtuoso first-time director on a shoestring budget and always perched on the edge of disaster, nothing else mattered, or even existed. It felt like we were the center of the universe.

While we were filming, some people working on another film that had just wrapped in Montana drove through La Junta to visit friends of theirs on our crew. I remember being amazed, thinking, *Somebody's making a film somewhere else?*

In this rarified world, two life-altering things happened to me: I learned that filmmakers can be artists. And I fell in love with Jack Fisk.

Terry Malick had been telling me all about this great young art director for weeks when I finally met him during preproduction. I was coming down the stairs at Terry's one day, when I saw a tall, thin man with long, nearly black hair and an equally shaggy black dog at his feet. I was wearing my favorite tapestry boots, snug overalls, a Cub Scout shirt, and a tiny toy car dangling from a silk cord around my neck. I remember thinking, *That's the brilliant art director that Terry's been talking about?* He wasn't much older than me. But he was very cute, and so was his dog.

Jack remembers thinking, *She doesn't look like Caril Ann Fugate.* That's the girl my character was based on. We said a few words to each other, but I was still seeing someone else, and we didn't meet again until Colorado.

In the meantime, it was beginning to dawn on me that someone I currently thought of as my boyfriend didn't think of me as his girlfriend. Or at least not his only one. I visited him once when he was staying at the Chelsea Hotel in New York. The Chelsea was the place where the über-cool stayed, and you had to be careful not to step on people passed out in the hallways from drug overdoses. He had a meeting that morning, so he left the room before I did. He was gone for about two seconds when he stuck his head back inside and said, "Oh yeah, and don't answer the phone while I'm gone, okay?" That was like saying to me, "Oh, and don't eat the chocolate cake you're holding." So as soon as the phone rang, I dove for it. "Hello," I said in my most seductive voice. There was a woman with a French accent on the other end of the line. "No, he's not here right now," I said. "He just stepped out. Who should I tell him called?" I heard a click and then a dial tone.

Another time we were driving through Topanga Canyon outside LA, when out of the blue he said, "So, what do you want to do with your life? Find a man, or what?" I don't think I said a word, but it was a moment of epiphany for me. NO FUTURE IN THIS RELATIONSHIP began flashing like a neon sign inside my head.

WHEN I ARRIVED in La Junta, Jack had already been at work for weeks, scouting locations and building sets out on the prairie. I knew he was supposed to be the art director, but at first it looked like he was pretty far down on the food chain, because he was doing all the work. He was always walking back and forth hauling wood and props and furniture and hammering and painting things, while his assistant art director was sitting in the shade having a cigarette and telling us all what was going to happen next.

We were staying at the Capri Motel in La Junta, which was the only motel for miles in any direction, and it had seen far better days. But the Capri had a restaurant attached to it, the people were friendly, and almost every room was filled with cast and crew. It became our home away from home. I was happy to have Janit Baldwin there for company. She had been cast as Holly's best friend (sadly, all her scenes were cut from the film), and her mother, Dona, was hired to do makeup and hair. Dona also played the part of a deaf maid who is spared by Kit. Janit and I had a scene under the bleachers where the two girlfriends practiced kissing each other so they'd know what to do if they ever had boyfriends. But Terry said the scene turned out to be a little weird. Janit and I certainly thought it was weird while we were shooting it—but then, what did we know?

It was that kind of film; everybody pitched in. Terry even had a tiny speaking role after an actor didn't show up. It wasn't the only time he's acted in one of his own movies, although it's always uncredited and he's incognito. Terry is warm and funny and engaging with his friends, but he is an utterly private person who shuns all publicity about himself. Which has, of course, just added to his mystique.

. . .

WE STARTED SHOOTING in mid-July, with temperatures hovering around one hundred degrees. One afternoon Janit and I were sipping cold milk shakes through straws, when Jack and one of his friends walked by. I offered Jack the rest of my shake and he took it from me with a grin. It felt like a primal act, a "stranger in a strange land" moment—sharing water in the hot desert. I learned that he was an artist from back East, a trained painter and sculptor who had moved to LA and started working as a grip and set dresser. When he was still in art school, Jack created huge environmental sculptures in his studio, but longed to see people moving through them and interacting with them. While in Philadelphia, he began designing sets for the Theater of the Living Arts, which led to his work in film. It was a natural evolution.

Badlands was his first serious film as an art director. His previous experience was on exploitation films and biker movies, one of which had an art budget of $300. Jack went to the hardware store and bought $100 worth of plywood, $100 worth of black paint, and $100 worth of chain. That kind of austerity turned out to be good training for *Badlands*.

Terry only had a budget of $250,000 for his entire film, which was tiny, even for an independent feature back then. Jack did his best to stretch things out. When he arrived in Colorado, he found an abandoned house that had belonged to a junkman who'd recently died. He paid the man's family $100 cash for everything in it. To Jack it was a diamond mine, filled with amazing things like jars of black widow spiders and balls of string the size of pumpkins, an old iron bed, and a Sears and Roebuck catalogue from the early 1950s. There were rusty tools and beat-up furniture, perfect for "Cato's shack," an important location where Kit visits his old buddy (and then shoots him). Jack and I found out right off that both of us loved going to flea markets; our idea of a perfect date was rooting around at the town dump.

We were all in awe of Jack's ability to incorporate these junk-store finds into the set to help develop the characters. I could only marvel when I walked into the house he had created for Holly and her father to live in. I spent hours in Holly's bedroom, preparing for my role by imagining myself in her world. And everywhere I turned, there was some kind of treasure Jack had left for me. He had found an old stereopticon just like the one my grandparents Momsy and Pops had. Terry later shot a scene of Holly looking through it. The closets and drawers were filled with trinkets and books that Jack thought my character might have liked: a horned toad made of plaster of Paris, a tiny lead soldier on a three-legged horse, a door knocker shaped like a butterfly with painted enamel wings. I loved them so much; I still have them. I'd lay on Holly's bed and hold these gems in my hands, feeling like I was Scout in *To Kill a Mockingbird* and Boo Radley was leaving me gifts in the hollow oak tree. And, also like Scout, I had the eerie feeling that I was being watched, even though there didn't appear to be anyone else around.

Jack later admitted that he often was quietly watching me from another room while I explored the set. *Badlands* was like an enormous art project for him, and Terry and I were his grateful beneficiaries.

Terry Malick only shoots in natural light, so Jack would build several identical sets with skylights and windows facing different directions so that Terry could keep shooting as the sun moved across the sky. Terry rarely saw the sets before they were finished. He told me that working with Jack was like being on an Easter egg hunt—he never knew what wonderful things he would find when we arrived at a location. Usually, Jack would have just left, leaving behind an abundance of riches, and a complete environment for us to work in.

Terry and Jack never mapped out exactly how a set should be built. They didn't use storyboards or even color sketches. Instead they would have a conversation about what each scene might entail, but they didn't have to talk much. Jack and Terry's work together is very instinctual. They were already developing a kind of shorthand with each other, one that has intensified and deepened with each film they've done together. On *Badlands*, when they were discussing Kit and Holly's hideout in the woods, Terry mentioned the two fugitives might have built a wickiup or lean-to made of sticks, and Jack just nodded his head.

What we found the next day on the banks of the Arkansas River was almost beyond belief. There was a magnificent tree house built up among sprawling old cottonwood trees, made out of branches and twigs braided together with rope. It had ramps and rope swings, and a crow's nest where Jack had placed a copy of *Kon-Tiki* for Holly to read. That had a lot of meaning for me. It was the book my mother read to my brothers and me to keep us occupied during one long car trip to the Rio Grande Valley and back. There were other wonders Jack had imagined for us: a framed Maxwell Parrish print hanging on the tree house wall, soft pillows and blankets that made a bed; chickens living beneath a woven basket; booby traps and a covered pit that Kit could use to hide from bounty hunters. As soon as Martin and I saw the set, we started acting like children romping in a playground.

While Jack set the stage, Terry gave us the words to say and the freedom to inhabit our characters. Martin and I both loved working with Terry. We trusted him completely, and he coaxed the most nuanced performances out of us by trusting us back.

By now my relationship with Jack was in full bloom. When I arrived in Colorado, I was still sort of seeing that "Oh yeah, and don't answer the phone while I'm gone" guy back in LA. Once I left town, he started sending me messages. But I was so involved in the filming and having so much fun with Jack that I never answered them.

I'd found my soul mate, and didn't try to hide it. But Terry didn't realize what was going on until well into the summer. We were filming a scene where Martin and I were dancing in the dirt beneath the tree house, while "Love Is Strange" played on the portable radio. It was a beautiful but bizarre moment in the film, and Martin was being playful. We were shuffling and spinning around when he decided to ad-lib a move and kick me in the behind with his boot. All of a sudden, Jack walked into the shot while the camera was rolling and said, "I don't think you need to do that." They were all shocked. Jack has an almost Zen-like calm about him, and this was a side of him that none of them had seen before. But I got the joke. Jack's humor is deadpan; he was kidding around. Terry just shook his head and kept rolling.

One day after filming at the tree house, Jack invited me on our first official "date." He wanted to take me by boat down the Arkansas River back to the Capri Motel. That sounded like fun to me, so the crew left us out in the cottonwood grove and drove on back to town. Jack's dog, Five, went everywhere with him, and this time was no exception. So off we went, the three of us. No sooner had we launched that rickety little boat than it started taking on water. We sank fifty feet downstream. Luckily the Arkansas is shallow in the summer, and we made it to shore . . . just as a massive thunderstorm blew in across the prairie. There was all kinds of thunder and lightning and pelting rain. But we were so mad about each other that Jack and I just figured it was part of the adventure, and we started walking back to town in the storm. When we didn't show up at the motel, alarmed crew members sent out search parties to find us and bring us in. But we didn't want to be found and would jump into wet ditches whenever we saw a car coming.

By the time we made it back to the Capri, our friends were about to call the sheriff to start dragging the river. It never occurred to us that anyone would be worried. And some weren't.

We were still soaking wet and covered with mud when we walked into the restaurant, hoping for a hot cup of tea. Terry was eating dinner and looked up at us with a beatific smile.

"Oh, you're back," he said. "How was your boat ride?"

· · ·

BEFORE LONG, JACK AND FIVE moved into my motel room. I had everything all neatly arranged, with my clothes lined up in the closet and toiletries carefully laid out in the bathroom. Jack carried in a cardboard box stuffed with jeans, dark blue shirts, paintbrushes, and spare motor parts. Five ate human food, mostly chicken, sometimes bones and all. Sometimes Jack liked to feed her in the parking lot. It was a bit of an adjustment for me.

Jack and Five had to move out again a few weeks into the filming because my parents decided to drive up from Texas in their brand-new Buick to visit me. They wouldn't have understood our living arrangements. My parents got a room at the Capri and drove out to the set with us. They loved meeting Terry and his first wife, Jill, and they seemed to like Jack, who was introduced as our art director. After seeing us together for a while, they must have figured out that something was going on. And Daddy even thought enough of Jack to let us borrow the Buick one afternoon, but probably regretted his decision after Jack drove it off-road to check on one of the locations and brought it back covered with dust and dog hair. The next morning, when my dad was backing out of the motel parking lot, he got a flat. When we saw him later he said, "You won't believe this, but they found a chicken bone in my tire!" I looked at Jack, and Jack looked at Five. My dad never suspected a thing.

Jack and his dog moved back in after my parents left, but the motel room was getting awfully cramped. We decided to pool our living allowances and rent a small single-wide in the trailer park across the street for $55 a month. We decorated our new home with props from the film. This was my chance to impress Jack with my domestic skills, so I decided to cook him dinner. I wasn't eating meat at the time, but he loved it. So I made him a hamburger. It was so memorable he saved the recipe:

HOW TO MAKE A HAMBURGER

Ingredients:

ONE HALF POUND LEAN GROUND BEEF.

10 SALTINE CRACKERS.

1 ½ CUPS WESSON OIL.

1. Crush crackers and mix with lean ground beef.
2. Form into a softball-sized sphere.
3. Add Wesson oil to iron skillet.
4. Put ground beef softball in the center of the skillet.
5. Turn on stove.
6. Cook until done.

Jack never said a word when I mixed that prime ground beef with crackers. And he didn't even snicker when I plopped it into a skillet of cold oil. All he did, when I decided the meat was done, was wad up a huge ball of paper towels to try and soak up some of the grease. And then he ate the whole thing. Now, that's love.

Food was never very important to me. I was like my mother that way. She made wonderful, healthy meals, but she never liked to cook. When we were little, lunch would be sliced tomatoes, a wedge of lettuce, and a hard-boiled egg. She could make all the standard Southern dishes, like fried chicken, corn bread, and beans with ham hocks, but she never really enjoyed it. I remember when the space program was in the news, she said to me, "Sissy, one day we won't have to cook at all! We won't even have to eat! We'll just take a pill."

When I was little, my favorite snack was a sugar sandwich. I'd sneak into the kitchen and climb up on the counter to get out the sugar and white bread. I always thought I'd hidden the evidence, until Mother would walk into the kitchen and feel that telltale crunch under her shoes. "Sissy! Who's been into the sugar?"

My dad was the real cook in the family. He loved making sweets, especially fudge and popcorn balls and pulled taffy. It must have come from his Moravian ancestry, where food was the centerpiece of every family gathering and sharing a meal was the ultimate expression of love. I think that's why I tried so hard to cook for Jack, but most of the time, Five was the only one who really enjoyed my efforts.

At first I was afraid that Five would be jealous of me, because she was so devoted to Jack. He had gotten her three years before as a puppy in a pet shop in Pennsylvania Dutch country. Nobody could tell him what breed she was. She had long, shaggy hair that covered her face, like an English sheepdog, but she was much smaller and pure black. Her unusual name was decided long before she was born. When Jack was in seventh grade and delivering newspapers at five o'clock one morning, it just came to him: *One day I'm going to have a dog and name it Five.* He must have had a thing for numerals; Jack had also had a cat called Two-and-a-half. Five was so smart and well behaved that she never ran around or made a sound while we were filming. She did whatever Jack asked her to do, and she followed him like a shadow. Five always sat between us in the front seat of Jack's truck, and she'd lean against me. At first I thought she was trying to push me away from Jack, but that wasn't the case. She leaned on the people she liked, and it meant that she had accepted me.

Maybe she was also grateful that I saved all of our lives one night when we were riding around in that van.

Much of the story of *Badlands* is told in voice-over by my character, and one scene called for Holly to describe seeing the distant lights from the oil fields around Cheyenne. Since there were no flaming derricks nearby, Jack had built enormous bonfires out on the prairie to create the effect. When the sun went down, Jack lit the fires and Terry started filming. We were sitting in Jack's van, watching the fires and listening to Terry and the crew on our walkie-talkie, when Jack noticed that one of the burning piles had started to go out. "Got to go stoke that fire!" Jack said, as we suddenly went tearing across the desert at top speed. Of course he didn't turn on his headlights, because that would have wrecked the shot. We were bouncing along at fifty miles per hour, which normally would have seemed like fun to me, but we were off the road and couldn't see a thing in front of us in the moonless night. I started yelling at him to stop, but he kept going. Finally I screamed so loud there was nothing he could do but slam on the brakes.

Then we heard Terry's voice over the radio. "Cut!"

Jack switched on the headlights. We were teetering inches away from a twenty-foot drop into a ravine. If I hadn't screamed, we would have sailed off the edge and landed facedown, with no seat belts or air bags to save us. After that Jack was afraid not to listen to me.

BOTH JACK AND TERRY had this idea that the prairie was as flat as it looked, and they always took crazy risks driving around on it. One afternoon Terry wanted to shoot some scenes of Kit racing around in a stolen car on the open range. The crew turned a Corvair into a camera car because it had a rear engine and a trunk in the front. They removed the trunk lid and strapped Terry inside with a camera in his hands and a football helmet on his head, then someone drove the Corvair across the desert at top speed while Terry filmed. I'll never forget the image of him zooming across the plains in a cloud of dust, wearing that silly football helmet.

It quickly became clear to everyone that Terry would die to get things right. He was—and is—an artist and a perfectionist. We'd be shooting one scene and he'd look over and the moon would be coming up, so we'd all drop everything and rush to get that shot. We were running around like the Channel 5 News Team, Terry later joked. Jack and I thought it was a brilliant and exciting way to work, but the crews tended to disagree. One morning Terry came out of his motel room with all the actors in tow. The production team had set up ahead of us down the road somewhere, but Terry liked the light where we were, so he said, "Okay, we're gonna film here." The producer said, "We can't do that! We've already sent all the equipment over to the location!"

"I don't care," Terry said in his soft drawl. "I'm shooting here."

There was a lot of eye-rolling among the camera operators and grips. Terry had never completed anything longer than that short in film school, and most of the crew figured they knew more than he did. Which may have been true. But Terry never lost sight of his vision, and he fought for every foot of film he shot. And he shot a lot of film. Thousands and thousands of feet; he was insatiable. By midsummer he was already over budget and behind schedule. It seemed like every day the production was about to be shut down for lack of funds.

The low point came when a special effects man named Roger George flew in from Hollywood to stage the fire in Holly's house. Rather than build special sets to burn, he decided to film the fire inside an abandoned house—which seemed risky to Jack. But since George was the pro, everyone went along with him. Roger liked to coat everything with rubber cement and then light it up for dramatic effect. He and his team were walking around the house in gum boots, pouring rubber cement on piano keys and slathering it on walls. Everybody was getting light-headed, including Jack, who stepped outside the house for some fresh air. The idea is to wait for the fumes to dissipate and then set a controlled burn in each room. But Roger's young assistant apparently didn't get that memo, because as soon as they were done, he lit the match. Roger was screaming, "Nooooooo!" when the house went up in a fireball. The crew, the cinematographer—everybody started diving out the windows. Roger ran outside, engulfed in flames. He had to be medevaced to a hospital in California, where he recovered from serious burns. It was a miracle that nobody was killed. The house burned to the ground, along with the equipment and the cameras.

After that, most of the crew quit, figuring they wouldn't be paid. Only the actors and the art department lasted for the whole shoot, which went on for sixteen weeks. What remained of the crew operated out of my dressing trailer, which was the only vehicle left behind. I ended up catering their meals, which shows how desperate things had become. Luckily they enjoyed peanut butter and jelly.

But we soldiered on. Edward Pressman, one of the producers, needed to borrow more money to complete the film. He asked for $100,000 and the bank turned him down. Then Ed's mother, a colorful and savvy businesswoman who ran the family toy company, stepped in to help. "Never think small," she advised. So she went to the bank, asked for $1 million, and they gave her the $100,000 we needed to keep going.

By the time we wrapped, Jack was painting the leaves green at some of the locations, because the season had changed to fall. He and I rented a small U-Haul trailer and filled it with some of the treasures we'd saved from the set. Then we loaded Five into the red van and pointed it west on the interstate, heading back to Los Angeles and a new life together. As we were pulling out of La Junta, we passed Terry's Volkswagen bus on the side of the road. He stood smiling next to it with his wife, Jill, his Great Dane, and an Aeroflex camera. He had about twelve rolls of film left, and he wanted some more nature shots.

IT TURNS OUT that Terry Malick liked editing even more than he liked shooting film. *Badlands* took ten months to cut, and he decided to write an extended voice-over for my character to help knit together the narrative. He stapled quilts to the walls of one bedroom in his house, and we recorded the voice-over there. It is some of the most beautiful language ever written for film, and I still get chills hearing it. But it also contains the funniest, most deadpan lines I've ever read. "Kit shot a football. He said it was excess baggage." Or, while looking out at the bleak, featureless landscape, Holly says, "Kit told me to enjoy the scenery, and I did." The genius of *Badlands* is that Terry somehow made it possible for the audience to forgive Holly for her complicity in the murders because of her innocence and pliability. Or, as she puts it, "When Kit says 'frog,' I jump."

When *Badlands* was finally finished, I went along with Terry to present it at the New York Film Festival. We were both exhausted, living on nerves and excitement, when we finally took our seats at the Lincoln Center premiere. Terry and I grabbed each other's arm like kids as the film rolled along on the big screen. But we were shocked that the audience watched in utter silence. *Badlands* is by no means a comedy, yet there are many funny parts; but nobody even chuckled. There was applause at the end of the screening, but we had the sinking feeling that the audience didn't get the film. Or maybe they thought it was inappropriate to laugh at a couple of killers, no matter how ironic or funny the lines.

But no matter. The critics loved *Badlands* and instantly recognized it as a landmark in American cinema, even though it would never be a hit at the box office. The studio didn't know what to do with it, how to market it. But I realized even then that I had been a part of something great. I'd been a part of making a nearly perfect movie, and if I never did another film again, it would be okay, because it was enough to have done *Badlands*.

Terry Malick went on to direct a succession of brilliant, complex films, from *Days of Heaven* to *The Tree of Life*, always with Jack by his side as production designer. But nothing has ever really matched the magic of discovery we all felt that summer in the Colorado desert, when we learned how a film could be a living, breathing, collaborative work of art.

"What's the man I'll marry gonna look like? What's he
doing right this minute? Is he thinking about me
now, by some coincidence, even though he doesn't know
me? Does it show on his face?"

— Holly Sargis, *Badlands*

J UST LIKE HOLLY IN TERRY'S SCRIPT, WHEN I WAS A GIRL, I
used to daydream about the man I would spend my life with. What
does he look like? What's he doing right now? It turns out that while I
was looking up at the sky in Texas, trying to imagine my dream partner,
Jack Fisk was growing up in Illinois and Virginia, watching the same
moon and wondering the same thing. How lucky we were to have found
each other, and at just the right time. If we had met a few years earlier,
when I wanted to be a rock star and he was a painter, we might have
sailed right by each other. But now all either of us wanted to do was
be artists and make films. It was already impossible to imagine a life
apart.

We were a perfect match. I always fell for the tall, dark, handsome
guys. And Jack had always dated strawberry blondes, starting with his
first grade girlfriend, Maude, who I'm told looked a lot like me. When
we showed each other the childhood photos we carried with us, both of

us proudly holding up fish we had caught, it looked like we could have grown up in the same neighborhood. We would have been friends. Jack was like my brothers: kind, straightforward, with a great disposition and a sense of humor—and more than a little mischief. Most of all, when I was with him, I felt like I could be myself. I didn't have to pretend I knew things I didn't, or be cooler or smarter than I was. He thought I was beautiful and intelligent, and he liked me the way I was. And if that was okay with him, it was okay with me, too.

JACK AND I SPENT hours and hours telling each other stories about our childhoods and our families. Jack Alan Fisk Jr. was born in Ipava, Illinois, a small village tucked into the cornfields between Peoria and the Mississippi River. His ancestry is German, Swedish, French, English, and Cherokee Indian, a heritage that expresses itself in his high cheekbones and dark hair. His grandfather owned and operated Ipava's only funeral home and furniture store, and his dad, Jack Sr., was expected to go into the family business. He met and married Geraldine Rosalind Otto while they were both in college, and their first child, Susan, was born in 1941. Jack Sr. was in undertaking school in Chicago when the Japanese bombed Pearl Harbor, and he immediately signed up with the army air corps. After pilot training, he was assigned to the 475th Fighter Squadron, flying P-38s in the Pacific theater. He rose through the ranks to captain and earned a Distinguished Flying Cross as an ace pilot with seven confirmed kills. According to family lore, Jack Sr. flew on a combat mission with Charles Lindbergh, who was then a civilian, training U.S. pilots how to conserve fuel. When they ran into a Japanese warplane in the skies over New Guinea, Lindbergh shot him down. Because he wasn't supposed to be shooting at anything, Lindbergh wanted to award the kill to Jack Sr. "Let Fisk take it," he said. But word

149

of the dogfight got back to the army brass, who grounded Lindy and sent him home.

After Jack Sr. returned from the war, the family lived together in a house across from a small park, and he reluctantly went back to work as an undertaker. Jack was born in December 1945, and nineteen months after that came another daughter, Mary. Jack was a happy, imaginative little boy. I loved the story he told me about sitting on the front steps of his family's house in Ipava, watching a man mowing the grass in the little park across the street. Jack could hardly believe his eyes; the man had a pet monkey that rode on the top of the mower. So every Saturday Jack would sit patiently on the front steps and wait for the man with the monkey on the mower to cut the grass. He loved that monkey and would watch it for hours. Finally one day, he couldn't stand it any longer, and he ran across the road to get a better look. But when he got up close, the monkey was gone. Jack was crestfallen. The monkey on the mower was just a big, black gas-powered engine. So Jack ran back across the street, sat down on the steps, and there was the monkey again, riding on top of the mower.

Later that year he learned the truth about Santa Claus, too.

Jack Sr. still loved the air corps, and kept up his skills piloting planes out of Chanute Airfield whenever he could. He was flying to Washington, DC, to petition for reinstatement into active duty when his plane was caught in a thunderstorm and crashed in a cornfield in Indiana. Jack Jr. was just shy of his third birthday when his father died. He has only hazy memories of his dad, what he looked like, what they did together. What he does recall is that his world felt warm and complete and safe when his father was alive; and then things were not very good at all.

Gerri was left with three young children and working for her in-laws. Hoping for a better life, she remarried. Charles Luton was an executive who set up and managed brass foundries all over the world. He adopted Gerri's children and changed Jack's first name to John. So for all of his school years, Jack was known as John Luton. Jack was sent to a Catholic military boarding school when he was in the third grade. I have trouble imagining a military academy run by nuns, but Jack did well there, even though he was a little homesick. He was the highest ranking officer in third and fourth grade, which meant he got to lead the cadets when they marched on the parade ground. For some reason Jack could never remember the drill routine, but he was so popular that his fellow cadets always covered for him. The most important thing he took away from that school was something Sister Mary Bartholomew told him. "Think of your every action as a prayer," she said. The notion that you were speaking to God in everything you did, both good and bad, and that praying was more than just repeating words in church, made a deep impression on Jack. One's whole life can be a manifestation of God, a continuous act of love. Of course she also told him that because he wasn't Catholic, the best he could ever do was purgatory.

The family moved constantly. Charlie Luton's job took them to Michigan, to Virginia, and even overseas. In Lahore, Pakistan, Jack used to play with another American boy named Bill, whose father worked at the embassy. Years later, Jack was surprised to run into his childhood playmate again at the release party in New York for a PBS film called *Verna, USO Girl*. My costar in that film, William Hurt, turned out to be the little boy that Jack had known in Pakistan. They hadn't seen or thought about each other for decades. Talk about a small world.

Jack's family ended up in Alexandria, Virginia, and Jack enrolled in public high school. He was still going by the name John Luton, and the student alphabetically assigned to the seat next to him in homeroom was a boy from the Northwest named David Lynch. A few years later, after he left home, Jack changed his name back to Jack Fisk. But if he had done it sooner, he might never have met David, and his life might have taken a very different direction.

David's father was a research scientist with the Interior Department who had transferred to Washington after years in Montana and Idaho. David was a handsome, all-American-looking kid who seemed perfectly conventional, at least on the outside. Like Jack, he had already decided he wanted to be an artist.

They shared a rented studio in Alexandria and painted side by side. After graduation, David went to college at the Museum School in Boston, which he hated, and Jack went to Cooper Union in New York City, which he found too commercial for his taste. David and Jack both decided to drop out and travel to Europe, where they planned to study with the Viennese painter Oskar Kokoschka. But they didn't think it out very well. They managed to get free tickets over the Atlantic by signing up as chaperones for a group of teenage girls on their way to a summer vacation. But once they landed in Europe, they quickly realized that the couple of hundred dollars they had saved up wasn't going to last long. It was much more expensive than they'd imagined, especially since David insisted on drinking real Coca-Cola and would only smoke American Marlboro cigarettes. After a series of misbegotten adventures— including a wild train ride on the Orient Express and getting stranded in Athens—the young artists ran out of money and had to wire their families to help them get home. The trip that was supposed to have lasted several years lasted two weeks.

Shortly after that debacle, Jack transferred from Cooper Union to the Pennsylvania Academy of the Fine Arts, which he decided was a true artists' paradise. Some of the finest young painters in the country were there, including James Havard. When David heard Jack's stories, he packed up and moved to Philadelphia.

There, Jack and David were living the "art life," staying in dangerous rattrap apartments, showering at school, buying all their clothes and furniture at Goodwill, and eating when their dieting girlfriends gave them their school meal tickets. Rumors circulated that Jack and David were really from very wealthy families. To some people it seemed they were far too happy to be truly indigent. Jack started experimenting with sculpture and other media, creating the large constructions that would later inspire his production design. One of his pieces was a fiberglass sculpture of a man who had fallen asleep in a chair reading a newspaper. The figure had a rubber stomach embedded with a battery-powered device that moved his belly up and down under the paper, like he was breathing. Jack stored it in the basement of his apartment building, where it nearly gave the gas meter reader a heart attack. The meter reader came to love the sculpture so much that Jack gave it to him when he moved away.

David Lynch's latent eccentricities flowered in Philadelphia. He would work all night, then sleep until five o'clock in the afternoon, just in time to head next door to Pop's Diner for a cup of coffee before it closed. The diner was also popular with workers from the city morgue across the street, and David befriended them. They would take him on tours of the facility and show him the "parts" room," where they kept unidentified body parts. He'd get dressed up for these occasions in at least two ties—one regular and the "lucky tie" that he wore everywhere.

In 1967, David married a fellow art student and moved into a house in an even rougher neighborhood. He also bought a used Bolex camera for $400 and started making short art films. For his first piece, he projected an animated film onto a three-dimensional, white, sculpted screen. Before long, David's quirky vision earned him the attention of the American Film Institute, which gave him funds for a short film called *The Grandmother*, about a boy who plants a seed in the ground that grows into, well, his grandmother. In 1970, David was accepted into AFI's Center for Advanced Film Studies—the same place Terry Malick was honing his skills.

That August, David moved out of his house, rented a U-Haul truck, and drove to Los Angeles with his brother John and his best friend, Jack. Initially, Jack had no particular interest in moving to LA, but he decided to come along for the ride. "Let's just say it was time for me to get out of Philadelphia," he told me, offering no explanation other than a mischievous, gap-toothed grin. Once on the road, he decided to make the most of it. He had just been to a James Rosenquist show at New York's Metropolitan Museum and had been inspired by the eighty-foot paintings of spaghetti and jet airplanes. Jack was attracted by the scale, and he was bored painting by himself in a studio. Since Rosenquist had worked as a billboard painter, Jack got an idea: Maybe Los Angeles would be an interesting place, with good weather, to start painting billboards. He also thought he might try his hand at acting, since he had appeared in some of David's short films.

It turned out that his acting skills were not as good as he'd thought once he had actual lines to say. And because the studio system was collapsing in Hollywood, all the best scenic artists were working as sign painters. But Jack was fascinated by the film business and got his first job directing traffic for a biker movie being shot in Topanga Canyon. He graduated to gaffer and grip jobs, and eventually art directing and production design. During the filming of *Badlands*, he fulfilled one of his art school dreams: Terry Malick made Holly's father a sign painter, and Jack got to create the most wonderful billboard ever seen on the Colorado plains.

JACK HAD GIVEN UP his small rented house in Laurel Canyon while we were on location for *Badlands*, so when we arrived back in LA we stayed with Janit and Dona for a few days. We wanted a place that felt like living in the country, so we rented a little stone house just off the main road in Topanga Canyon. We furnished it with $300 and the props from *Badlands*. The first person Jack wanted me to meet was his younger sister, Mary, who had also moved to Los Angeles. Mary met us at the door looking very cool in a Hawaiian shirt, but she was in a bit of a tizzy because the soufflé she'd made for dinner had fallen. She apologized all evening, but I thought it was delicious. I had no idea it was supposed to be fluffy. What she didn't know was I'd never even seen a soufflé before and wouldn't have recognized one if I'd tripped over it. I haven't had one since, so I can honestly say that Mary's was the best soufflé I've ever eaten.

The next person I met was Jack's best friend, David Lynch. David was living in what had been the horse stables of the twelve-acre estate in Beverly Hills that the American Film Institute was leasing as its headquarters. David had turned the stables into a makeshift soundstage, where he was filming his first feature, *Eraserhead*, a film about "dark and troubling things." He was surreptitiously living behind a padlocked door in the stables, sleeping during the day and working all night.

ALTHOUGH WE HAD been together for months, it wasn't until I met David that Jack really started making sense to me. Together they were like two alien Eagle Scouts on a mission from Planet Art. For them, filmmaking was an expressive form that synthesized all of the creative elements of painting and sculpture, light and music. It's what they talked about, and all they wanted to do. I felt lucky to be included, and I found that I fit right in with them. This was the place I had been looking for. For the first time in my life, I felt a part of the conversation. I finally had my own seat at the table.

Soon after we met, David started imagining a role for me in one of his future films. "We'll call it *Ronnie Rocket*, Sis," he said in the funny, clipped way that he speaks. "We'll shave your head and dress you in dungarees with a wide belt and heavy work boots. It will be great!" Thanks, Dave.

While he was making *Eraserhead*, David was always broke. His only source of income was his paper route, delivering the *Wall Street Journal* in his Volkswagen Beetle. The film consumed every dime he made, and the production lurched along in fits and starts. The delays have become famous. It's true that the lead character, played by Jack Nance, walked through a door one day and walked out of it a year and a half later.

Jack helped David however he could, by collecting material for sets and even appearing in a small role as "Man in the Planet," which involved having his face and torso slathered with latex. It took days to get the gunk out of his beard, and Jack still jokes with David about it. Whenever Jack had extra money, he would invest it in the film. There was a time when Jack cashed in every paycheck he got from one film job and handed it over to David.

When *Eraserhead* was finally released in 1977, it became an instant cult classic. It also caught the eye of Mel Brooks, who was producing a dramatic film about John Merrick, the deformed sideshow performer known as the Elephant Man. By then David had married Jack's younger sister, Mary, and had come up in the world. Instead of locking himself in the stables, David and Mary lived in a garage that they converted into an apartment. David still worked at night, spending all afternoon drinking milk shakes and coffee at Bob's Big Boy and jotting ideas down on paper napkins. After he was nominated for two Oscars for adapting and directing *The Elephant Man*, he and Mary finally moved into a real house. His lucky tie was working.

EVEN THOUGH *BADLANDS* WAS A HIT with the critics, it was not my ticket to instant stardom. I was getting some roles, but a lot of the time, I was helping Jack. I would run errands and help dress the sets and paint flats. It was the hardest work I ever did. I got shin splints running from one prop house to another. I wasn't very good at it, but I was learning, and everything I did with Jack was fun.

A few months after we arrived back in LA, Jack had the chance to work with another up-and-coming director named Brian De Palma, who was filming *Phantom of the Paradise*, a rock 'n' roll remake of *The Phantom of the Opera*. I had auditioned for the film and lost out to Jessica Harper, a talented actress with an enormous voice. But I was happy to pitch in and help with the sets—and Jack needed help. The day before filming was to begin, he fired his entire art department because they hadn't gotten the first set ready on time. Then he had to scramble to finish decorating the sets by himself. We stayed up all night sewing together a black satin bedspread that was designed to look like a 45 record. Jack's construction crew had built a huge skylight over a big round bed for an important scene that takes place in a thunderstorm. Unfortunately, one of the crew members used water-soluble caulking on the skylight, which fell apart during the rainstorm and ruined the set. It was only the first of many disasters on that film.

The next location was in Dallas, Texas, where we took over the old Majestic Theatre and dressed it like a gothic opera house for the concert scenes. Jack had no time to assemble a real art department, so he took what he could find—me and my teenage cousin Sam, who had long curly hair and wore a beaver top hat. The closest Sam had ever gotten to an art project was helping his mother with her decoupage. But he was smart and funny, and he was willing to work hard.

Brian De Palma, the son of a New Jersey surgeon, had studied physics before becoming a director. Although Brian is a very talented filmmaker, he is also a famous curmudgeon. It is not easy to make him laugh. If and when you ever did, you felt like you'd won the lottery. I would say to him, "Good morning, Brian," and he'd growl, "What's so good about it?" It didn't take long to realize that his gruffness was part of a razor-sharp sense of humor and a huge part of his charm.

Brian came to rely on Jack to fill in the gaps in the production. When they realized they needed to create a new record label for the film, Jack designed the classic "Death Records" logo. His inspiration came when he walked out the door one morning and stumbled upon a deceased songbird. He picked up its stiff little corpse and took it to work, where it was photographed and immortalized as the Death Records mascot. (You can still find the T-shirts online.)

One day Jack was busy with something or other at the next location so he left Sam and me in charge of the set. "There's nothing much happening today. They'll be on this scene through most of tomorrow," Jack told us. "Just watch the set. If they need any props, put 'em in."

The minute Jack left, Brian decided that the scene wasn't working, and he wanted to shoot a different scene. There were no cell phones back then, and no way to reach Jack to ask him what to do. The script supervisor saw that I was starting to panic. She came over to me and said, "Don't worry, it's the same set. You just have to repaint and redress it." So I said, "Okay, no problem."

We moved the props around as fast as we could and then started putting a new coat of paint on the walls. Brian was sitting in his director's chair with his arms folded, watching us, which was a little disconcerting. Sam and I didn't know enough to realize that we had to paint the set with white primer before changing the color. Before you could say presto chango, the blue we were trying to cover began bleeding into the pink, and we ended up with a blotchy magenta mess. I'm sure that if he could have, Jack would have fired us, too. And from that point on, Brian De Palma would think of me as the worst, no-talent set decorator he'd ever worked with.

Despite the difficulties of the shoot, it was great being back home in Texas. I made a few trips to see my folks, and Jack's mom, Gerri, flew down from Washington to visit us on location. We'd had an instant connection from the moment we met. I loved her for being so smart and down-to-earth, and she could tell how much I appreciated her son, which was what mattered to her. When she arrived in Dallas, she spent one whole night, all dressed up, sitting in the middle of the empty Majestic Theatre, watching Jack clean and sweep the stage.

One of the best things that happened to us during that shoot was finding Twerp. We were rummaging around in a storage shed filled with props one day, when we heard the faint sound of a little bird singing. We followed the peeping to a tiny blue parakeet hopping around in a box of broken mirrors, trilling happily at his many reflections, probably thinking he had lots of little blue friends. Jack and I found a cage for him and named him Twerp.

When we wrapped the film, Twerp traveled home with us to California. By now Jack and I had moved into another rented house deeper in Topanga Canyon, a rugged, twisting passage through the Santa Monica Mountains connecting the Pacific Coastline with the San Fernando Valley. I loved it there. Unlike the more cultivated, shabby-chic grottoes of Laurel Canyon, Topanga had a rustic, back-to-the-land vibe, and the mountains there were filled with miles of trails. I would hike for hours in my flip-flops; you could go barefoot to the grocery store. And I loved living with Jack Fisk. He woke up every morning thinking, *Oh boy! What do we get to do today?* We were happy as could be with each other, but neither of us was interested in marriage. We thought, *Why mess up a good thing?* My mother, however, saw it differently.

"If you love each other and want to live together, why not get married?" she said.

"Oh, Mother!" I said. "What's the big deal about getting married? It's just a piece of paper."

She thought for a minute and said, "Well, if it's not such a big deal, why don't you just go ahead and do it?"

I had to laugh. I said, "Okay, Jack! Let's get married!"

We took the blood tests everyone needed to get married, then we forgot about it until the day before they were about to expire. When we realized we'd either have to do the deed or get another blood test, we thought, *Another needle? No way. We'd rather get married.* We called the Cottage Chapel in Santa Monica and set a time for that afternoon. It was April 12, 1974. We didn't tell anybody what we were planning. I wore old blue jeans, for something old and something blue, and I was carrying a bright new penny. . . . I think I may have borrowed the penny from Jack. We loaded Five into the car and threaded our way down the canyon to the Pacific Coast Highway, then headed east on Santa Monica Boulevard toward the chapel. At a light, we looked over, and there was David Lynch in his Volkswagen Beetle, stopped right beside us. We honked and waved, and David waved back. "Hey, Jack! Hey, Sissy!" That chance meeting made David our best man; Five was the maid of honor.

There was music playing when we arrived at the chapel, so we waited outside the door for a long time, thinking someone else must be getting married. Then a nice minister in a suit opened the door, welcomed us in, and began to read the service. Suddenly he pulled back a curtain to reveal a very small organ being played by a very petite woman who craned her neck and gave us a great big smile without missing a note. It was like a vaudeville routine. The wedding was lovely, except for one little slipup by the minister . . . "and obey." After that was corrected, we exchanged our vows, then pressed Five's ink-covered paw onto our marriage license to sign as our "witness." (Sometime later we got a lovely letter from the minister, talking to us about the sanctity of marriage, and with a P.S.: "And hello to your well-behaved black dog.") On our way home, we stopped at the A&W for a couple of root beers. And that was our wedding day.

As conservative as my father was, I was surprised when he encouraged me to keep my birth name. One day he handed me a *Time* magazine with an article about that very thing. I hadn't considered changing it anyway; I'd worked too hard for the name I already had. And Jack couldn't care less about that sort of thing. But I was touched that my father wanted me to keep my identity, which was an advanced idea at the time. In those days, women still couldn't serve on juries in some places, and in at least one state there were laws on the books giving husbands complete control of joint property as "head and master" of their households. (I swear I'm not making this up!) My dad had always encouraged me to be independent and to manage my own money, have my own career, and be an equal partner in a relationship, so that I'd never be completely dependent on anyone. Jack not only agreed with this, he encouraged it. Eventually he and my father developed a deep respect and admiration for each other (even after he found out about the chicken bone).

The only time I was ever given any trouble keeping my own name was when I applied for a passport after I was married. For some unknown reason, the woman behind the desk in the passport office felt threatened. She did *not* want to give me a passport in my birth name. She said I was married now, and that meant my name had legally changed. I could not have my birth name on my passport; no way. I tried to explain that things had changed. I quoted the *Time* magazine article. I kidded. I cajoled. It didn't help. I begged. I threatened.

"Look," I said finally. "If it doesn't bother my husband, why should it bother you?"

She just looked at me.

"He's out in the car." I said. "I'll go get him and you can ask him yourself!" And so there I was, like a little kid, having to get my husband's permission to put *my own name on my passport*! It was 1974, but it felt like the Dark Ages.

· · · I I · · ·

I HAVE TO ADMIT THAT I WAS KIND OF BAFFLED WHEN THE
excellent reviews we received for *Badlands* didn't translate into good
jobs. I thought I was going to have to keep a big stick by the door to beat
people away, but sadly, that was not the case. (Although I did keep my
baton handy, on the off-chance someone asked me to twirl.) I made a
couple of forgettable films for low pay, and waited for my next big break.
Jack was working all the time, but he couldn't get into the art director's
union, which was a real closed shop, so his options in Los Angeles were
limited. One of the movies he worked on was a blaxploitation parody
set in Watts called *Darktown Strutters*. It wasn't exactly an artistic challenge, but the money was good. And one of the crew members, a teenager from Fort Worth named Bill Paxton, became a lifelong friend.

When we met Bill, he had shoulder-length hair and wore a top hat
(just like my cousin Sam—it must have been a Texas fashion state-
ment). He was living with his brother, Bob, and another friend in an
apartment in West Hollywood, paying the rent by doing odd jobs in the
movie business. Like David Lynch, and Jack before him, Bill had a paper route, although his newspaper was the *Los Angeles Times*. They used
to compete about who could throw the paper in the most perfect, accurate arc. Bill had been working on a Roger Corman film as a set
dresser when Jack hired him for *Darktown Strutters*. He was as handsome
as the movie star he would later become, and charming as the day is

long. Bill was an industrious worker, but he was still a goofy kid who loved to drink beer and listen to music all night when he had the chance. We all became great friends during that movie. And when Jack and I decided we could finally afford to take some time off for a belated honeymoon trip through Europe, we asked Bill, his brother, Bob, and another friend to stay in our house in Topanga and take care of our pets.

By then we had Five and Twerp and a cat named Strutter, who came from the rough neighborhood where Jack and Bill had been working. They were standing on the sidewalk when somebody pitched a kitten out the window of a moving car. Jack brought him home. Strutter must have been scarred by the experience, because he grew up to be the meanest cat in the world. He would bite your hand and then run away. That is, if you were lucky he ran away. If he thought you were special, when you walked up to the front door he would leap from the roof onto your head and try to tear your face off. So, you see, we couldn't let him stay with just anyone. Still, looking back, I wonder what on earth we were thinking, leaving our house for five weeks with a bunch of teenage boys and a psychopathic cat.

THE TRIP WAS GREAT. Jack and I traveled all over Europe and the Middle East. His sister Susie was living and working in Beirut with her first husband, an Egyptian named Hosni Iskander and their young son, Nasif. It was a beautiful city, right on the Mediterranean, with the clearest, bluest water I had ever seen. Everything seemed so exotic in Susie and Hosni's apartment. Even simple things, like light switches, bathroom fixtures, drawer pulls, toilets, were like nothing I had ever seen before, certainly nothing I'd ever seen at Lumber City. (See, I was even starting to think like an Art Department P.A.) But I was most captivated by a huge self-portrait of Jack hanging on their dining room wall. It was an incredible drawing, done by Jack while he was in art school. I coveted it for myself, but I was too polite to ever mention how badly I wanted it.

As we were preparing to leave the States, my parents worried about us traveling to Lebanon, because fighting had broken out there. I wasn't at all concerned. But then, I was young and naive, and not very interested in international news. I'm afraid my world revolved around what was happening in the entertainment section of the *LA Times*. Susie had told us it was safe in Beirut; we would be just fine. But after we arrived we learned that even though there was supposed to be a cease-fire, the streets were still dangerous. Large sections of the city were off-limits, and there were many routes that we couldn't take. We saw buildings and whole neighborhoods pockmarked by bullets and badly damaged from mortar fire. But Hosni, a tall, handsome, gentle man, was fluent in English and Arabic, and had relatives living in the city, so he was the best tour guide imaginable. We saw the country as few tourists could, and we were always greeted with warmth and hospitality—even though I made some grievous cultural mistakes. I had no idea that it wasn't proper to wear short shorts all over the Middle East. Fortunately, Susie made sure I was covered up when we were in public places.

Jack and I drifted through the first leg of our honeymoon in blissful innocence, untouched by the events erupting around us. I only remember hearing gunfire one time, while we were lying on the beach enjoying the sun. On the news that night we learned that troops had been landing just down the beach from us. We had no idea we were in the middle of an invasion, right there in our bathing suits.

We left Beirut just before the cease-fire collapsed and the whole country was caught up in a full-blown, bloody civil war. A few months later, Susie and Hosni had to flee Beirut in the middle of the night. Their apartment was occupied by Lebanese troops, and the soldiers vandalized the huge self-portrait of Jack. That made me want it even more—the layer of graffiti would have made it an even more amazing piece of artwork. But the war dragged on for years, and I never got the drawing out of the country.

After we left Beirut, Jack and I slowly made our way across Europe.

The rest of our vacation was wonderfully uneventful. We had the time of our lives traveling by train on Eurail passes and staying in lovely pensions along the way. We hiked mountains in Switzerland, rode Vespas through Italy, toured museums in Paris, and spent what money we had left shopping in England.

Then we sent word to Bill and the boys that we were on our way home.

As soon as I ran into the living room to say hello to Twerp, I knew something was terribly wrong with the bird. He wasn't singing happily. And he looked different. "Jack?" I said. "Isn't Twerp blue?" Jack threw Bill a look that was sharp enough to cut his throat. All Bill could do was stammer, "It was Strutter!" Then he told us a half-baked tale about how they kept piling our mail on a stool beneath the bird cage, and that the cat was finally able to climb all the way up and get to Twerp. They had thought it would ease our hearts if they bought us another parakeet.

It sounded kind of suspicious to me, but I was relieved that Five and the cat were in good shape and the house was relatively clean. "Not Sissy clean," as I pointed out. But good enough for forgiveness.

The full details of what happened while we were in Europe remained shrouded in mystery for the next thirty-four years. Bill Paxton would guard his secret well, even as he became an accomplished art director, working on big pictures with his friend the director James Cameron. He uttered not a peep when he switched to the other side of the camera, starring in *Twister* and *Apollo 13*. It wasn't until he was starring in the HBO show *Big Love*, and I had joined the cast for a recurring guest part one season, that Bill finally spilled the beans.

"Oh, Sissy, I'm still so sorry about Twerp!" he said, shortly after I arrived on the set. Then he proceeded to spin the story of Twerp's demise, except it was different from the version I had heard in 1974. Bill is a great storyteller, and a group of cast and crew members gathered around as he set the scene.

"Strutter was the meanest cat in the world and he was always trying to kill Twerp," said Bill. "He would just sit all day under the birdcage, staring up and twitching his tail. So it wasn't a safe situation for the bird, anyway. Meanwhile, my brother Bob and I and our friend Danny were really enjoying living at the house. We would stay up all night messing around and blaring music as loud as we wanted, and then by the time it was getting light, we'd be wanting to go to bed. But Twerp would just be waking up, the bird was like a rooster in that house. He'd be whistling and chirping and we couldn't get to sleep. So, we thought, the solution would be to hang the cage in the downstairs shower and close the door. Let that bird just sing its heart out. That worked out great for a while, until one night Strutter got in there. The next day we found feathers everywhere, and Twerp was gone.

"We panicked. Here we were, entrusted to take care of this beloved pet, and it was eaten. Then we thought, hell, parakeets kind of look alike. So we drove over to a pet shop in Tarzana and bought a parakeet that we thought looked sort of like Twerp. We figured that it had been a while since Sissy had seen it, and maybe she would think it was molting. So we brought it home. That bird just dropped dead, overnight. We didn't know why. (Twerp #2 probably took one look at Strutter and had a heart attack.) So we went back and bought another bird, Twerp #3. We got him set up in the cage just as Jack and Sissy walked in the door. . . ."

Bill looked over at me and saw the look on my face. I think he went a little pale. He may have even glanced around to see if Jack was going to pop out of the shadows and fire him. Then we both doubled over laughing. The truth was out.

"It was a cover-up!" I said.

"Aw, Sissy," Bill said. "We just made up that story about the mail to make it look like we weren't completely negligent."

I forgave him again. I just hope Twerp went quickly, without any suffering.

And Bill forgave me for the first time he hosted *Saturday Night Live* and, because he was my friend, they dumped a bucket of pig's blood on his head.

AFTER WE GOT BACK from our honeymoon, Jack and I went house hunting. We found a simple ranch house on a ridge at the summit of Topanga Canyon. It only cost $55,000, but we needed help guaranteeing a loan, so we asked my dad to come out and have a look at it. Daddy walked through the house, inspected the foundation, and took a stroll around the property. It was an ugly yellow stucco tract-type house, but sound. Jack already had big plans for the place. Best of all, you could see all the way across the canyon, over pine, eucalyptus, and chaparral-covered peaks. "Well, Jack," said my dad. "What you've got here is a $5,000 house . . . with a $50,000 view." He agreed to help us buy it.

Not long after we moved in, Jack started renovating. One weekend, using only a hatchet and a crowbar, he gutted the house and tore down three of its four walls. How it was still standing, I don't know. The only room he didn't tear up that weekend was our bedroom, so I went in there to get some sleep. When I woke up, I found Jack in what used to be the living room, sitting cross-legged like an Indian on top of a huge pile of rubble, reading a book titled *How to Build a Wood Frame House*. Of course, this was a man who could build anything for a film set, from windmills to dungeons. Before long, he turned that little tract house into a hilltop paradise, with vaulted ceilings and skylights and stained glass, an outdoor dining room and a wraparound deck with a hot tub and sauna.

The only disadvantages of living way up there were the steep roads and the constant threat from wildfires. Some nights we would sit on our deck and watch the orange glow creeping along distant ridges. We had some close calls in our part of the canyon. In the beginning, we would evacuate whenever a fire was near. I learned to keep the guitars and family treasures handy, and to hang all my clothes in one direction, so that I could scoop them out of the closet in a single motion. Then I would take a trick from Pancho Villa's playbook and pile all my belongings on the bed and haul them off wrapped in sheets, just like the bandits did in the Rio Grande Valley back in the day. I figured you could learn from anyone, even criminals.

Many times we would load our most precious possessions into our cars and sleep in the house, ready to leave at a moment's notice. Then it dawned on us: LA County used convicts to fight wildfires, while we were placing all our valuables in ready-to-be stolen vehicles left conveniently by the road! We also noticed that the more seasoned homeowners weren't panicking and running every time there was a fire. Jack and I took a cue from our neighbors and ended up staying behind most of the time, sitting on top of the house drinking margaritas while dousing our roof with the garden hose.

The steep road up to our house was a daily challenge. For a while we had my brother's Austin Healey, which Jack and I had driven out to Los Angeles from Texas during an ice storm (but that's another story). It was scary keeping that car in gear climbing up the mountain. There were places where it felt like we would flip over backward, or slide back down, like my father sometimes did trying to drive out of the spillway at Lake Lydia. Eventually we got used to it, but some of our friends never did. We had a tax accountant who was afraid of heights. We would have to pick him up at the bottom of the hill and blindfold him while we drove him up to our house to do our taxes. Once there, he sat with his back to the windows.

Jack was always finding interesting used cars for us, and the only requirement was that they make it up the canyon. The worst was a 1968 Ford Fairlane station wagon that was so awful I wouldn't even let him park it in front of the house. But he redeemed himself when he showed up one day with a pea green 1950 Plymouth in cherry condition, with only thirty thousand miles on it. It even had the original white sidewall tires. The car had only had one previous owner, a studio contract actress named Virginia Grey, who used to date Clark Gable. Her Pall

Mall cigarettes were still in the ashtray, stained with red lipstick. We left them there, untouched. This car was so awesome that people would stop on the street to stare at it. When Jack and I drove it to film premieres, and we'd pull up along with the usual Mercedes and Rolls, the valet parking guys would squabble over who got to park the Plymouth. Then one night, driving on Hollywood Boulevard, some jerk rear-ended us and then sped away. The impact knocked Five right into the front seat. We were all okay, but the accident crumpled the trunk and bent the chassis. We managed to drive the Plymouth back to Topanga, where it sat in a field for two years. When a house painter came up to give us an estimate and saw the Plymouth parked in a patch of weeds, he said, "Hey, I'll paint your house for free if you give me that car." Jack took the deal, but he felt bad. He hated to take advantage of anyone. But to everyone's astonishment, he only had to turn the key once and it started right up.

We eventually sold the Austin Healey, too. It was always a persnickety car, and the fuel injection often stopped working. My dad gave me a little hammer to carry whenever I drove it. When the car stopped on the freeway, I'd have to jump out in the emergency lane in my long hippie skirt and tapestry boots, then kneel down behind the back wheel and tap a little box. That would get the fuel going again. It finally got too dangerous for me to drive the Austin Healey, and we sold it to a collector. Now I wish I had kept it in the family, but back then I was still too young to be sentimental.

BRIAN DE PALMA LOVED working with Jack, and he hired him as art director for his adaptation of a Stephen King novel called *Carrie*. By now Brian was one of the hottest directors in Hollywood, and all the young actors in town wanted to be in the picture. I read for all of the female parts, but I wanted the title role of Carrie White, the bullied, alienated daughter of a religious fanatic, who unleashes her telekinetic powers on her high school class. Even though I was twenty-five years old, I still looked like a kid, and I thought I'd be right for the part. But Brian and the studio had a different idea. In fact, they didn't even want to give me a screen test, because they had already decided on another actress to play Carrie. I didn't know that Brian had argued with the studio to stop them from canceling my screen test.

I was unaware of what was going on behind the scenes when I called Brian the night before my scheduled screen test. I had just gotten my first television commercial, a big job for Vanquish headache medicine, and it would pay good money. The only problem was that it was shooting on the same day as my test. I was hoping Brian would say, "Are you crazy, Sissy? Of course, do the test!" Instead there was a short pause on the line and then Brian's scratchy, deadpan voice.

"Do the commercial," he said.

That made me so mad that I canceled the Vanquish job. Now I wanted this part so badly, I could taste it. I was convinced that Brian only thought of me as Jack Fisk's wife, the no-talent set decorator, and I was going to prove him wrong. I stayed up all night and reread the whole book. In the morning, I got ready for the test by not showering and smearing Vaseline in my hair. I rummaged through my trunks and found a pale blue sailor dress that my mother had someone make for me when I was in seventh grade. I looked like a total dork, and that was the point. When I got to the studio, the hair and makeup people started swarming around me, trying to fix me up for the screen test. I ran away from them, yelling, "Nooooooo!" I was already channeling Carrie. She reminded me of a timid girl I knew in school who dressed in hand-me-downs and had a reclusive, skittish personality. But there was a sweetness that I could see underneath her facade. It made you want to save her. That's what I took with me in front of the camera that day.

After the film was processed, Brian, the producers, the casting director, and Jack got together at the studio to watch all the screen tests. I had ridden along with Jack, but stayed outside waiting in the car. I was feeling awkward, crouched on the floorboard, thinking, *What am I doing here?* Then Jack came running out to the parking lot. "Ask for whatever you want!" he shouted. "You've got the part!"

The studio had been so sure that I was wrong for the role that they never bothered to make a deal with me before I tested, which is standard procedure. Brian was shocked as well, because he was so fixated on this other actress. But Jack told me that as soon as I came on screen, they knew they had finally met Carrie.

WE FILMED ON LOCATION all over the LA area, from the desert suburb where Jack and his team found Carrie White's house, to the track at Pacific Palisades High School, to the back lot at Culver City Studios where *Gone with the Wind* was made. The cast and crew were wonderful. Piper Laurie was over-the-top great as Carrie's mother. Then there were my classmates: Amy Irving, William Katt, P. J. Soles, Nancy Allen, and John Travolta, who I knew from my New York days. John was already becoming a big star with his television show, but he had signed up for an ensemble role in *Carrie*, and he never showed a bit of attitude about it. They were all young and beautiful, and I could see that they were having a great time together on the set. But I was doing my thing, inhabiting the character of Carrie. I kept myself separate and lurked in dark corners of the soundstage, brooding, while everybody else had fun. I decorated my dressing room with religious tokens and played heavy classical music on the stereo. Jack had a book of Gustave Doré's Bible illustrations that I pored over every day, studying the body language of people being stoned by their persecutors or tortured for their sins. I tried to start or end every major scene in one of those melodramatic positions. Some of Dore's figures were looking up at the sky without lifting their heads, and I practiced staring up and down like that, so that only the whites of my eyes would show. I was pretty serious back then; I was young and thought I had it all figured out.

THE FIRST DAYS OF SHOOTING were the hardest for me, because Brian started with the sequences in the high school girls' shower room. My scene called for Carrie to be standing naked under the shower, then panicking when she discovers she's bleeding, which she doesn't understand is her first menstrual period. I was wracking my brain, trying to come up with a sense memory or an experience in my life that I could draw on to make the scene feel real. I went to my director and said, "Brian, tell me about the scene."

He thought for a moment, then said, "It's like getting hit by a Mack truck."

"Got it," I said. "Like getting hit by a Mack truck . . ."

I wandered back to my dressing room, trying to imagine what it's like to be hit by a truck. Jack was there, and I told him my dilemma.

"Well, I got run over by a car once," he said.

"You did?"

Jack told me that he was walking home from school one winter evening and it was snowy and icy outside. He found an abandoned sled along the side of the road, and he decided to carry it home with him. It was getting dark and all the Christmas lights were on in the neighborhood. He thought they were so beautiful, reflecting off the snow. With the sled in his arms, he looked at all the houses along the way, with their colorful trees in the picture windows and sparkling lights on the eves, thinking how lovely it all was in the quiet and the snow . . . when he glimpsed a flash of light. He looked up and there was a set of headlights coming straight at him. He looked away, then back again, and now the lights were right on him. He pulled the sled up just as the car hit him. He went down and the car rolled over him, pinning him to the ground. The sled was splintered, but it had probably saved his life. He tried to get up, but he couldn't. He imagined that there was a four-hundred-pound man in that car, keeping him down. Then suddenly he heard the car start up again, and he thought, *Oh my God. He's going to back up and run over me again.* He thought he was a goner, but when the car moved, he was able to scramble out from under the tires. He was badly bruised, but not seriously injured.

I listened carefully to his story. And that's what I used when it was time for the shower scene.

Brian cleared the set of everyone who wasn't needed. I took off my robe and stepped under the spray while the camera rolled. Jack was sitting at my feet on the shower room floor, ready to pour fake blood into my hand when the time came. The water was warm, and I thought how Carrie would have enjoyed the feel of a hot shower, because she probably didn't get one at home. If you think of something, it will register on your face. Then I imagined: *I'm walking home from school, and all the Christmas lights are twinkling along the road. They're so beautiful and I'm thinking how beautiful they all are. . . .* I am soaping my arms and torso and my thigh. . . . *And then I see a flash of light. The headlights are right on me. I can't bear to see, so I look away.* There is blood all over my hands. *The car hits me with all its force. . . .* I start to scream. And scream. And then . . . I run.

All the beats in that scene matched the rhythms of Jack's story. It worked perfectly. I was so relieved.

Then Brian said, "Okay! Great, Sissy. Now let's try that again."

I spent the whole day in that shower. By the time we were finished, I looked like a ghost and felt all shriveled up, like when you've stayed in the bathtub way too long.

I wasn't the only actor having trepidations about that opening sequence. The script called for all the high school girls to be partially nude as they romped around the locker room at the end of gym class—a fantasy scenario that only a man could dream up. When it came time to actually shoot the scene, some of the girls were balking. According to Brian, there was a lot of weeping and hand-wringing among the cast. That is until we all watched the rushes from my shower scene.

I had it written into my contract that I would not appear fully nude on screen. But that was a trick of the editing room; the camera saw everything. And as it happened, every time Brian shot another take of the shower scene, the clapper board was placed directly in front of me. And each time the board was pulled away, the camera was right where my contract said it couldn't be. Now, I'm not a shy person—you can't be in this business!—but by the time the rushes were over, I didn't know if I should laugh or crawl under my chair. I decided to laugh.

"Thanks a lot, Brian!" I said, as sarcastically as I could, as I left the screening room.

After that, Brian later told me, the female cast members stopped complaining about their topless locker room scene.

PIPER LAURIE WAS SO MUCH FUN to work with. We had a fabulous time playing everything big—big gestures, big emotions, outrageous scenes. And she was such a good sport. For her death scene, I had to telekinetically impale her with a hail of kitchen cutlery, crucifying her like St. Sebastian. But those were the days before computer-generated imagery, so we had to shoot the scene the old-fashioned way. First the special effects guy put her in a harness with all the trick knives and forks already in place, then they attached them to different locations in the kitchen with wires. On cue, the special effects person would yank each wire and the utensil would come spinning out of her, while she jerked her body in the same direction. Then the editor would reverse the film and paint out the wires, and it looked like she was being stabbed. It was so much fun to watch, but it was time-consuming. The crew had to break several times during the filming. At one point Piper was seen walking to lunch with knives, forks, and potato peelers sticking out of her and her nightgown drenched in fake blood. She casually waved hello to David Janssen, who was filming an airplane disaster movie, while he dined on lobster in his trailer. David waved back without missing a bite.

JACK WAS HAVING A GREAT TIME designing the sets for *Carrie*. Like Terry Malick, Brian De Palma loved how Jack would create a world for the actors to inhabit, often working around the clock to stay just ahead of the camera crew. Brian said, "Jack's sets were always wet." (That came to be known as Jack's calling card.) The biggest and trickiest was the apocalyptic prom scene where Carrie is voted queen, which was shot on the same sound stage in Culver City that was used for *Citizen Kane*. The night before Brian started filming there, Jack's team of "elves," including Bill Paxton, were busy fashioning tinfoil stars and painting glitter on the decorations for the freshly built high school gym set.

It wasn't hard for me to get into this scene, because I'd been to a few proms in my time. I'd even been homecoming queen my senior year at Quitman High School. The lights and music were so familiar to me, and I could easily imagine how Carrie would have been dazzled by the attention. Of course, anyone who has seen the movie knows that Carrie's moment of glory is destroyed when her enemies drop a bucket of pig's blood on her head and all hell breaks loose—literally. They filled the bucket with Karo syrup and red food dye. Of course we had to film the scene twice, from every angle. At first the "blood" felt like a warm blanket, but it quickly got sticky and disgusting. I had to wear that stuff for days. And when they lit the fires behind me to burn down the gym, I started to feel like a candy apple.

The scene where Carrie is buried in the rubble of her house was my first big death scene in films, and I wanted to make the most of it. It was a tricky setup. Jack had built a tall, narrow closet with the roof cut out so the camera could shoot down on me. I was thrashing around on the closet floor, causing an earthquake with my anger. The crew was shaking the closet walls while Jack stood next to Brian and the cameraman, throwing Styrofoam rubble on top of me. I was writhing in agony, focused on the sensation of being buried alive, but evidently I was taking too long to expire. I was almost completely covered up by debris when I heard a familiar, laconic voice calling down from above.

"Die, Sissy! Just die!"

JACK ALSO BUILT a quarter-scale model of Carrie White's house, which was used when the earth swallowed up the flaming ruins at the end of the picture. Now, don't read this if for some reason you haven't seen *Carrie* and don't want it spoiled for you. In the final scene, Amy Irving's character visits the spot where the house had stood and where Carrie lies buried. As she kneels to place some flowers on the grave, Carrie's hand shoots up out of the dirt and grabs her.

To set up the stunt, Jack dug a hole and built a plywood chamber beneath the soil, with a breathing hole and a piece of Styrofoam for Carrie's arm to push through. When I heard that Brian wanted to bring in an extra to do the hand scene, I objected.

"Please, Brian, I want to do it myself."

"But Sissy, we'll have to literally bury you in a coffin in the ground," Brian said. "Let me hire someone."

"No, Brian, I do all my own hand and foot work!" I was joking, but I was also serious.

He looked at me and then turned to my husband.

"Jack," he said. "Bury her."

AFTER *CARRIE* WRAPPED, Jack and I invited Brian De Palma out to have dinner with us in Topanga Canyon. Despite his grumpy demeanor, he is a lovely person and we have always been so fond of him. I wanted to make it a really special evening. I planned a wonderful roast chicken with vegetables, followed by scrumptious ice cream sundaes. On the day of the dinner, a freak winter storm blew into Los Angeles, with freezing temperatures and gale-force winds. Brian, a city boy from New York, managed to make the white-knuckle drive up Topanga Canyon, but by the time he arrived, we had lost electric power. The stove went off, but the bird was nice and brown, so we figured it had to be done. We were all bundled up in our warmest clothes when we sat down to eat. I served our lovely dinner, but when we cut into the chicken, it was still raw. Brian sat there shivering in his great big coat and wool cap, staring down at his plate of cold, bloody chicken.

Then he looked up at me balefully and said, "What's for dessert? Ice cream?"

NOW BRIAN DE PALMA KNEW I was a terrible cook as well as a worthless set dresser. But all was forgiven after *Carrie* was released in the fall of 1976. The film was Brian's first blockbuster, and it earned Academy Award nominations for Piper Laurie and for me—something unheard of at the time for a "horror movie." I even won the National Society of Film Critics award for best actress.

Around that time, Jack and I flew back to visit my folks in Texas. We were driving along the Central Expressway in Dallas with my brother Ed, his wife, and their two young sons, Mark and Stephen, chatting away, when we passed the biggest drive-in movie theater I had ever seen. And what would happen to be playing on that screen the size of Mount Rushmore? The shower scene from *Carrie*. I clamped my hands over my nephews' eyes, which were growing wide as saucers as it slowly dawned on them that it was Aunt Sissy up there—with no clothes on.

Did I say I was everywhere? *Newsweek* put my freckled face on the cover and featured me in a story about the "new actresses" of Hollywood. Around the time I was shooting Carrie, I also had a supporting role as a spaced-out housekeeper in Alan Rudolph's *Welcome to LA*. The film was produced by Robert Altman, who noticed me in the dailies and cast me in his next film, *3 Women*.

There was nothing ordinary about working with Bob Altman. He came up with the idea for *3 Women* one night in a dream; the next morning he stopped by the Fox studio and made a deal. Shelley Duvall, Janice Rule, and I began filming in the desert outside of Palm Springs with only a treatment and Bob's direction to guide us. I played Pinky Rose, a vacant waif who shows up looking for work at a low-rent physical therapy spa. Shelley's character, the super-efficient Millie Lammoreaux, takes Pinky under her wing, until their roles reverse and Pinky starts assuming Millie's identity.

We started each day's filming with a briefing from Bob, who would outline what he wanted in each scene. Then we'd improvise the dialogue. And each night, the script supervisor would type up her notes and hand out a page or two of what we had shot that day. By the end of the shoot we had a whole script, and a film that was as surreal and dreamlike as its origins.

As actors, we were all thrilled to be working with such an innovative director, and we gave the film everything we had, even when we weren't sure what we were doing. In the climactic scene Shelley's character delivers Janice Rule's baby in a lonely motel room while I stand by, watching. Bob set up the camera a long way off, to film with a long lens through an open doorway. The scene was emotionally wrenching, with a lot of thrashing and moaning and Shelley staggering around covered in blood. We all thought we must really be on to something when we noticed the whole crew gathered around Bob Altman. Instead of wandering around the set, everyone was staring intently at the monitor.

When the scene finally ended, Shelley and Janice and I walked over to talk to Bob, eager to find out what brilliant thing we had done to draw so much unexpected attention. We soon discovered that the "monitor" was actually a portable television set, and everyone had been watching the World Series!

·　·　·

WHILE I WAS WORKING on *3 Women,* Jack was on location in Canada with Terrence Malick, filming Terry's second feature, *Days of Heaven.* It was an exciting and creative time for us. The only thing missing from our lives was Five.

Five had broken her leg when she was young, falling out of a truck, and she died from complications years later, when she was about seven. We were shattered. For Jack, it was like losing his best friend and his guardian angel all rolled into one. Five had taken care of Jack for years, and now she would entrust him to me. To help fill the hole in our world, we adopted a cute little mutt named Heidi. In the years to come, Jack and I would always surround ourselves with dogs and cats and birds and horses, completely willing to let them break our hearts again and again for the privilege of having them share their too-brief time on earth. We've loved them all, but Jack would search for decades before he found another dog like Five.

· · · 1 2 · · ·

I'VE NEVER LIKED BEING TOLD WHAT TO DO. WHEN I WAS
about three years old, I climbed high up into a tree and wouldn't
budge. My dad said, "Sissy, are you gonna come down from there, or do
you want a paddling?" I looked him straight in the eye and said, "I want
to eat an orange."

In the summer of 1977, Loretta Lynn started telling the world that
I was going to play her in a movie based on her autobiography, *Coal
Miner's Daughter*. I was slightly dumbfounded because I'd never even met
Loretta, and I'd certainly never agreed to be in her film. I had been approached by Universal, which had the rights, but what little I knew
about the project seemed wrong to me. It was a big-budget studio production, a rags-to-riches story with a country music theme—all things
I'd been trying to steer away from in an attempt to minimize my "country" image and open myself up to different kinds of roles. (Recently, I'd
even made myself stop wearing cowboy boots.)

And I wasn't exactly sure I trusted Hollywood to keep Loretta's
story out of that dreaded but familiar territory: clichéd and corny. Besides, I was already committed to another film, a more artistic film, I
thought, being directed by the former cinematographer Nicolas Roeg,
who also directed *Don't Look Now* and *The Man Who Fell to Earth*.

But Loretta wasn't taking no for an answer. Universal had shown
her a stack of eight-by-ten glossies of all the young actresses in Holly-

wood, and when she "got down to one of a little ol' strawberry blonde with a freckled face"—me—she said, "That's her. That's the coal miner's daughter!" Before long, she was telling the audiences at her nightly concerts that I was going to portray her. Gossip columnists picked it up. She announced it weekly on daytime and late night talk shows. Loretta was a regular on Johnny Carson in those days; she was popular and funny, not to mention entertaining. But it was driving me crazy because she'd always mention the movie and say, "Little Sissy Spacek, she's gonna play me." I thought, who is this woman, and why is she saying these things about me? Finally, I couldn't take it anymore. I decided to tell her in person that I didn't want to do the film, and would she please stop saying that I was.

Jack and I were visiting my parents in East Texas and staying at their lake cabin near Quitman, when we found out Loretta was performing in Shreveport, Louisiana, only a few hours away. This was my opportunity to meet the woman face-to-face. My brother, Ed, who was still deeply involved in the music business and knew both Loretta and her manager, made some calls and arranged a meeting. So we loaded into the car and headed east. I was careful to look as different as I could from this country music star, so there would be no confusion. I wore my hair up. I wore John Lennon wire-framed glasses. I wore pegged pants, high heels, and a shawl. I looked like an urban hipster, and I was going to show Miss Loretta Lynn that I was my own person, I made my own decisions, and I'd already made mine about this movie.

Finally, we arrived in Shreveport and turned onto Fisk Street. *Fisk Street!? That's weird.* I shook it off. I just needed to get to Loretta. We could see the auditorium in the distance, but it was quiet. The parking lot was deserted. We were late, so late we'd missed the whole thing, managing to arrive after the concert was over and the auditorium was empty. But Loretta's tour bus was parked out back, and we were invited on board. All of a sudden, the door to the living quarters of the bus flew open and out stormed a tiny woman in a flaming red chiffon dress. Some of Loretta's band members were following right behind her like a covey of quail, and she was angry and shaking her fist in the air and hollering, "BAM BAM BAM! BAM BAM BAM! I couldn't hear nothing but them dat-gum drums a'beatin' in my ear!"

At that moment I thought, *Oh my God, I have to play this woman!*

WE VISITED A BIT that evening, and I was captivated by Loretta. She was tired after the show, but as gracious and kind as could be. She had this regal kind of beauty—high cheekbones and jet-black hair that made her look like Indian royalty. And there was a glint of steel in those hazel blue eyes of hers. I felt at home with her right away, like we'd been friends for a long time. She was a grounded person, and still a tomboy and a country girl who hoed her own garden and grew her own butter beans. She opened her hands to show me great big blisters. "Looka here, Sissy," she said. "I got these puttin' in my garden." When she told me she had twenty-seven goats back at her farm outside Nashville, I was a goner.

Still, I had big misgivings about signing on to *Coal Miner's Daughter*. By then I had read Loretta's book and admired her for all she had over-come to get to where she was. Her story was already an American leg-end: She had grown up dirt-poor in Butcher Hollow, Kentucky, where her father worked in the coal mine and her mother raised their babies in a house so far in the backwoods there wasn't even a road to it, just a trail. When she was only thirteen, she married a brash young army vet-eran named Doolittle "Mooney" Lynn, who took her away with him to a logging town in the Northwest. She'd had four children by the time she was nineteen, and no skills to speak of except raising babies. But she had an old guitar that she taught herself to play, and she started writing songs and singing them to her kids. From those humble beginnings, she built a career as the top female country star of her day. Her husband was a rough but good-hearted character who managed her in the early days and then, after she became a superstar, retreated back to their farm at Hurricane Mills, Tennessee, to raise the children and ride around on his beloved bulldozer.

It was an inspiring story, but I wasn't sure I could play a real person who was still living and working. Should I try to imitate her, look and sound like her? Could I get away with an impression that wasn't letter-perfect? And the subject matter, if handled the wrong way, could easily cross the line into camp. But on the strength of Loretta's personality, I agreed to meet with the director who was, at the time, attached to the project.

It did not go well.

As soon as I walked into the meeting, he pointed to a *Time* magazine with Loretta's picture on the cover and said, "This is what we're dealing with. Everybody knows what Loretta looks like, and you don't look like her."

I said, "You're right, it's a bad idea."

It was a short meeting. As I was walked out, I bumped into Sean Daniel, the producer from Universal, and Michael Chinich, the casting director, who had both been huddled against the door, waiting to hear what happened. They really wanted me in the picture.

"How'd it go?" they asked in unison.

"Not good," I said. "I don't look like her."

But Sean and Michael were not about to drop it, and neither was Loretta Lynn.

Meanwhile, the Nicolas Roeg film kept getting delayed. Months went by, and I didn't know which way to turn. At this point I hadn't worked on a film in nearly two years, since *3 Women*. I was getting a lot of offers, but I felt strongly that I needed to step back and choose my next project very carefully. I wanted to play a grown-up for a change—I was in danger of being typecast after playing a succession of teenagers like Holly Sargis, Carrie White, and Pinky Rose. The Roeg film, in which I would play a mysterious woman caught in an obsessive love affair with a psychiatrist, felt like a step in the right direction. And so did the role of Carolyn Cassady, the brilliant and long-suffering wife of Neal Cassady and companion of the beat writer Jack Kerouac. I wanted that part badly. The script was called *Heart Beat* and was set in the 1940s and '50s. I had read every book about the Beat Generation that I could get my hands on, and I was so into it that I was shocked when the film-makers didn't want me for the part.

One night in LA, Jack and I were invited to dinner with the producer, Ed Pressman, and the director, John Byrum. They told me I was perfect for the role, but they were holding out for Diane Keaton, who had just won an Oscar for *Annie Hall*, and who basically had her pick of any movie out there. Outwardly I seemed completely calm while I tried to absorb the news that I might not be playing Carolyn after all. I was smiling and nodding as Ed and John spoke, not realizing how tightly I was squeezing my glass of wine until it literally shattered in my hand. Glass and wine flew everywhere. I got the part of Carolyn—and when we started filming in San Francisco, Ed Pressman gave me a gift: a piece of the broken wineglass. "That's when you clinched it," he said.

Meanwhile, the folks at Universal were still pressuring me to sign on to *Coal Miner's Daughter*, in spite of the director's misgivings. My manager, Bill Treusch, was advising me not to make a country music movie, while my agent was saying, "Do it! You'd be a fool to pass this up!" In the middle of this mental tug-of-war, Jack and I flew to Washington, DC, to visit his mom. She lived in a high-rise apartment building outside of the District, from which she would commute to her job in real estate in a big white Cadillac. Gerri was not a country music fan, and her car radio was always tuned to a classical station. She didn't know much about Loretta Lynn, but she did recognize my dilemma. When she saw me tearing my hair out, she said, "Sissy, why don't you ask the man upstairs?"

"What? Oh, right, the man upstairs." So I said, "All right, God! Give me a sign!" I was kind of joking.

Later that night we were watching *The Tonight Show* in her apartment when Loretta came on, and sure enough, she told Johnny Carson that Sissy Spacek was going to play her in that movie. I thought I would scream.

"C'mon," Jack said. "Let's just go for a drive."

So we got in the elevator and rode twenty floors down to the basement parking lot. We climbed into Gerri's Cadillac, and as soon as we drove through the metal gates and out onto the street, the radio started up and I heard Loretta singing the refrain to "Coal Miner's Daughter." It seemed that Gerri's classical station turned into a country station at night. That was enough of a sign for me.

"Stop the car, Jack! I'm doing the movie!"

Not long after I agreed to do the film, my longtime manager and I parted ways. It was a painful time because Bill Treusch and I dearly loved each other and still do. Meanwhile the director who didn't think I was right for the project was replaced. It turned out that Loretta wasn't sure about this director, either. She thought he made good films, but she didn't think he understood her life, and she was afraid he might make fun of her. So the studio bought out his contract. Then the producers and I began looking for another director. We screened as many films about musicians as we could find. We looked at *The Buddy Holly Story* and *Payday*, the story of a shady country star, starring my cousin Rip Torn. But the one that truly caught our eye was *Stardust*, directed by Michael Apted, about the rise and fall of a fictional sixties rock idol. The film had the mixture of realism and grittiness that we wanted for *Coal Miner's Daughter*, and we felt that Apted was the perfect choice to direct. The soft-spoken British director happened to come from a coal mining area in England. And we thought that, being an outsider, he might bring less cultural baggage to the production. After meeting him, we were convinced he would see Loretta and her family and fans as real people, not cartoonish hillbillies.

I started following Loretta around like a puppy, trying to capture her body language and her accent. She doesn't have a typical Kentucky accent. In fact, I never found anyone else in Kentucky who sounded like her—she has a completely unique rhythm, the way she breathes and talks. I met her while she was playing some shows in Lake Tahoe and spent an afternoon tape-recording her while she told stories. She had me rolling on the floor laughing half the time. We even used some of her stories in the script; like the time a fan ran up behind her and snipped off a piece of her hair for a souvenir. "That was before I was a-carin' about the back of my hah-r," she said, as only Loretta could say it.

When I got back home from our visit, I videoed myself sitting in a chair with my tape recorder in my lap, playing and replaying Loretta telling stories. I would play that recorder and repeat those lines over and over until I kind of got my own version of her. Somewhere around my house, in a storage room or closet, is a video of me learning to "speak Loretta." And once I "got" her, I decided I should stay in character all the time, on and off the set. When we started filming, people working on the set who hadn't known me before thought that was the way I always talked. I knew I had it down when Jack brought our little dog, Heidi, to visit me on location. She came running as soon as she saw me, and I greeted her in Loretta's voice, "Well, I'll be! If it ain't my little dog, Heidi! C'mere, girl!"

Brrrrrrrppp! As soon as Heidi heard that voice, she put on her brakes and started backpedaling. And I thought to myself: *Yes!*

GETTING LORETTA'S VOICE and character was one thing; learning to play and sing like her was a whole new challenge. I could already play guitar, since I'd started out as a singer, but the producers at Universal still weren't sure whether or not to dub Loretta's vocals over my performance. That was a sticking point for me, and one that I knew might blow the whole deal, because in the best movies I'd seen about singers, the music had always been done live. It added realism and authenticity. In the end, Loretta was the one who encouraged them to let me do all the music, "Let her sing," she said. So I sang.

I spent about a week with Loretta in Nashville, at the Spence Manor, a hotel on Music Row with this crazy guitar-shaped swimming pool. I could look right out my window and see it. Everybody from Elvis to the Beatles to Frank Sinatra had stayed there, and so it was an inspiring setting to learn Loretta's music. We would write out the lyrics to songs on scraps of paper and fasten them with bobby pins to lampshades all around the suite. Loretta would walk around with her guitar, singing, and I would walk behind her with my guitar, doing my best to copy her, note for note. Sometimes we'd go into the bathroom, where the acoustics were fantastic, and sing together, our voices blending in a way that rarely happens outside of families—it's that sibling thing. We started to joke that we must have been twins in another life. Loretta and I ended up writing music together. She told me I was a quick learner. Mostly I didn't want to do anything that would embarrass either of us.

Once I learned the songs, Loretta turned me over to the legendary record producer Owen Bradley. Owen had worked with all the greats, and he was quite a guy—warm, funny, and extremely talented. First he set me up in the studio with her actual recordings, but with the vocal tracks removed so I could sing her part. Then he brought in Loretta's band to work with me. He also told me great stories. One day I said, "Owen, Loretta has all this vibrato in her voice. I don't have any vibrato."

"Don't worry, Sissy," he said. "Loretta doesn't have any vibrato in her voice either!"

"What do you mean? I can hear it."

"No," he said. "She'd just hold that note for a long time and then shake her arm while she was holding it."

I still don't know if he was pulling my leg, but I did try it, and it worked!

Finally, Loretta made the ultimate gesture of faith: she invited me to sing with her at the Grand Ole Opry. I knew that it was an incredible honor, and an opportunity to complete my transformation into her character. But I was more than intimidated. In fact, as I stood in a corner of the stage, watching Loretta and her band, I was scared stiff. Literally. I could see her beckoning me to join her at the microphone, but I was kind of frozen in place. Then I felt a gentle nudge in the small of my back, followed by a slightly bigger nudge. Suddenly Doolittle Lynn was pushing me out on the stage, just like he had done to Loretta the first time she played at the Opry. I joined Loretta onstage and we traded verses of one of her songs—I can't even remember which one, I was so terrified. But she later said that Opry members couldn't tell when she left off and I began, we were that close. I started to tease her, telling her that someday I was going to hijack her bus and wear all her dresses and go out on the road as Loretta Lynn. Looking back, I wonder if it wouldn't have been a relief for her. She was still working two concerts a night, staying for hours after the lights came on to make sure everybody who wanted an autograph got one. "I never forget," she told me, "it's the fans that gave me this career."

Loretta and I became as close as sisters during those months. I drew on what we had in common, the mutual love for our families and a deep sense of our roots. "Take me as I am," she would say. "Never change. If you have to change to be something, why do it? It's hard enough to be yourself, why be somebody else?"

She is a wise woman.

Loretta's support was crucial for me, and for the production. Everybody in Nashville and the country music world loved her so much that they welcomed me and the movie with open arms. She was the reason we were treated so royally. She made it happen.

ONCE MICHAEL APTED was on board as director, the production started coming together. Michael had the brilliant idea to cast Tommy Lee Jones as Mooney Lynn. I hadn't known Tommy Lee before working with him on this film, but I grew to love the man dearly. At first he seemed like the good old Texas boy that you'd expect him to be: smart and funny and more than a little wild. But underneath all that is a sophisticated scholar who graduated cum laude from Harvard. I can honestly say he's always the smartest person in the room. Tommy Lee had great instincts about the film. He was the one who brought in his friend Levon Helm to read for the part of Ted Webb, Loretta's coal miner father. It was an inspired idea.

Levon was a founding member of the Band, and although he's a world-class musician, he'd never acted a day in his life. But he knew that character in his bones, and his portrayal has such dignity and grace that it literally anchors the film. To play Loretta's mother, Clary, Levon in turn recommended the mountain singer Phyllis Boyens, who was also incredible in her first acting role.

As the locations were being chosen and the sets constructed, Tommy Lee was hoping to develop a relationship with Mooney along the lines of the one I had with Loretta. But he got off to a poor start.

A limo was sent to the Spence Manor in Nashville to drive Tommy Lee and Levon out to Hurricane Mills to meet Mooney for the first time. Tommy Lee brought along his Australian cattle dog, Travis, who went everywhere with him. Along the way, Levon wanted to stop at a recording studio to visit some friends, so they left Travis in the car with the limo driver. The way Tommy Lee tells the story, the driver was "a little bit goofy"—whatever that means—and all he could remember was that he was supposed to be in Hurricane Mills at a certain time. So he left Tommy Lee and Levon behind and drove to Mooney's place with Travis.

Mooney had been waiting around with some of his ranch hands, expecting to meet the movie version of himself, when the limo driver pulled up and out stepped Tommy Lee's dog. By the time Tommy Lee finally got there, Mooney had gone. One of the ranch hands pointed to a hill behind the house, and Tommy Lee could see him on a bulldozer, knocking down one tree after another.

It took a while, but the two eventually became good friends. Mooney taught Tommy Lee how to drive the old bulldozer used in the film, steering it with brakes. He also showed him how to get the most speed out of the WW2-era jeep that Tommy Lee drives in the scenes where he is courting me. Tommy Lee got so good at it that he about scared me to death careening along rutted roads and crashing through creeks. I dreaded hearing Michael's smooth British voice saying, "Okay, let's try that again." And after a day of getting bounced around and splashed with mud, I was so mad at Tommy Lee, I could spit. He must have been doing it to get a rise out of me, just the way his character did. That's part of what made it so great to play scenes with him. Sometimes all I had to do was react. He elevated my performance in every way.

We were all so lucky to work with the cinematographer Ralph Boda, who gave the film much of its visual richness and realism. Michael would rehearse a scene with the actors until we were all happy with it, and then he and Boda would watch the final run-through and design the shot around what we had done. It sounds ordinary, but many directors do the opposite: they design the shot first and then have the actors play the scene within their parameters. Michael Apted trusted his actors. It felt extraordinary—even revolutionary.

The first part of the film was shot on location right where it took place, in the mountains where eastern Kentucky, West Virginia, and Virginia converge. It was a close-knit cast and crew, made even closer because there were so many musicians among us. The production was based in Wise, Virginia, about seventy miles, as the crow flies, south of the real Butcher Hollow, and we stayed in a historic white clapboard hotel called the Wise Inn. I had a room on the very top floor, filled with antiques and a claw-foot bathtub where I could soak off the mud and dirt I'd be covered with at the end of a day's shooting. All night long we could hear coal trucks rolling through town, rattling the hotel's old glass windows. Levon took over the basement taproom most nights, filling it with guitar players and banjo pickers, singing the old mountain songs that sprung straight up from the land that surrounded us. It was pure magic, and the music washed over us, spilling back and forth, in and out of the production.

I'll never forget the funeral scene, where Loretta comes back to Kentucky to bury her daddy. Ted Webb was waked right in his cabin, and the scene called for Levon to lie in an open casket while his family gathered around him and sang. Levon had a touch of claustrophobia, and at first he was a bit spooked by the scene. To reassure him, Michael Apted laid himself in that coffin for the rehearsal, just to show him it would be all right. Finally, Levon settled in for the scene, and the cast and extras all stood around in mourning, then started to sing "Amazing Grace."

Suddenly, Levon bolted upright from his coffin in full death-mask makeup.

"Cut!" Michael shouted.

"You're singing it wrong," said Levon. "It's got to be done the old-fashioned, traditional way."

Luckily, we had Phyllis Boyens there playing Loretta's mother, and she had brought along her father, Nimrod Workman, one of the most revered traditional musicians in Appalachia, and a famous union organizer. In the film, you can hear Nimrod's voice in the background, calling out the lines of "Amazing Grace," while we sing them back to him.

Having Phyllis and Nimrod in the cast went a long way in helping the mountain people accept the production company in their midst. One of the wonderful things about being a filmmaker is that you get to live all these different lives, in different places, sometimes for three or four months. You get to experience an area, not as a visitor, but as somebody who's trying to sink down into the bedrock of the community and get to know what it's like to be a local. People are pretty good about sharing and helping you figure that out as long as they know you're sincere. Michael and the producers and set designers bent over backward to make sure the film was an honest and accurate portrait of life in the coal towns and hollows. They weren't going to sugarcoat or romanticize the poverty, but they made sure they didn't fall into the clichés about ignorant hillbillies living in squalor, either. The costumes were perfect and the sets were exquisitely accurate, from the corn cribs in back of Loretta's home place to the newspapers used for wallpaper inside the cabin to keep out the drafts.

The people of Appalachia have been misused and misunderstood for generations, and they are rightfully wary of strangers poking around their business. The production team took great pains to make sure all the advance work had been done before we arrived to film in various locations, but they couldn't always reach everybody ahead of time. And there were some locals who were downright hostile.

The roads in eastern Kentucky wind through the mountains and coil along creek beds so that it can sometimes take hours to go three miles as the crow flies. One day we were moving the whole unit, with a big generator the size of a city bus, crawling up along twisted, rutted mountain roads, until we finally reached the place where we were supposed to shoot. Out of the woods stepped a rough-looking man with a shotgun who shouted, "Get off my land!"

"But we're shooting a movie, sir!" explained the assistant director.

"I said, get off my land!" the man repeated.

We were all remembering a local legend that had been told in the taproom of the Wise Inn a few nights before: An old man from the holler was riding to town with his wife in his horse-drawn wagon. The horse stumbled on a rock. The old man stopped the wagon, looked down at his horse, and said, "That's once." The horse walked on, and after a while he stumbled again. The old man gripped the reins in his hands. "That's twice," he said. He told the horse to walk on. But after a while the horse stumbled again.

"That's three times."

With that the old man pulled out his gun and shot the horse dead. His wife was stunned, but after a moment she began to scream and holler, "Are you out of your mind? How could you do such a thing, you crazy old man!? Now how are we supposed to get home?"

The old man looked over at his wife. "That's once," he said.

So while the AD and the mountain man stared each other down for a moment at the entrance to the holler, we all started shouting from our cars, "Come back! Come back! He's already said it twice! Don't let him say it again!"

We finally got the generator turned around and nobody got shot.

WE FILMED MY CONCERT scenes at both the Ryman Auditorium and the Grand Old Opry with as many of the real performers as we could. I was backed up by Loretta's band members, while Minnie Pearl, Roy Acuff, and Ernest Tubb made cameo appearances. Tubb, "The Texas

Troubadour," had recorded duets with Loretta back in the early sixties. He was a full-blown country legend, famous in Nashville for his habit of getting drunk on his tour bus, firing his band members, and throwing them out, one by one, on the side of the road. Eventually his manager learned to follow in a car to scoop up the stranded musicians and drive them to the next gig. Luckily, he had quit drinking by the time we made *Coal Miner's Daughter*.

My parents visited the set while we were filming at the Opry, and they struck up a friendship with Ernest Tubb. He was from Crisp, Texas, a small town thirty-five miles southeast of Dallas, so they felt like neighbors. Daddy told him to stop by and visit if he was ever passing through Quitman, and sure enough, a year later Tubb's tour bus pulled up in front of their house. It stretched the length of our front yard, from Edna Lipscomb's to George Tom Shaw's place. People stopped their cars to gape at the spectacle while Ernest and his band were inside drinking coffee.

Mother and Daddy took all the attention in stride. They were proud of me, along with the whole town. In fact, after the release of *Coal Miner's Daughter*, Quitman declared May 31, 1980, Sissy Spacek Day. Jack and I flew in for the celebration in Jim Hogg Park that featured a country-western band, a presentation by the reigning Dogwood Queen, a performance by the Curley Q Square Dance Club, and a host of games and competitions. My favorite notice: "Children participating in the frog and turtle races are reminded to bring their own frogs and turtles."

People brought baskets of fried chicken, coleslaw, and homemade fruit pies, and spread them out on picnic tables in the shade of the old oak trees. I spent all day visiting with friends and signing hundreds of autographs. But before all of this had a chance to go to my head, a drive to Mineola brought me back to earth. The Select Theater, where I'd spent so many teenage date nights, was showing *Coal Miner's Daughter* as part of the celebration. But when I looked up at the marquee, I saw they had billed me as "CISSY SPACEK." The theater had run out of S's.

· · ·

DECIDING TO DO *Coal Miner's Daughter* changed my life and the trajectory of my career. The film was a commercial and critical success, and between us we won a slew of awards, including a Golden Globe and an Oscar for me as Best Actress. Loretta sat in the audience at the Academy Awards and cheered as loud as my own mother would have when I walked out onto that stage. Her only regret, she said, was that Tommy Lee didn't get a nomination, too. I agree. He was so good in that role, and I'm convinced that without him, I wouldn't have gotten any awards at all.

I had written out an acceptance speech, just in case, but it's true that your mind does go blank as soon as you hear your name called. Luckily, I think I thanked everybody I wanted to, but most of all, Jack. I also thanked my parents, who were watching it on television back home. I've never been much of a party person, but we did go to quite a few of them that night. When we got home early the next morning, I found dozens of yellow roses waiting for me at my front door, sent from all of my friends in Quitman. It made me feel like I had won for the whole town.

But perhaps my favorite accolade of all was a telegram Dolly Parton sent me shortly after the film opened. It read, "Dear Sissy, I hope you make millions of dollars from *Coal Miner's Daughter* so that you can get a boob job and do the Dolly Parton story."

THE OSCAR RECOGNITION made me a bona fide movie star, which is a weird thing to be. It can be a lot of fun—I mean who doesn't like flying first class when you can do it?—and the fact that you're considered a box office draw brings whatever roles are out there your way. There's also the ability to get a project made just by attaching your name to it, not to mention getting the best table in a restaurant. But it's harder to stay grounded when everybody suddenly recognizes you on the street, they want to do you favors; they know your work and your face, so they feel they know you.

The loss of privacy unnerved me at first. I was having lunch with my mother at a restaurant in Texas when one person after another came over to ask me for an autograph or to pose for a snapshot. I was hungry and trying to finish my salad, and I must have rolled my eyes or muttered something to my mother because she reached over and touched my arm and smiled.

"You are so lucky," she said.

"What are you talking about?" I said, feeling more besieged than blessed at the moment.

"Well, all you have to do is smile or sign your name, or look somebody in the eye, and you can make them happy," she said. "Isn't that wonderful?"

I'll never forget that moment. Sometimes you just have to hear it spoken to make the obvious clear.

IN THE END, the hardest part about *Coal Miner's Daughter* was giving it all up. It was kind of sad to go back to my old self. I was so funny as Loretta! I had my own bus and band and millions of adoring fans! I loved being her.

The film's success transformed Loretta's life as much as it did mine. It opened up her music to audiences that might not have listened to her before, and helped keep her in the spotlight. We knew while we were making the film that it might be pretty good, but we didn't know it would be so beloved. Thirty years later, people still come up to me on the street and tell me they've seen it ten, twenty, thirty times or more. They've connected with the film in such a personal and enduring way, and they've kept it alive for new generations. That is a testament to Loretta.

Loretta Lynn, like many country stars, gives so much to her fans that she often loses the distinction between her public and her private lives. Loretta collected all the props and sets from the movie and had them hauled to Hurricane Mills to create a museum and tourist attraction called the Loretta Lynn Ranch. She and Mooney rebuilt the house from

Butcher Hollow and the church where they were married in the film, and rent it out for weddings. Tourists pour in by the busload and hitch up their RVs in the campsites. Visitors can view the Cadillac where Loretta wrote her hits, and see all the fabulous flouncy dresses I wore in the movie, along with her own costumes and memorabilia. Until his death in 1996, Mooney and Loretta lived in the same white-columned antebellum mansion where we did a lot of the filming. It was also opened up to daily tours, like the White House, and still is, although Loretta now has built a separate place on the property where she can have more privacy. She says that if anything is out of place in the mansion, different than the way it was in *Coal Miner's Daughter*, the tourists kick up a stink, they know the picture so well.

Loretta loved the movie, but she's said she can't watch it anymore. The scenes of leaving her father and mother are just too painful to relive, she told Michael Apted years later. "There's too much real in it." It was also hard for her to watch the scene of her nervous breakdown, when she collapsed onstage after touring nonstop for years. She had missed watching her children grow up, missed out on her own life while she was stuck on the spinning merry-go-round of fame and obligations. The lessons weren't lost on me. I saw how easily it could happen. And I didn't want to give up all that she did for my own career; I wanted to keep some privacy. It's been important to me to live a regular life, around regular people, because these are the characters I portray in films: regular people, like me.

But after *Coal Miner's Daughter* came out and offers started rolling in, I was faced with more dilemmas. Do I keep making big studio movies and build on this new momentum? Do I stay in Los Angeles, in the belly of the movie beast, stoking my career, or find a place of sanctuary, a place where I can live a real life? I wanted to stay up in that tree, and I wanted an orange. So I waited for a sign.

··· V I R G I N I A ···

$$\cdots \quad 13 \quad \cdots$$

A N ACTOR'S WORK DOESN'T END WHEN THE FILM WRAPS.
We are expected to support it by attending all the red carpet
events and giving interviews to the media. Dozens and dozens of interviews. I enjoy meeting journalists, but it's hard trying to answer the
same questions over and over in new and interesting ways. By the end of
a publicity tour, I'm usually staring off into space, in a corner of my hotel room, unable to remember my own name. Once, after a very gruel-
ing press junket across Europe, I had an out-of-body experience on the
most popular nighttime talk show on English television. Every day I
did countless back-to-back interviews. Every night I flew to a different
country, and every morning I started the daylong interview process all
over again. I was exhausted after several weeks of this on top of fractured
sleep and terrible jet lag. I loved the studio press people I was traveling
with, but by the time I arrived in London, I was fried. So when they
asked me to do one more, very important talk show, I knew I wasn't up
to it, but I hadn't the strength to even refuse.

When I arrived at the live show, I was thrilled to meet Gloria
Swanson, a great actress and movie icon. She was a tiny woman, but
formidable. She was there to promote her memoir, and we chatted for a
while backstage. I'll never forget how kind she was to me. She could see
how exhausted I was, and she was concerned that I was in no shape to
do the show. She went on first, and I waited my turn. When I heard the

music swell and felt a tap, I walked out to take my place beside Ms. Swanson. After that, things got strange. The host appeared to be talking, but I couldn't hear what he was saying. I felt like I was watching television with the sound turned down. I could see his lips moving, and then he would cock his head. I assumed he was waiting for an answer to a question that I hadn't heard. I had answers—but unfortunately none that went to any of his questions. I think he must have thought I was on drugs, which was not the case at all. Apparently he was ripping me to shreds. And although I appreciated what appeared to be Ms. Swanson's attempt to defend me to the host, I couldn't understand anything she was saying, either. I was too far gone. The next day at the airport, as I walked up to the long line of Americans waiting for the flight back to the U.S., they looked at me with sympathy and concern. I even heard a few of them murmur, "Awwww. . . ." It must have been pretty bad.

So when I was asked to fly to Brazil for the opening of one of my films in South America, I was feeling more than a little trepidation. I called my mother to tell her the latest news.

"Yeah," I sighed. "It looks like I've got to go to Brazil and do a bunch of press."

"Oh really!?" she said, her voice filling with excitement. "You get to go to South America?"

"Well sort of," I said, "I don't really *get* to go; I have to go."

"Oh, Sissy, that's the chance of a lifetime!" she said.

"It is?"

"Well yes, of course it is! You'll have so much fun!"

"I will?"

"Of course you will! Just think of all the things you'll get to see."

I thought for a moment. It was beginning to sound like fun.

"Do you want to go?" I asked.

So off we went to South America to meet the press. With her, I saw everything in a different light. Even the long flight to Brazil seemed amazing: "How luxurious!" she said. "We get to go on a plane and stretch out on a seat that's just like a bed!" And once we arrived, she was right.

We had a blast. We were all dressed up one day and looking lovely, when our young host suggested we climb to the top of the most popular mountain in São Paulo. It was a challenging climb, especially in our high heels, but Mother and I were both game, and we made it to the top without too much trouble. After that, I don't know what came over me, but once atop São Paulo's highest peak, standing on a large wooden ramp used to launch hang gliders, I felt compelled to jump off that mountain holding on to nothing but the harness of some very handsome young Brazilian. I was one step away from flying into the abyss, when fortunately, my mother grabbed me by the collar and wouldn't let go. "This is not a part of the plan," she said through a clenched jaw. "You are here to talk to journalists!" Well done, Mother!

Once I reached my thirties, I appreciated my mom more than ever. We were long past the push and pull that daughters go through with their mothers as they assert their independence and adulthood. I realized that so much of what I had, I owed to her. She was my confidante and my friend. And when it came time for me to play Nita Longley in *Raggedy Man*, she literally became my role model.

JACK HAD HONED HIS CRAFT as a production designer while working with some of the best directors of our generation. He knew filmmaking inside and out. And he had always wanted to do a film about a woman like his mother, Gerri, who had struggled to raise small children on her own. So when a writer from Austin named Bill Wittliff showed us his original screenplay about a divorced mother raising two young sons in rural Texas during World War II, we both knew it was the perfect match. In 1980, we spent six months on location in Texas, making *Raggedy Man*.

Actually, we hadn't expected to spend that much time on one picture. But that summer the Screen Actors Guild went on strike for three months. We had to shut down on the first day of production. There was nothing to do but wait around until we could go back to work. For me, it was heaven to be back home. Jack and I had rented a place on Lake Austin, not too far from our location in Maxwell, Texas. The lake is actually a dammed section of the Colorado River, cut through lime-stone, winding its graceful way through Austin. We spent every day water-skiing nine miles up to the dam and then nine miles back down. At the time I was also running five or six miles a day and following a strict vegan diet. Sugar didn't touch my lips. I was so fit, you could bounce a quarter off me. (Although I was occasionally known to break rank and have a margarita or two.) When the strike was settled and it came time to start shooting again, I weighed about ninety-five pounds, and I was afraid I would look too skinny in the one scene where I took my clothes off to bathe.

Times had changed, and we were no longer as nonchalant about nude scenes. The sixties and seventies were definitely over. During the actors' strike, Jack and I had nothing but time, so we rehearsed in the little house where my character, Nita Longley, lived. I was sitting in the galvanized tub, and Jack used a video camera blocking out the cam-era angles so that we could suggest nudity without actually showing anything. It was going great when we heard a knock on the front door.

"Yoo-hoo! Anybody home?"

It was a group of neighborhood women, coming to bring us some fresh garden vegetables to welcome us back to town. They took one look in the house and scurried away, leaving their carrots and cucumbers on the front porch. But the people of Maxwell rolled with the punches. We also had fabulous luck finding the boys to play Nita's young sons from a local radio casting call. Neither eight-year-old Henry Thomas nor five-year-old Carey Clyde Leebo Hollis ("I've got four names!") had ever acted before, but you would never have known it. In a scene at the din-ner table, Henry was so angry that he raised one eyebrow at me. I thought, *Oh great, blown off the screen by an eight-year-old.* What was it W. C. Fields said? "Never work with children or animals." (Later, when Jack was editing *Raggedy Man*, he showed Steven Spielberg some footage of Henry Thomas, and Steven cast him immediately for the lead role in

ET. We were thrilled for Henry. We'd known he was a star from the moment we met him.) I loved watching Jack work with those boys. He expected them to deliver like seasoned actors, and they did. He added little things for them to do that came right out of my childhood, like playing with cutout cardboard wings.

In *Raggedy Man*, Nita Longley is a plucky, lonely young woman, doing her best to get by in a dead-end job as a telephone operator in a small town where people look down on her for being divorced. Then Teddy, a handsome young sailor on leave, played by Eric Roberts, wanders into her life and turns her world upside down. To play Nita, I reached back into my grab bag of memories for the voice of Ganelle Rushing, Quitman's telephone operator. I drew on what I knew about Jack's mom and the screenwriter's mother, but most of all I used my own mother's spirit and her gestures to create the character. Sometimes, Mother would eat her meals leaning over the sink to save dishes and catch crumbs, so Nita did that, too. And I wore my hair up like my mother did during the war. In my favorite scene in the movie, I am pinning laundry onto the clothes-line, just as I had seen Mother do it a thousand times. (We even have a home movie of her at the clothesline, dressed so femininely, shyly trying to shoo away my father, who was filming her.) When Teddy and the boys beg Nita to come fly a kite with them, at first she says no, brushing them off with a friendly wave that says "don't be silly." Then she gives in and runs to them, but not before stealing a glance at herself in the reflection of a window and fluttering her hands over her hair to make sure her pins are in place. It's a gesture I'd had seen my mother use many times, and I knew it by heart. My entire performance was an homage to her.

AFTER WAITING SO MANY YEARS for just the right film projects, great parts came tumbling in one after another. I was finally portraying real, flesh-and-blood women in serious, thought-provoking roles. The day after I won the Academy Award for *Coal Miner's Daughter*, I flew off to Mexico to film *Missing* with the director Costa-Gavras. It was another script based on a true story, this one set in 1973 during the military coup in Chile. I played the wife of a young journalist, Charlie Horman, played by John Shea, who disappeared in the violence following the overthrow of Salvador Allende. Jack Lemmon played Charlie's father, Ed, who flew to Chile to search for his son.

I have to admit that I knew next to nothing about the political turmoil going on in South and Central America during the 1970s. But preparing for this film was a quick education. I was shocked and disillusioned when I learned of our government's complicity in so much brutality and suffering. What really got to me was a short film I watched about the Chilean folk singer Victor Jara. He had been swept up by the military in the aftermath of the coup and was held prisoner with thousands of other Allende supporters at the National Stadium in Santiago. For days, Jara was tortured by his captors. They smashed his fingers then taunted him to play his guitar; instead he sang a song he had written for Allende. He kept on singing until they shot him dead. That was the kind of cold savagery the Horman family was up against.

Costa-Gavras was a fascinating director, full of surprises. Once he had someone fire a gun off camera while Jack Lemmon was doing a scene, without telling him beforehand. Jack's startled reaction was real, and exactly what Costa was hoping for. Then there was an even bigger surprise—for all of us: Someone on the street fired back at us with a real machine gun. We dove for cover, then scrambled to get out of there. Sometimes Mexico City felt like the Wild West.

We were lucky that gunman wasn't around when we were filming a huge outdoor night scene. The camera was shooting down a very long street and there were lots of extras and soldiers, along with the principal actors. In the scene it is supposed to be getting near the evening curfew in Santiago, and everyone is rushing home to get off the streets. Many, including my character, are afraid of being caught out after dark and are scrambling to find refuge. People are running, guns are firing, helicopters are flying overhead, and a beautiful white horse runs loose through the streets. It's a very dramatic moment in the film, and many things had to be coordinated for everything to work. Finally we heard "Roll camera!" I was waiting to hear "Action," when suddenly Costa called, "Cut!"

The director ran across the street to an old man, who had been on his hands and knees scrubbing the sidewalk. Costa leaned down and helped him to his feet, took away the scrub brush and handed him a broom so he would be standing upright in a more dignified position. Then Costa walked back to the camera and we began again. The AD shouted, "Horse in place again, actors ready, roll camera." I was bowled over by Costa's compassion; there are very few directors who would delay a major action scene to preserve the self-respect of one extra.

Costa was born in Greece but had lived in France for many years and spoke beautiful French, Spanish, and English, but still there was a slight language barrier between us. After one particularly harrowing scene, he came up to me to ask if I was okay. "I need a hug," I said. He looked at me quizzically, then turned and walked away. I thought, *Uh-oh, maybe I've offended him.* But the next day when I saw him, he threw his arms around me, and every few minutes throughout the day he would walk over and give me a big hug. Sometime later a friend, an American costumer named Pam Wise, also working on the film, told me that Costa had walked up to her and said, "Please, could you tell me . . . what is a hug?"

I needed a lot of hugs during that film. It was emotionally exhausting, trying to imagine what these characters were feeling. I worried myself sick. I was amazed at how Jack Lemmon could turn his acting on and off at will. Jack would be telling us all a joke and stop in the middle when the director yelled "Action!" Then he would deliver an incredible, emotional performance. And as soon as he heard "Cut!" he would finish the joke. I, on the other hand, would stew all day long if I had an emotional scene coming up. If the scene was at five o'clock in the afternoon, I would start winding myself up hours before, getting ready, and by the time the scene finally rolled around, often I would already be spent. Jack sat me down one day and offered some advice. "You know, you're really good, kid, but you should trust yourself more," he said. "The scene will either work or it won't, and no amount of thrashing and flailing around will help. Go easy on yourself. You know what to do. So just do it." He was an inspiration to me, and living proof that all great acting doesn't have to involve suffering.

Nevertheless, I still relied on some of my time-worn tools to get myself into character. One time I was flummoxed by a scene that called for me to face down a table filled with American diplomats who weren't doing enough to find my husband. I was supposed to be in control of the scene, but I felt like I didn't have anything to draw from. I sat there for a while, feeling intimidated by all these men in dark suits. *Suits*, I thought, wracking my brain, *dark suits, dark suits*. Then it dawned on me. *Of course! Suits! These guys look like agents.* After that, I thought, *Okay! You're working for me! This is what's going to happen now!*

I BECAME FRIENDS with the Horman family while we filmed *Missing*, and I've kept in touch with Charlie's widow, Joyce, the model for my character. She has never given up her quest to bring his killers to justice. Joyce credits our film with helping to keep his case in the spotlight. New evidence keeps turning up, including once-classified State Department documents indicating the possible complicity of the U.S. government in Charlie Horman's death. A judge in Santiago ordered the arrest of a Chilean intelligence officer in connection with Charlie's execution, and in 2011, a former U.S. naval officer was indicted for his alleged role in the killing. But nearly forty years after his death, the full story of what happened to Charlie Horman is still unknown.

ANOTHER REASON THE SHOOT was so difficult was that my mother had become seriously ill. In fact, she was undergoing treatments in Texas for a malignancy while I was accepting my Academy Award. As soon as we wrapped *Missing*, I flew back home to spend as much time with her as I could. I had no illusions anymore about finding miracle cures. I understood now that for all of us here on this earth, our days are numbered, and I didn't want to waste a moment. I wanted to be as close to my mother as possible, for as long as possible. So I would crawl onto her bed and curl up next to her, like I had done as a child, when she read me to sleep for my afternoon naps.

Jack and I were traveling in early November 1981, when we got a call that we'd better come quickly. She had taken a turn for the worse.

When we arrived at her bedside, Mother had already begun the journey. I don't know if she could always understand what we were say-ing, but she knew we were there. One of the last things she said was "Where's Jack?"

"Oh, I'm right here, Gin," Jack said, and Mother smiled.

Daddy told us about the morning he took her to the hospital, when it was clear that was where she needed to be. My father was saying, "C'mon, Gin. It's time to go, sweetie." But she kept walking around the house, looking at everything. This was the place she'd loved best. This was where so much had happened. All those chickens she'd fried and the scrapes she'd bandaged. Susan and Peggy and Imogene at the kitchen table drinking coffee, hearing the morning school bell and rushing us into the car and off to school. The laundry she'd hung out while the marching band played . . . and all those sugar sandwiches. I'll bet that's what was flooding through her mind that morning, all those sweet memories. She stood in the living room for a long time, Daddy said, just taking it all in. Then she took a breath and turned to go.

All her life, my mother had believed that our minds are the builders of the universe. She never put it in those exact words, but she believed that we are responsible for our every thought, word, and action, both good and bad, and all that it sets into motion. She encouraged us to be positive and loving, and to find the good in all things. And if we be-lieved deeply enough, we would see all those we'd loved, who had gone before us, again. She'd say, "Oh, I'll see Mama, and Robbie, and the babies I lost." While she lay dying, she could see, although she wasn't seeing what was in the room. Instead she'd look up and say, "Ahhh," with a big smile, and then reach out as if to hug someone. I sat beside her, and I knew what she was seeing. It was a beautiful transitional state. She was starting her new life. I hope that's the way it is for me. I'm going to believe deeply that I'll see her and all my loved ones again, and maybe that will make it so.

I found out I was pregnant the week my mother died, but she never knew. She was already on her way, and I didn't want to risk doing anything that would make it more difficult for her to leave this world. I just wanted her to be surrounded with love and to go peacefully.

My mother died when I was thirty-one and she was sixty-two. That is my age now, as I write this. When I think of her, I remember the words of wisdom she left for me, and her favorite verses of scripture, which she wrote down in a little notebook. "Fix your thoughts on what is good and true and right," she wrote. "As a man thinketh in his heart, so he is." And best of all: "And now abideth faith, hope, and love, these three; but the greatest of these is love."

ONCE I LEARNED I was pregnant, I researched the subject as if I was preparing for a major film role. I read every book and article I could get my hands on. I wanted to change my diet to add more protein, so I started eating chicken and fish. I had been running every day for years; everything I read said I could continue whatever I had been doing, but not to start new sports. I assumed they were referring to show jumping and skydiving. I figured that jogging would be fine. My doctor, a handsome Beverly Hills obstetrician named Mark Surrey, had other ideas. He told me all the typical reasons I shouldn't jog while pregnant. But after I showed him my research on the subject, he started jogging with me. I loved being pregnant—or maybe I just decided I was going to love it. I was lucky because I didn't have morning sickness or any unhealthy cravings. I decided I was going to crave pineapple and watermelon, and so I did. For years after that, we'd go into any grocery store in the area, even in the winter, and the stock clerks would sidle up to me and whisper, "Ms. Spacek, we have watermelon in today!"

·   ·   ·

THE *COAL MINER'S DAUGHTER* soundtrack had done well, with me and Beverly D'Angelo, who played Patsy Cline, doing the singing. Now I was offered the chance to make my own album. I recorded *Hangin' Up My Heart* in Nashville with the amazing Rodney Crowell as producer. Rodney was a Texas boy from the rough side of the tracks in Houston, who made it big in Nashville as a singer-songwriter and a member of Emmylou Harris's band. He felt like family the instant we met. Rodney brought in his wife at the time, Roseanne Cash, and his friend Vince Gill to sing on a few tracks. It was like a fantasy from my younger years come true. We even got a hit single on the country charts with a cover of "Lonely But Only For You." Three decades later, if you search for my music on a website like CD Baby, you're apt come up with an obscure electronic band that calls itself Sissy Spacek—ironically I'm sure—best known for a catchy number titled "Remote Whale Control." (Could this be the new measure of immortality?) But making my record with Rodney Crowell was a high point in my career. While we were recording, he laid his hands on my pregnant belly and blessed my growing baby, hoping the sound waves she was receiving would make her a musician.

"Okay, Rodney, we've marked this baby," I said. And boy, was I right. Schuyler has grown up to be a fabulous singer-songwriter (if I may say so, myself!), and I can somehow picture her floating around, moving her tiny translucent fingers in time with Rodney's guitar licks.

Jack and I had decided on our baby's name long before she was born. There is a town called Schuyler—pronounced "Skyler"—in the foothills of the Blue Ridge Mountains, with a rock quarry where local artists get their stone for sculpting. We always loved the way the name sounded, and thought it would be a good name for a boy or a girl. We didn't know of any other Schuylers then, so we may have started a trend.

When I was eight months pregnant, in May of 1982, the producers of *Missing* asked me to appear at the Cannes Film Festival for the film's debut. "I can't go, I'm too far along," I told them. But I agreed to check with my doctor. "You can go!" said Mark Surrey. "But only with your doctor. And that would be me!" We flew over on the Concorde, which had narrow seats and rattled like crazy when it broke the sound barrier, but we got there fast. As soon as we arrived in the South of France, we checked out all the hospitals near Cannes, just in case. Mark kept a close eye on me. When we arrived on the red carpet, I was with two gorgeous men, Jack Fisk and Mark Surrey, one on each arm. Mark was so handsome, he looked more like a movie star playing a doctor than an actual doctor. And since he was a bachelor, every night he would bring a different European model or actress to dinner, none of whom spoke any English. There was a lot of nodding and sign language going on.

We stayed at the famous Hotel du Cap, which was always sur-rounded by hundreds of paparazzi. One morning I came out with Mark to go for a jog. We started running, and all the photographers thought they could easily keep up with a pregnant woman. They sprinted around us and then ran backward, snapping pictures, but I was too fast for them and they tumbled like dominoes over a hedge. We hopped over them, laughing like crazy, and continued on our run.

That night Jack Lemmon won a well-deserved award for Best Actor, and Costa-Gavras won the Palme d'Or for best picture in the festival.

WE FLEW RIGHT BACK to Los Angeles, where Mark would be stand-ing by to deliver when the time came. My dad was staying with us at the house in Topanga because he wanted to be close when Schuyler arrived. He was also good company. So we all waited for the baby. And waited. Finally, in early July, I started getting my first contractions. I had been through Lamaze class with Jack, and I had done a lot of reading, so I thought I knew exactly what to expect. I was wrong. It was shocking to me how much something could hurt without actually killing you. We called Mark, who told us to meet him in his office first thing in the morning, since the contractions were still pretty far apart. So Jack

February 14, 1977 / $1.00

Newsweek

The New Actresses

Sissy Spacek

After *Carrie* came out I was everywhere—even on the cover of *Newsweek*. A reporter came to Quitman, Texas, to interview my parents. When the article came out, my dad bought up all the magazines in town—if anyone else wanted to read it, they had to come to our house.

Mattie Darrow,
Get Low.

Pinky Rose,
3 Women.

Rose Straight,
The Straight Story.

Ruth Fowler,
In the Bedroom.

Carolyn Cassady,
Heart Beat.

Missus Walters,
The Help.

Carrie White,
Carrie.

Nita Longley,
Raggedy Man.

Holly Sargis,
Badlands.

Some of the characters that I found inside me. When I was younger I always wanted to play someone my own age; now I'm finally getting to. You've got to watch what you wish for.

Jessica Lange, Diane Keaton, and I had a great time being sisters in *Crimes of the Heart*. We shared a house on the set where three-year-old Schuyler gave Diane first aid with her new play doctor kit.

With Jack Lemmon, who played my father-in-law in *Missing*. Jack could be telling a joke, stop, play a dramatic scene, and then finish his joke. He told me to "just act" and forget the "Method."

I worked with Tommy Lee Jones on *Coal Miner's Daughter*, and then in 1995 he directed me in *The Good Old Boys* (left). Here he is telling me all the reasons I shouldn't be galloping sidesaddle across "Cemetery Field."

Richard Farnsworth and me (below) in Iowa for *The Straight Story*. Richard was nominated for an Oscar; I cut my hair and wore prosthetic teeth to play his daughter.

Lee Marvin (left) unexpectedly took off from the set of *Prime Cut* with me in the back of the car wearing nothing but a horse blanket. What a sight I must have been walking into the hotel lobby.

Me as Loretta Lynn with Ernest Tubb at the Ryman Auditorium.

Loretta and me after I won the Oscar for *Coal Miner's Daughter*. She believes we were sisters in a past life. For two years Loretta told everybody that I was going to play her in the movie. I wasn't so sure . . . until I met her.

With Brian De Palma on the set of *Carrie*. I'm wearing the sailor dress my mom made for me in the seventh grade.

Here I am on the set of *Heart Beat* with John Heard and Nick Nolte. David Lynch painted the artwork for this scene and played the artist.

The kite scene in *Raggedy Man* with (left to right) Carey Clyde Leebo Hollis, Henry Thomas, and Eric Roberts. I was channeling my mother in this scene.

I always liked tuxedos more than gowns.

Me in Beirut, dressed rather inappropriately, during our honeymoon.

This was taken in Quitman on Sissy Spacek Day, 1980. The whole town came out to celebrate.

Me and my girlfriends Janit and Monica. I got that Hawaiian shirt in a thrift store.

Jack and me on our first visit to Cannes. The next time we came back I was eight months pregnant.

On the set of *Phantom of the Paradise* with Five.

I've always loved Jack's gap-toothed smile.

Jack and Five a few years before we met.

Jack, Five, and David Lynch at art school in Philadelphia. David was making short films; Jack was building large sculptures.

Schuyler had a great time in Texas while I worked on *The Good Old Boys* with Tommy Lee Jones and Sam Shepard.

Little Bit taking Schuyler for a ride around the farm while our dog River follows along behind.

Schuyler played the lead in *Annie* in her school play. Soon kids were running past me to get her autograph.

Schuyler singing at Joe's Pub in New York City.

Schuyler in the hunt field.

Schuyler at the barn on her ninth birthday.

Madison's affinity for animals started early. It's a good thing we live on a farm.

Madison has always been an insatiable reader . . . who loves to draw and paint and build things, like her dad.

Little girl, big horse.

Madison sits under one of her many creations.

Madison helped teach her friend Natasha how to ride a bike.

Madison and Jack hiking in Telluride, Colorado.

My father in his *Coal Miner's Daughter* cap going off to fish. He loved getting out on the lake.

My mother: my confidante and favorite traveling companion.

Our daughters came along at just the right time in my life.

Jack and me on the farm with our dog Patch and our cat BB.

Our dog family on the farm. Rigby visits from California and Maude visits from Texas. Nigel thinks he's a dog.

drove me to Beverly Hills, and of course we got caught in traffic. My dad was riding along in the backseat. He was so sweet, and he wanted to be in on this. But because he was sitting there, I couldn't cuss! Every time that wall of pain hit me, I wanted to scream horrible things, but I couldn't do it in front of my dad. I didn't want to worry him, so I pretended I was fine.

Mark took one look at me in his Beverly Hills office and sent us home. I wasn't anywhere near ready to have this baby. He said to come back later, much later. I was so fit that when I got my first contractions, my whole body just flexed. I was just one mass of muscle, and that baby wasn't going anywhere. Or so we thought. Wouldn't you know, as soon as we got to Topanga, it was time to turn right around again and go back to the hospital, but this time in bumper-to-bumper traffic.

The hospital was surreal. I felt like I was descending into underground catacombs, with doors on each level clanking shut behind me, as if I might never get out of there. Women were screaming as they wheeled me to the maternity floor. It's hard to believe there are so many people in the world, if they all get here like this! We checked into a private room, where Jack could stay with me overnight in a chair that folded out into a bed. My labor lasted the rest of the morning and into the evening. I just kept doing my Lamaze breathing and, in between, a little bit of cussing. Jack's sister, Mary Lynch, was pregnant at the same time with her and David's son, Austin. She came into the hospital to bring pillows for me when I was in hard labor, and I'll never forget the look of fear in her eyes. She knew she was up next, and this was what she was in for. So I smiled at Mary and didn't make a peep, pretending everything was just fine. That's when I did my true Academy Award performance—trying not to frighten my family.

I wanted a natural birth without any drugs, but this was getting ridiculous. When they offered me an epidural, I took it. Suddenly I was calling out to strangers in the hall to come on into the room. We were having a party!

Schuyler was born at 8:30 P.M. on July 8, 1982. She had red hair and brown eyes, and she was healthy. We kept her in the room that night, in a bassinet right next to the bed. My agent, Rick Nicita, and the producer Sean Daniel, both our good friends, stopped by the hospital room to bring flowers and good wishes. As a joke, Rick had a contract for Schuyler already drawn up from Creative Artists Agency, ready for her signature.

I was completely exhausted, like I'd run a marathon, so as soon as everybody left, I fell into a deep sleep. When I woke up in the middle of the night, I scooted over to see the baby, and she was gone. I looked over at Jack in his fold-out bed and saw that he had put her on his chest like a puppy, and they were both sound asleep.

The next morning the hospital had a little class for all the new mothers. The first one said, "Hello, my name is Marie, I got here on Tuesday and had a baby boy. We're going home in two days!"

Next was Shirley. "We had our daughter three days ago, and we're gonna be leaving tomorrow!" Then it was my turn.

"Hi, my name's Sissy. I had my daughter at eight-thirty last night and, oh—there's Jack! Gotta go!"

We couldn't see the point in sticking around a hospital when we could go home and get some rest. But after we filled out the release forms and the nurse handed Schuyler to us, Jack and I turned to each other with the same thought: *Yikes! You mean they're just gonna let us take her?*

We had no clue how to be parents, but we figured it was now or never.

As soon as I met our daughter, I realized I'd had no idea it was possible to love somebody so much. After we settled in at home, Jack quietly walked into the bedroom where I was holding Schuyler and caught me saying, ". . . and you're *all* mine!" I've never lived that down.

While I was pregnant, Jack gave me a book called *The Womanly Art of Breastfeeding*. I threw it across the room "It's my body and I'm not going to do that!" I snapped. Even though I was into natural foods, I had no intention of relinquishing control of my body to some tiny, demanding, ravenous human just because everybody else said it was such a great idea. Two and a half years later, the doctor said, "Relax, she'll wean herself!" By then I was worried I'd be going to first grade with her . . . as her lunch box.

I used to think that when you gave birth, that was the hardest part of it. But I was wrong—the hard things just keep coming. You quickly realize that you have brought into the world a complete, separate human being who is not going to listen to you unless she wants to. When she was a toddler, I would dress Schuyler in boots and jeans and all the things I had to fight to wear when I was a little girl. She wanted to wear frilly dresses and paint her room pink! I was horrified. How could I have given birth to this child? I kept trying to bring out the tomboy in her until one day she looked at me and said, "Mom, I'm not a little you!"

I finally got it. Children are just who they are. There are always going to be power struggles. Your job is to feed them, shelter them, give them room to grow, teach them manners, and make sure they don't run in front of trucks or fight with sharp objects. The rest is loving, and letting go.

··· 14 ···

A FEW YEARS BEFORE SCHUYLER WAS BORN, JACK AND I
bought a farm in the foothills of Virginia's Blue Ridge Mountains. There was an old white clapboard farmhouse and lots of out-
buildings scattered over acres of rolling green pastures ringed by forest.
At first we'd only stay in Virginia for a couple of months at a time. Jack
and I would ride horses and swim and hike in the woods, amazed that
we had a place where we could pick apples and rake leaves and watch
foals being born. Then we'd go back to LA, which seemed less and less
like paradise all the time. One day as we were heading to the airport,
and our farmhands were waving good-bye to us, Jack turned to me and
said, "You know, we're paying them to live our lives."

After we learned I was pregnant, we decided that the farm would be
a quiet, healthy place to prepare for our baby, so we started spending
most of our time there. Schuyler was born in Los Angeles, but when she
was five weeks old we were back on a plane, headed to Virginia. For a
while we lived on both coasts.

One afternoon on the farm, Jack and I noticed a pair of otters swimming in the pond behind our house. We could hardly believe it; we had
never seen otters there before. We sat quietly on the back porch, careful
not to disturb them, and were rewarded with the most enchanting performance. It was like watching an Esther Williams film choreographed
by Busby Berkeley. Their movements were so perfectly synchronized.

The otters swam side by side, doing the backstroke in lazy circles, then suddenly diving and somersaulting to the surface. They chuckled and squealed as they chased each other through the water like carefree children. We hoped they would stay forever, but they were only passing through. We watched as they scrambled up the bank, shook themselves off, and continued purposefully on their way—to who knows where. We never saw those little otters again, but knew we had witnessed pure joy.

It may have been the moment we decided to move to Virginia for good. We wanted to live in a small town where our children could have roots. I wanted them to grow up with dogs and horses and dirt between their toes, like I did. And I needed a place where I could live a real life among real people and not be tethered to the phone, waiting for my agent to call. Even though I had always tried to keep myself grounded, I'd seen how easy it is to get swallowed up by the "star maker machinery"—as Joni Mitchell put it—and spend your life trying to stay "king of the mountain." I figured that if you heard your name being whispered all the time, pretty soon you'd start hearing it whispered even when nobody was whispering. I didn't want that. The parts in films that interested me were never the glamorous characters, but ordinary people. I wanted to live and raise my children in a place where I could know the name of the neighborhood grocery clerk, and host my daughters' birthday parties, and stretch my bare feet on my own grassy lawn. The hills and piney woods around our farm in Virginia reminded me of the place where I grew up, and it felt like home.

Our decision to move east seemed even wiser when we got back to the house in Topanga and discovered we had been robbed. The place was ransacked and my guitars were stolen—including my Martin twelve-string that I'd already saved once on the streets of New York. But thank goodness, my mother had visited before she got sick and said, "Let's clean your silver and wrap it up and put it in the attic. If somebody breaks into your house, at least they won't get your silver." I should have put my guitars up there, too.

We were kind of spooked after the burglary. And we'd begun to notice that little things were missing from around the house. One night we heard a commotion in the back and thought for sure someone was breaking in. We shouted out, but the racket didn't stop. So we tiptoed quietly and followed the noise to the laundry room, and saw a big bag of cat food being tugged through the kitty door. When we looked out the window, we started to laugh. There was a little raccoon with his foot braced against the door, trying to pull the bag outside. I said, "Oh my God, Jack, now they're coming in pint-size! We're getting robbed by raccoons!"

Not long after that, the phone rang and Jack picked it up. "I'm calling about the Harley-Davidson motorcycle that you have advertised in the *LA Times*," the caller said.

Jack started to tell him, "Oh, you must have the wrong number . . ." but before he could finish, a deep voice barked, "Get off the line, this call's for me!" This was strange because we weren't on a party line. When we called the phone company, they figured that someone living nearby had probably worked as a lineman and had climbed up the pole and tapped into our phone. We guessed it had to be one of the motorcycle gang members living down the street. We also discovered he'd run up a bill for more than $3,000 in one month while we were away. It was the last straw. In the fall of 1982 Jack put the house up for sale and we started packing.

I HAD SPENT SO MUCH TIME in the public eye that I needed a sanctuary, a place where nobody could see me from the road while I was walking around in my pajamas, watering the garden. The farm gave me that solitude. But when we wanted visitors, we didn't have to go that far. Our next-door neighbors, Hugh and Winkie, lived at a farm called Highground, where they trained and "finished" some fine Thoroughbred horses on the mineral-rich grass of the Piedmont. When Hugh wanted to visit, he'd just trot on over. He descended from a bloodline almost as rare as some of his horses, but he liked nothing better than riding around on a tractor all day with a can of Budweiser in his hand. Hugh and Winkie were just two of the dozens of incredible characters we met in our new hometown.

The first person we met was Magruder Dent, our real estate lawyer. Mac might have stepped right out of a Southern novel. He looked like a country squire and had a mind like Clarence Darrow. He had a wry sense of humor, too, and was known to greet newcomers with a friendly "Who the hell are you?" (Although he never said that to us.) Once you got past the feigned gruffness, Mac was a courtly, warm, and very wise man. His wife, Posy, was also remarkable. She was tall and athletic, with sharp blue eyes, and a ferocious curiosity about the world. Posy loved entertaining and filled her house with writers and artists and colorful local characters—like the woman who claimed to be the long-dead Russian princess Anastasia, and the elderly man who only dressed in safari clothes and lived half the year in Kenya, where he left his Land Rover chained to a tree. (Posy's choice of guests probably inspired Mac's standard greeting.) I admired Posy most of all for her tenacity and courage. One terrifying afternoon Posy was driving her two very young grandsons around her farm and left them strapped in their car seats in the back of her Jeep while she got out to open a gate. When she turned around, she saw that one of the boys had climbed into the driver's seat and the Jeep was rolling down a hill toward a deep pond. She was in her late sixties, but she sprinted after the car and reached it just as it plunged into the water and sank. Posy dove in after it. She pulled one boy out of the Jeep and then dove in after the other one. Posy saved both of her grandchildren that day, and there's no doubt that she would have drowned herself before she gave up on rescuing those boys.

When I saw her after the incident, I hugged her and said, "Posy, you're such a hero."

"Oh, no," she said. "And I'm just heartsick that I let it happen in the first place."

She was a great lady.

· · ·

WHEN WE MOVED TO THE FARM, it didn't take us long to realize that our part of Virginia has more in common with rural England than the rest of America. There were not one but two active fox-hunting clubs in our county. Posy and Mac, Hugh and Winkie, and a lot of our new friends were members. Hunting with hounds is a tradition in Central Virginia dating back to the days of Thomas Jefferson. In fact, some of Jefferson's relatives—many of them with bright red hair, which made me feel at home—still lived in a family compound on a lovely, venerable farm just down the road. It's the only place I know of that still belongs to the same family that was given the original land grant from the King of England and has never been sold.

Even our farm has a connection to "Mr. Jefferson," as he is still known around here. It was part of a much larger land grant given to Dr. Thomas Walker, a physician and explorer, who was Jefferson's guardian after his father died. Dr. Walker was a pioneer who loved living on "the edge of the wilderness." But he is most fondly remembered in our neighborhood for bringing some of the first foxhounds—now known as Walker hounds—from England to America.

Not long after we arrived, Jack was off working on a film when I was invited to a dance at the local hunt club. The party was held in a humble wood frame clubhouse surrounded by porches at the end of a leafy gravel road behind the railroad tracks. A young man named Barclay introduced himself and asked me to dance. We spent the next hour dancing and talking. Barclay came from one of the oldest families in Virginia, which only meant that he had more pedigree than money. He introduced himself to me as "a blacksmith, tinsmith, and wordsmith." He had graduated from Harvard, was a wonderful writer, and made his living installing metal roofs on houses and barns. Barclay had a handsome, angular face, impeccable manners, and was one of the most accomplished horsemen in the area, which was saying a lot. He seemed to have stepped out of an earlier century.

When I got home that evening, I called Jack, breathless with excitement.

"Jack, you won't believe the night I just had!" I told him. "We're gonna love it here. I was dancing with someone who was just like a ... a ..." I looked for the word to describe an erudite fox hunter with a scratchy voice and calloused hands. "He was like a prospector!"

Jack and I don't go out very often, but we were invited to join the hunt club and started attending some of their events. One of the most interesting was a buffet dinner of game meat in its various forms, from braised venison to Brunswick stew to roasted partridge, sometimes served with shotgun pellets.

"It's perfectly all right to spit them on your plate," Winkie told us. "Even the Queen of England does it." And she would know. The queen had visited the area in the past.

Every March, at the end of hunting season, the hunt club puts on a formal ball in the same rustic clubhouse. Male guests traditionally wear tuxedos and women black evening wear—which is right up my alley. I prefer black suits and reasonable heels. I always want to be ready to run if I need to. Some gentlemen of the hunt who have been awarded their colors wear "evening scarlet" tailcoats while we all enjoy cocktails by the massive stone fireplace. The meal is sometimes served by candlelight. It always amazes me, getting all dressed up for an elegant evening out in the woods in the middle of nowhere, without a camera anywhere in sight.

We were often entertained by stories of some of the club's previous members, the most colorful of which was probably John Armstrong "Archie" Chanler, an heir to the Astor fortune and also a madman. At least that's what the State of New York declared when he was sent to an asylum. Archie escaped and returned to Merry Mills, his farm in Virginia, where the head of the hunt club helped organize a new trial to certify him sane. He was famous for throwing huge parties for everyone in the county, and would toss his drunken guests into a jail he had on the property if they got too rowdy. One evening, while defending the wife of his farm manager from a beating by her husband, he shot dead the offender. (Or, as rumor has it, he ordered his black butler to do the deed.) The next morning, Archie was found wearing leather pajamas, calmly eating a breakfast of roast duck and ice cream, while the corpse lay undisturbed a few feet away. Archie confessed to the shooting, but was absolved of any crime. When we visited the farm in recent years, the new owner pulled back the dining room rug and showed us the spot where the killing took place. Archie had marked it with a copper star.

We enjoyed the wonderful variety of people in our county. One of my favorites was Blue, proprietor of a filling station and garage at a fork in the road that leads to our farm. I would sometimes stop for gas when I didn't need it, just to talk to Blue while he topped off the tank. Schuyler and Madison (our second daughter) would run inside the store to buy gum and candy, like I had done at Mr. Butler's store when I was little. Blue was a good neighbor, too. One time Gerri's car got stuck in the mud on the farm, after she and I and the girls decided to drive to the chicken house to feed the chickens and gather some eggs. We had just come back from a shopping trip in town and were wearing our brand-new shoes. We'd had several big snows over that past week, but things had warmed up considerably, so when we pulled off our farm road to get closer to the chicken house, we could feel the car sinking down into the mushy earth underneath the melting snow. We were stuck. So we called Blue from the car and he came right over and pulled us out. He saved our new shoes, and he even fed our chickens.

When Blue finally retired, his family threw a party for him in his service station garage. It was an evening I will never forget. When we drove up, we could see that twinkling Christmas lights had been strung up inside the building. The automotive equipment was pushed back and tables full of barbecue and biscuits and scrumptious cakes and pies had been set out right over the covered repair bays. The place was transformed into something magical, and the whole town came out to celebrate. The room was filled with Blue's friends, black and white: horse trainers, investment bankers, teachers, store clerks, and school bus drivers. We were all there. It reminded me of why I loved the place so much.

It didn't take us long to fit right in to the local scene. Maybe our neighbors thought we were characters ourselves (but without the firearms or leather pajamas). Mostly we've tried to keep a low profile and get in step with how things operate here. I got the best compliment of my life from a carpenter and builder who was a mainstay of the community. "Sissy Spacek?" he told our friend Barclay. "Why she's just as ordinary as an old bar of homemade soap." (At least I hope it was a compliment.)

OF COURSE, RURAL LIVING isn't for everyone. And big farms require constant upkeep. I always say it's cost me a fortune to give my girls the simple life I had as a kid. From the start, Jack loved working on the farm and did most of it himself. He spent many an hour hammering fence posts, painting trim, and renovating barns. For him, it was part of the big art project of life. But there were a few other newcomers in the neighborhood who didn't last. We would watch them buy farms for what a tear-down house would cost in LA, thinking they had gotten such a great deal. Little did they realize that their expenses had only begun. The wife would remodel the house, and the husband would buy a new tractor. We would see him out in the fields mowing for a few weeks. Then we'd hear they were selling the place, getting a divorce, and heading back to the city.

Around the time we moved to Virginia, a famous musician bought himself a large farm through an old real estate firm in town that was owned by one of three brothers, all of whom slightly favored Ichabod Crane. The musician told the realtor, "Look, I've come here to be left alone. I just want to enjoy my land and I don't want anybody coming around and bothering me."

"Oh, no sir," said the realtor. "That shouldn't be any problem at all."

A few months later the musician bumped into the realtor at the post office.

"Hey," said the musician. "How do you meet people around here?"

He eventually put his farm on the market and moved back to New York.

WHEN WE MOVED TO VIRGINIA, Jack's mother, Gerri, came with us and Jack fixed up a cottage for her on the farm. It was wonderful having Gerri living here full-time. She ran the farm, handled our business, and helped take care of Schuyler (and later Madison) while we juggled our work schedules. She gave us the freedom we needed. I don't know how we would have managed without her, or without Alberta Mahanes. As soon as I met her, I knew I needed her help. There was something so patient and kind about her, I found myself following her around the house, trying to pick up nuggets of wisdom. I had recently lost my own mother, and I had so many questions about raising a child. Between Gerri and Alberta, I was covered. The three of us became great friends.

Alberta traveled everywhere with us. When Schuyler was still an infant, I had to attend an event in New York, and Alberta came along to take care of her. The plane left early in the morning, and we were late leaving the farm. So we decided to take a shortcut over the mountain. It was the dead of winter. As we pulled out of the driveway, it was still dark, and the clouds were threatening rain. The road kept getting narrower and steeper, and as we gained altitude, the rain turned to ice and snow. We were slipping and sliding, and Jack finally stopped the car at the top of a very steep hill, got out, and peered over the other side. It was a sharp drop covered by a sheet of ice, and we had to turn back. But it was too narrow to turn around, so Jack got out and manually spun the car around on the ice. Alberta and I suddenly realized how hazardous this was. I covered my eyes and said, "Berta, this is too dangerous! I think maybe we should get out!" Then I heard Jack get in and slam the door. He put two tires in the ditch to give us traction as we slowly skidded our way back to the bottom of the hill, the car complaining in low gear all the way. After it became clear that we would make it down safely, Jack said, "Wow, Berta, that was a close one, wasn't it? I can't believe we made it. Can you?" We heard nothing coming from the backseat. "Berta?" Berta?"

That's when we realized we'd left Alberta and Schuyler on the top of the mountain. She must have stepped out and closed the door just as Jack got in. Jack clambered back up the hill on foot, staying in the ditch to keep from sliding backward. He found Alberta by the side of the road, still holding Schuyler under that blanket, softly singing her favorite song.

I don't know how she put up with us.

AS THE YEARS WENT BY, it got harder and harder for us to tear ourselves away from the farm. Especially for formal events. One year when Ronald Reagan was president, Jack and I were invited to a fancy event at the White House. We drove to Washington and checked into a nice hotel. I started putting on my evening clothes while Jack got into his tux. Then we looked at each other and one of us said, "I wish we were at home in our blue jeans."

"Yeah, me too," said the other.

"Do we really want to do this?"

"No, do you?"

"No, let's go home!"

It wasn't a political thing. We'd met President Reagan before and liked him. But we were supposed to meet with Schuyler's kindergarten teacher in the morning, and that seemed more important.

Over the years, there were other White House functions that we managed to get it together to attend. The first time I met Bill Clinton, he and I had been chatting for a while when he said, "Wait, you've got to meet Hillary." He beckoned to her from across the sea of faces. "Hillary!" he said. "C'mere and meet the only other person in the room who doesn't have an accent."

. . .

NOT LONG AFTER WE ARRIVED in Virginia, Jack and I went out riding with Barclay and his brother, Sandy, a U.S. Parks Service ranger who was also a whip, or outrider, for the hunt. Watching the brothers ride was to behold a thing of beauty. It was a gorgeous day in May, and the hills were lush with green grass. The four of us reached the top of a rise overlooking a gently sloping valley. Jack and I just looked at each other and said, "Yee-hah!" We went galloping down into the meadow and up the other hill at full speed. When we looked back, Barclay and Sandy were still on the other side of the valley, perfectly collected atop their Thoroughbreds, no doubt wondering what kind of rednecks they had let into the club.

I thought I was a long way from riding cows with Vickie Johns, but apparently I wasn't.

SCHUYLER WENT TO HER first horse show when she was just a few weeks old. Little girls in riding clothes came running up to us and said, "Has she been on a horse yet?" She hadn't, but that didn't last long. The riders around here literally attach basinets to their saddles, so newborns can ride in their first lead line class and not be left behind in this world filled with horses and dogs. Most babies are sound asleep in the basket, so they don't even know they're on a horse. That basket has been passed around for years to many a tiny equestrian. Schuyler and Madison both became good riders; they rode in competitions and lined their bedrooms with ribbons. But at the farm they used the horses mostly for fun and transportation, like I did growing up in Texas.

There was a tiny general store less than a mile from our house, owned by a woman we all knew as Mrs. Smith—or as Schuyler would say, "Smizz Smisses." One summer afternoon, I was away somewhere, probably in town running errands, while Jack was upstairs in the bedroom, recovering from hernia surgery he'd had the day before. Schuyler and her cousin Austin, both about eight years old, wanted to ride their ponies over to Mrs. Smith's store to buy an ice cream as they often did. Somehow they talked Jack into letting them go but he told them, "Walk. Don't take the ponies." He gave them all kinds of instructions, including to stop and look both ways when they crossed the street, which was a two-lane country road, but the cars moved fast. Feeling very old and responsible, Schuyler and Austin set off on their excellent adventure, trailed by a couple of the farm dogs, Buster and Lucky.

Twenty minutes later, Schuyler called Jack from Mrs. Smith's store, crying and hysterical.

"He got run over, he got hit by a car!" she sobbed. Jack jumped out of bed and took the flight of stairs in two leaps, despite his stitches. He jumped in the car and raced over there, making bargains with God to be a better person if Austin was spared. As he rounded the corner, his heart nearly stopped when he saw a crowd of people standing around a small form in the road. But when he pushed through the crowd he saw that it was our dog Lucky. Austin and Schuyler were inconsolable, but okay.

They had done everything right, waiting and looking both ways before they crossed the road. Buster had followed them, but Lucky had hesitated. They were calling her just as a big truck came over the hill.

It's a wonder that children survive their childhoods, and that parents survive their children. As long as there are trees and playgrounds and sharp furniture, emergency rooms will stay in business.

One summer a good friend of ours, Sue Kramer, was visiting us from New York. She's a screenwriter that Jack was working with at the time. She was terrified of horses after a traumatic riding experience when she was younger. She had fallen off and broken both of her arms, and was in double casts for months. Jack invited her to go riding on Simon, one of our gentlest horses, in the hope that she would be able to conquer her fear. Finally she mustered the courage to take a slow trail ride around the farm. Schuyler was about nine at the time and didn't understand how anyone could be so terrified of horses. She wanted to go on the trail ride, too. Jack was afraid Schuyler might go running around on her horse, jumping over everything, and scare Sue even more.

Schuyler was mad because she couldn't go, so she climbed up into a huge old oak tree and onto a tree house that wasn't quite finished. Jack was keeping an eye on her while he and Sue walked their horses slowly around the field across the pond. Suddenly Schuyler fell out of the tree and landed with a thud. Then she started to scream. Jack leapt off his horse and threw the reins to Sue, yelling, "Take the horses back to the barn," then sprinted to Schuyler's side. Poor Sue had to figure out how to get to the barn and what to do with the baffled horses while Jack took care of Schuyler.

It was a frightening injury; her arm had come unhinged at the elbow and was twisted in a way that arms don't normally twist. I heard yelling from across the pond and grabbed a tray of ice and my homeopathic kit and ran to help. I had been running about six miles a day for years and years, but I was breathless after running only a hundred yards to help my injured child. We bundled her into the car and picked up Sue, who had found someone at the barn to help her with the horses.

On the way to the hospital, we called the best orthopedic surgeon in town and alerted him we were on our way. Dr. Frank McCue was responsible for saving Jack's hand after an accident with a high pressure paint sprayer, and he'd set several of my broken toes. (He was the go-to guy for injured appendages.) As Schuyler was taken out of the van, Jack called to Sue, "Park the van!" A dyed-in-the-wool New Yorker, Sue was unfamiliar with driving large vehicles. But she had a job to do, so she forged ahead. Just as she was pulling into the underground parking garage, someone came running out, waving their arms for her to stop. That's when she heard the crunch and realized she was taking off the top of the van.

By the time we got to the hospital, I was feeling so queasy that I was ready to faint. After they had calmed Schuyler down and given her morphine for the pain, they whisked her away to surgery. She was lying down in the operating room and I was lying down in the waiting room.

When the doctors came out after the surgery, Jack and I jumped up, hoping to get to see her. The doctor said, "She's asking for . . ." "Me?" I interrupted. "No, she's asking for Sue." "Sue?" I said. "She barely knows Sue!" Sue stepped forward and offered an explanation: "I've been telling her stories all day. That's why she wants me." "Sure, sure, go ahead," I said. But I was thinking, *Hey, I gave birth to her. Doesn't that count for anything?*

Dr. McCue came by to see us and told us Schuyler was doing fine. The arm was not broken, but it was seriously dislocated and would be in a cast for several months. Good news. My stomach was starting to settle down and I wasn't feeling quite so faint. Then the anesthesiologist came over to give his report, and he recognized me and started chatting away about his brief career in the movie business. He said that before studying medicine, he had worked in the art department on a couple of films but had decided to change professions after a disaster on one film he'd worked on. Jack took a closer look at his face and then said, "Oh, I remember you now! You're the one who ruined my set! I fired you!"

The doctor was the person who'd worked on *Phantom of the Paradise* and who'd used water-soluble caulking on the skylight, which collapsed, ruining the set and delaying the filming. Jack still hadn't quite gotten over it. And now this same guy had put our daughter under for surgery. We were just praying he was a better anesthesiologist than he was a carpenter!

I CONFESS THAT I HAVE always been a fainter—it's a condition that runs in the family; my father also had it. I'm told it's an oversensitive vasovagal response to different triggers, such as pain, surprise, or watching your six-year-old have lidocaine injected into her gashed eyebrow. (But that's another story.)

My most famous fainting episode took place during a dinner party at the farm. I had the table set and candles lit and a beautiful bowl of pasta and fresh tomato sauce was ready to serve. We were just sitting down to dinner on the porch with a table full of guests when I saw a mangy stray cat that had gotten into the house jump up onto the kitchen counter and head straight for the turkey that was fresh out of the oven. I was hoping no one else saw it, and I quickly excused myself and rushed into the kitchen to remove the cat. As I hurried through the door, I smashed my foot into the doorjamb and felt a lightning bolt of pain shoot up through it, but I shook it off and grabbed the cat. Then I limped back to the table and sat down. The next thing I remember was waking up on the floor with a pillow under my head, both girls staring down at me, and hearing Jack's voice outside a dark red veil covering my eyes. Jack helped me up, and I apologized to our guests as he walked me up the stairs to bed.

"Jack!" I whispered. "My eyes are burning and I can't see!"

"It's okay, Sissy," Jack said mildly. "You just fainted into the pasta sauce."

I'd broken my toes before, but this was a bad one. My toe went sideways instead of straight ahead. I'd broken it in half. So Jack took me to see our ol' friend Dr. McCue to have it set. I was supposed to fly to New York early the next morning to meet with a Dutch director about a film he wanted to do with me, and I really didn't feel up to the trip. But a broken toe didn't seem like a good enough excuse to cancel the meeting. I told my doctor about it and he said, "Look, it's a bad break, but if it would make you feel better, why don't you just tell the director you broke a bone in your foot, and ask him to come down to the farm?" To make it more convincing, the doctor put on a full lower leg cast.

Sure enough, the director agreed to meet me at the farm. As soon as he arrived, he was helping me hobble around in my cast, serving himself tea, and being a complete gentleman. There were torrential rains that day, but we had a lovely time out on the covered porch, talking about his film, while Madison, who was about two at the time, played nearby. The porch was wet from all the rain, and all of a sudden I saw her slip and fall on her back all the way down a flight of stone steps. I jumped out of my chair, sprinted across the porch and down the stairs, and scooped my screaming daughter into my arms. The director almost had a heart attack. He looked at me quizzically. I was hoping he had read those stories about mothers suddenly developing superhuman strength when their children are in danger. But I think he probably just thought I was some kind of freak.

And Madison was fine.

A S SOON AS WE MOVED TO VIRGINIA, THE ENTERTAIN-
ment media decided I must have retired. I couldn't convince
them otherwise, so I just kept on working. But after I had children, my
choices were even more careful. I only wanted to make films that mattered to me, or with directors or actors I'd always wanted to work with.
And when I went on location, the whole family came along with me.

Gerri and I would fly to the location a month or so before filming
began. We'd find a house to rent and then visit the local schools to find
out which of their best teachers were out on maternity leave. We'd interview them and then hire a teacher who could bring her baby with her
while she tutored the girls for a few months. We'd set up a classroom in
the living room and usually would have classes in the mornings and
take field trips in the afternoons. We brought the girls' bikes and pets
and toys to make it feel like home.

AFTER A STRING OF SERIOUS FILMS, it was a relief to do a Southern
comedy like *Crimes of the Heart* in 1985. Of course my character, Babe,
tries to stick her head in the oven and kill herself, but not before realizing how hungry she is and eating some day-old popcorn on the stove.
I got a great note about her from the director, Bruce Beresford. He told
me to play the character straight; it made her so funny. I also asked

Beth Henley, the Mississippi playwright who wrote the script, "What can you tell me about Babe?"

"Well," she said, "Babe is the kind of girl who plans a big dinner party, has a gorgeous centerpiece, a fabulous outfit, and sets the table beautifully, but forgets to put the roast in the oven."

"Oh, I know her!" I laughed. "I *am* her!"

The scuttlebutt in Hollywood was that the director was going to have his hands full with so many major female stars in one production. Who was going to be the biggest diva? But Jessica Lange, Diane Keaton, Tess Harper, and I defied the industry stereotypes by getting along like, well, sisters. There were no divas on this set. Usually the cast members are given their own motor homes as dressing rooms. But on *Crimes of the Heart*, which was filmed on location outside Wilmington, North Carolina, the production took over a house next door to the set and fixed it up for us. We had the hair and makeup department and wardrobe right in the back of the house. Each of us had a bedroom and bath, we shared the kitchen and a television in the living room, and we all hung out together like a family—which is what our characters were supposed to be.

One day, Diane came into the house and saw Schuyler standing in the living room with her brand-new doctor kit. Without saying a word, Diane dropped to the floor, grabbing her knee and moaning, "Oh, my leg, my leg! Is there a doctor in the house?" Schuyler was only three years old, and feeling kind of shy. She stood there like a soldier, clutching her bag. Diane looked up at Schuyler, then looked at her bag. "Are you a doctor?" she whispered. Schuyler nodded solemnly, then kneeled down and opened her kit. Before long, Diane's leg was covered in bandages, and she had taken a sugar pill for the pain. It was a sweet, serendipitous moment.

I never realized how important my girlfriends were to me until I moved away from them. I hadn't been at the farm too long when I read somewhere that it takes seven years to develop a great friendship. This put me right smack in the dumps. It was before iChat and Skype, and really even before computers. Occasionally, one of my girlfriends would visit from New York or LA, but eventually she would have to go home and I'd be right back where I started—lonesome. But as time went by and I got into the routines of life, I began to make friends in Virginia. Then one day I woke up and realized that my dance card was full. I had some of the most wonderful girlfriends ever. And I met them in the most usual places—the grocery store, the school pickup line . . .

Diane (not Keaton, a different Diane) and I met in a grocery store. We were standing next to each other in line, both with little babies, and we started chatting. I had several hundred dollars' worth of groceries and diapers and household supplies in my cart. When I pulled out my credit card to pay, the cashier shook her head and told me they only took cash or checks. I had neither. I looked back at the fifteen shoppers behind me in line and I was near tears, thinking about putting everything back. Diane said, "Don't worry, I'll write you a check."

"You will? But we've just met."

She looked at me levelly. "Oh, I think you're good for it."

We've been friends ever since.

I met Aggie when she broke through the press line at the Virginia Special Olympics held on the side of a mountain in Wintergreen, Virginia. I had Schuyler in a backpack and it was snowing, but that didn't stop Aggie. She leaned close to me and said quietly, "I was wondering if you could give me an interview?" I smiled and explained that I wasn't giving any. To which she replied, "Oh, it's just a tiny paper in Nelson County. Nobody reads it anyway."

She was so disarming and open that I broke my own rule and gave her the interview. She became another good friend. She had been a competetive swimmer, and she taught both of our girls to swim. I also thought Aggie would be a great match for Barclay, the writer/roofer/prospector, and am happy to report that they married and raised two fine daughters on a farm they call Rock Bottom.

Aggie was a member of the Walnut Mountain Study Group, a collection of friends who got together to study homeopathic medicine and medicinal herbs. We met on my porch every month, just like my mother had her girlfriends over for coffee. I have been interested in herbal remedies, alternative medicine, and healthy living since I was in my early twenties. As a kid, my idea of a balanced meal was adding a pickle to my cheeseburger, fries, and Coke. But shortly after I moved to California, I gave up the occasional cigarette, became a vegetarian, and started running—all in one day. In for a penny, in for a pound, as my mother would say. I had heard a lot of older people joking that if they'd known they were going to live so long, they would have taken better care of themselves. I was determined to start early, and I did.

Instead of stopping by for a cup of coffee, my girlfriends join me for long walks around the farm. We share ideas and our favorite news stories, and sometimes even talk politics—but there's no gossip allowed. We laugh sometimes and I call them "church walks," because nature is my sanctuary. I can almost hear music in the leaves on a windy day And if I stand very still, I can hear the sound of geese flapping their wings as they fly overhead. The blue sky and the smell of fresh-mowed fields are a tonic for me, and fill me up like a prayer.

I've had many good friends walk with me over the years. My friend Mary is a fine arts photographer who looks like Grace Kelly and has a belly laugh you can hear across a crowded room. We got to know each other when she interviewed and photographed me with Schuyler for her book *Mother*. Mary always documents what's going on in her life, and motherhood was it at the time. Back then she and her husband, David, were raising three rambunctious boys, and Mary had become an expert. *Mother* was a follow-up book to *Giving Birth*, which I'm kind of glad I didn't see before having any babies. Ignorance is bliss, in this case. Mary grew up in Virginia Beach, and she spent her childhood surfing and beachcombing. One day she found a small, lifeless shark on the sand and threw it around her shoulders and carried it home, cheek to cheek, to show her little brothers. When her mother saw it, she said, "Mary, take that disgusting thing back to the beach." So Mary walked it back and tossed it in the water . . . and it swam away. My brother Robbie would have really liked her.

Whenever Mary arrives for one of our walks, she laughs and says, "C'mon, Sissy! Let's go count our blessings."

ONE NIGHT IN EARLY 1988, Mary, David, Jack, and I met for dinner at La Hacienda, a local Mexican spot with Formica tables and velvet sombreros nailed to the wall. I said to them, "We have some great news!"

"We have some, too!" said Mary,

"Ours is better!" Jack said.

"Nope, ours is better!" David said.

We all should have known something was up because Mary and I both skipped the 99-cent margaritas. Finally everybody blurted it out at once—we were both pregnant. We had found out on the same day.

After three boys, we were all praying Mary was having a girl. I was just happy to be having another baby. One child changes your life so much, you might as well have more. Who knows, Jack and I loved being parents so much we might have had a dozen if we had started sooner.

YOU WOULD THINK we'd have been better prepared this time around. One September morning, while we were out feeding the horses, I felt my first contraction. I looked at my watch. Jack went inside to take a shower. While I was taking off my boots, another one came. And then another.

"Jack, I think it's time to go!" I called into the shower.

"The contractions have to be twenty minutes apart," he called back.

"But they're two minutes apart."

He was toweling himself off. "No, we don't have to worry until they're twenty minutes apart," he said.

"Jack, I think it goes the other way. . . ."

While we were racing to the hospital, I called Mary. She still wanted to document all of her girlfriends' deliveries. And I wanted her there.

Jack and I had expected the contractions to go on forever like last

time, but I barely made it to the hospital. There is nothing more ferocious than a woman in labor, especially the second time around. I wasn't
worried about making noise this time, and I was mean as a snake. Some
poor young nurse came in to give me an injection and he couldn't find
my vein. His hands were shaking like crazy. "Get out of my room!" I
yelled, "And send somebody who knows how to give a shot!" He stumbled out of the room, terrified.

Mary arrived just in time. When the doctor walked in, she had her
scalpel ready.

"Put that down!" Mary barked like a drill sergeant. "Leave her alone!
She doesn't need it."

"Yeah! Listen to her!" I screamed.

What made the scene even funnier was that Mary was nine months
pregnant, standing up on two chairs, trying to balance herself while
yelling instructions and photographing the birth with a large Nikon
camera. The nurses were beside themselves; they didn't know whether
to help her or me.

The baby came moments later, and there was no need for any inter-
vention. After an hour or so I put my blue jeans back on, Jack scooped
up our new daughter, and we all drove home. We named her Virginia
Madison Fisk.

While Mary was photographing the delivery, she felt her own baby
begin to drop. And a few days later she gave birth to a girl, Natasha,
who would become Madison's best friend.

(I'd like to take this opportunity to thank Dr. Kay Halsey for
performing her duties with patience and professionalism while under
intense battlefield-like conditions . . . ambushed by two enormous, wild-
eyed pregnant women swearing and shouting orders.)

MADISON WAS THE SPITTING IMAGE of her father, with brown
eyes and a mop of dark hair. The apple didn't fall far from the tree. Schuyler and her cousin Austin considered her their personal plaything, so

235

she had to grow up tough. Jack was a wonderful father, but like most men, he was a little more lax around our girls than I was, and I always held my breath when I left them alone with him. My fears were confirmed when he showed me a video he'd made when Madison was a few months old. She was a pudgy baby and Schuyler, who was about six, was a peanut. But there, on tape, is little Schuyler carrying around and jiggling her baby sister, who is slowly sliding out of her arms. Then she hoists Madison up on the bed, leans all her weight on her, and coughs a wet, rumbly cough right in her face. It was like watching a Stephen King movie for mothers.

Somehow Madison survived her infancy, and grew to be a bright, precocious toddler. She always had a special relationship with her dad. One morning she came downstairs for breakfast and saw that Jack had shaved his beard. She had never seen him without a beard before.

She looked at him closely and asked, "What's your name now?"

"It's still Dad," he said.

Another time he wanted to get her up from a nap. She was still half-asleep and in her dream when she opened her eyes and said, "Did you know Beethoven was also a person?"

I always told Madison and Schuyler what my mother had told me: that the kingdom of heaven is within. When I did, I would place my hands over my heart. One Sunday morning Jack and I took the girls to the lovely old stone church down the road from the farm. Madison, who was about three, was listening intently to the minister's sermon. "Where is God?" the minister asked. "Where *is* God!?" Suddenly Madison piped up, loudly enough for all the congregation to hear, "God is in your chest!" she said.

I had to laugh. My mother would have been proud.

MADISON AND NATASHA were like me and Vickie Johns, always riding horses and getting into mischief together. Madison had a bay

Welsh pony she called Treasure and Natasha had a little chestnut Arabian named Mr. Pie. They taught their horses how to rear up and to jump hedges. They were such natural riders that I would let them go off on adventures, like riding bareback on the trails in the woods around the farm.

Not long ago, Madison asked me, "Mom, how could you let us ride up the mountain all alone? We were only, like, nine years old!"

"Well, I gave you walkie-talkies."

And I would do it again. I can't imagine having a childhood without being left on your own some time and being able to have some freedom. Jumping horses, riding bicycles and skateboards, and climbing trees all involve taking some risks. But how else can you know what you're made of if you're never allowed to test yourself? Our daughters both had plenty of mettle, but their personalities were very different.

Madison was a tomboy like me, always running barefoot or swinging off a tree limb with her clothes on backwards. Schuyler was a born performer. When she was about seven, she made her film debut in a dark comedy Jack directed called *Daddy's Dyin' . . . Who's Got the Will?* After that, she had stars in her eyes. She became convinced that we were ruining her career by not living in LA. During one visit to Los Angeles, she turned to me and said "Mom, why don't we live in LA like all the other actresses?"

I said, "Schuyler, honey, we moved to Virginia so you'd have a wonderful childhood like I did, riding horses, playing in the woods, swimming in the pond, running around the farm barefoot. We didn't want you to grow up in a city, with traffic and pollution. We wanted you and Madison to grow up breathing clean fresh air, not smog."

Schuyler took a great big deep breath of air, threw out her arms dramatically, and said, "But I LOVE smog . . . I LOVE traffic!" I realized in that moment that I'd met my match.

I explained to her that she didn't have to live in Hollywood to be an actress. If she wanted to learn to act, she should try out for her school plays. So that's what she did. (I assumed that she would soon tire of performing and lose interest. But as Loretta Lynn always told me: never assume.) She debuted in *Charlotte's Web*. We sat proudly with the other parents as she portrayed a bee with great flair. The floppy wings that her dad had made for her slapped all the other little insects and farm animals in the face as she danced around the stage. When she was in sixth grade, she played the lead in the musical *Annie*. I cleaned out the downstairs backstage area so the actors could have a safe, comfortable place to wait their turn to go onstage. I also volunteered to do hair and makeup, and curled up one of my movie wigs for Schuyler to wear as Little Orphan Annie. The show was so good that kids from other schools came to hear her sing, "The sun'll come out tomorrow." But we didn't realize what a star she was until Schuyler and I were strolling through a small shopping center in town at Christmastime. Some schoolgirls raced up to us waving papers and pens. We both thought they wanted my autograph until we heard them say, "Schuyler! Schuyler! Are you Schuyler Fisk? You were in *Annie*, right?" Her whole face lit up as she signed her first autographs.

SCHUYLER HAD SMALL PARTS in several of my films, but when she was eleven, she won a major role in *The Baby-Sitters Club*. Some mothers might have hesitated to let their child get into the business at such a young age, but acting was in Schuyler's blood and she had grown up around films. It was as natural to her as chewing gum. We made sure she was safe and kept up her schoolwork. Jack and I traded off traveling on location with her. The whole family moved to Ireland one summer when she starred in *My Friend Joe*. She played a circus performer, and I'll never get over the sight of her walking a high wire with a harness but no net. Madison, who was about five, was not in the film but had such incredible balance that the aerialist tried to talk us into taking her to France for training.

"I don't think so," I said. "She's going home to start kindergarten instead."

Schuyler was a fearless, tough-minded kid, like I was, and very precise about how she wanted things to go. Just as I had worn my father down to get a horse, Schuyler had used a similar technique to have her ears pierced when she was about nine years old. We finally relented and brought her to an ear-piercing booth in a local mall. The whole family got dressed up and came along for the occasion, and Jack took a video for posterity. It's painful to watch. The machine was supposed to punch a hole in her earlobe and leave a little gold stud behind. But the machine got stuck and the stud broke off. Soon the excitement on her face crumpled and she started to tremble. She was trying to be brave and not cry, breathing in little puffs to control the pain. But within minutes she'd regained her composure and got the second ear done. And she paved the way for her little sister, as all older siblings do for the younger ones. Madison got her ears pierced a short while later with hardly any begging.

OUR DAUGHTERS CAME ALONG just at the right time in my life, at the height of my success. Kids don't know you're famous, and they don't care. They'll kick you to the curb every time. You say frog, they don't jump; they say frog, you jump. When Schuyler cut most of her hair off with a pair of dull scissors when she was about four years old, it sent me into quite a tailspin. When Madison did the same thing at about the same age, I just shrugged and thought, *Well at least we have that over with.* (Of course neither of these episodes was nearly as bad as when my brothers cut off my ponytail right at the rubber band.)

It was not always easy combining career and family. In fact, it was kind of like patting my head and rubbing my stomach at the same time. I felt like the lady trying to keep all the plates spinning in the air. When I was making a film, I worried about the parent/teacher conference I was missing. When I was in the carpool line, I wondered if I'd ever work again. But I somehow managed to do both, and survived to tell the tale.

WE SPENT MOST OF 1994 in Texas shooting two projects back-to-back: *Streets of Laredo* and *The Good Old Boys.* Tommy Lee Jones was making his directorial debut with *The Good Old Boys,* a cable TV drama about cowboys trying to hold on to the ways of the Old West. Sam Shepard and Frances McDormand were in it, too, along with a newcomer named Matt Damon. The script called for my character to ride her horse side-saddle, and I wanted to make it look good. So I found a beautiful period Sears and Roebuck sidesaddle and took it to a leathersmith in Virginia who repaired and conditioned it. It was beautifully engineered and built for serious riding and jumping. I worked with a national side-saddle champion every day for months and before long I was cantering along the trails like I knew what I was doing.

I brought Schuyler and Madison with me for the filming, and they had a great time riding ponies bareback with the ranch kids who lived nearby. In fact, the whole movie felt like a family affair. Sam Shepard's teenage son, Jesse, was the wrangler on the movie, and he had a special horse and saddle ready for me when I got there. The horse was a handsome paint, but he was persnickety and had been schooled with an old Mexican parade saddle. When I got on him with my own saddle, he started bucking me across the field. I managed to stay on, and eventually got him calmed down. In the end, I came to love that paint horse. But I don't know if Tommy Lee ever trusted him after that incident.

This was a classic Western, and Tommy Lee and Sam were galloping their horses all over the place. I was only allowed to walk, or maybe trot if I was lucky. It started to bother me, because I had put in so much time learning to ride sidesaddle—and I wanted to *ride.*

"Tommy Lee, am I ever going to get to gallop in this movie?" I asked one day.

"See all the rocks in this field?" said Tommy Lee.

"Yep."

"Know what they call it?"

"Nope."

"Cemetery Field. That's what they named it after an old boy's horse threw him here one day, and he hit his head and died. Now, what would I do if I had to call Jack and tell him you got thrown off your horse, hit your head on a rock, and died?"

"Tommy Lee, where I live now, people jump four-foot fences in the woods riding sidesaddle in skirts. I worked hard to learn how to ride this way. I'd rather fall off and hit my head on a rock and die than go back to Virginia and tell everybody that I just walked into the middle of every scene!"

So he let me gallop in one time, but he shot it with me riding straight at the camera, so you missed the effect of my flowing skirts traveling east to west. And I thought, *Where's the drama?* It was a bit of a disappointment, but my only one. Tommy Lee Jones is a talented director. And I loved working with him.

In *Streets of Laredo*, shot on the same location, I got a little more drama than I'd bargained for. I drove a wagon filled with children through a raging dust storm and rode across the prairie at a dead run, shooting bad guys off their horses with a Colt .45 revolver. It reminded me that all my childhood experiences on the back of my horse had actually helped prepare me for something.

Madison, who was about four, wanted to be an extra in the film, so we dressed her up in an old-fashioned sailor dress that had been her sister's, her paddock boots, and a hat. She was so excited, but after hours of waiting in the heat she started to fade. By lunchtime, she was "over it." We had befriended one of the stuntmen who had also brought his children to the set. When he saw that Madison was losing her mind with boredom, he offered to put her on an old, gentle horse and walk around with her. She hopped right on. When it came time to eat, filming stopped and everyone headed over to the lunch tent, open on the sides because it was so hot. There were about a hundred people seated at the tables. Madison wanted to go faster, so she gave her horse a little kick. Even the mellowest horses have their moments, and this one took off at top speed. Right toward the lunch tent. We all stopped eating and turned to look, utensils frozen in midair, as we heard two set of hooves galloping toward us. Madison was in the lead, and way out front, on a direct path to disaster, when, from far behind, in raced the stuntman. He galloped alongside her, scooped her off her saddle, and pulled her horse to a stop just before it collided with the tent. Everybody applauded, then went right back to eating. Madison walked around with a smile on her face for the rest of the day.

··· 16 ···

IT'S NO SECRET THAT THE GOOD FILM ROLES DWINDLE when an actress reaches middle age. I don't even know who said it first, but the progression goes like this· At first the studio head says: "Get me Sissy Spacek!" Then it becomes "Get me a young Sissy Spacek!" Then it's "Sissy who?"

I have been lucky to find so many rich, nuanced characters written for grown women. One of the best was Ruth Fowler, the bereaved mother in *In the Bedroom*. It was Todd Field's first time writing and directing a feature, and it was shot for a budget of $1 million on location in Camden and Rockport, Maine, two idyllic little towns on the Atlantic coast. Everyone involved was passionate about the project. We always seem to have the most fun on films where nobody's getting rich and everybody's there for the right reason: because we love it. With financial limitations, everyone has to be more creative, figuring out ways to do things on a budget. The crew is smaller, and the unit is closer, and everybody pitches in. Schuyler, who was just eighteen, got her first experience in set decoration. Her job was to make a house into a home. She collected children's drawings (some of them her sister's) and painted some of her own. She came along with me to all the antique stores, asking if we could borrow furniture for the film. Todd and his wife had their own linens and paintings shipped out to the set, and many of us contributed some of our own clothes for costumes. It was like that scene in the Mickey Rooney musical, where he says, "Hey, kids, we've got a barn, let's put on a show!" We all worked together to make it happen.

Sometimes it felt as if I had come full circle in my career, reminding me of the days when I dressed sets for Jack. It made me proprietary about some of the props. I had chosen a perfect framed picture for my bedside table in the film. We were shooting a scene where I was lying on the bed, and I heard the camera operator say, "We've got a glare on that picture." Rather than change the angle, he sent an assistant over to take it out of the shot. I grabbed it, and a tug-of-war ensued. Guess who won? It was my contribution to what turned out to be an all-but-perfect film, a masterwork that paid off for all of us in every way.

IN THE LATE 1990S David Lynch directed a film that would bring us old friends together to work for the first time. *The Straight Story* is the simple, true saga of Alvin Straight, a retired farmer who drives his riding mower across two states to visit his dying brother. Jack signed on as the production designer, and David asked me to play Alvin's middle-aged daughter, Rose. It was a challenging part because Rose had a speech disorder. I needed to learn how to stutter through pages and pages of dialogue. I worked with a doctor of speech pathology and I listened to dozens of stutterers on tape. Then I had to learn to stutter with a Wisconsin accent. I used my old standbys, the tape recorder and video recorder. I gave myself headaches—for me it was all about the air being blocked and not flowing smoothly over the vocal chords. I had decided to wear some dental devices during filming to give Rose interesting teeth. So before I left LA, I worked with an Oscar-winning makeup artist named Matthew Mungle. He made me a set of prosthetic teeth and added plumpers, to fill out my checks, and a palate, which is sort of like a retainer, to change my voice and remind me to stutter. He was also able to lower my gum line with this device and give me one crooked tooth, which gave the illusion of a whole mouthful of crooked teeth.

The most important thing I did, once we arrived on location in Iowa, was spend days with Alvin's real daughter, Diane, absorbing her voice and learning her body language. She's a very funny person, and I enjoyed spending time with her. She didn't have a driver's license and had never driven a car, so we walked all over town together. She was quite an institution around Laurens, Iowa. One day she said, "I'm gonna take you to the cop shop." I didn't know what she meant until we walked in on a meeting of police officers and detectives at the police station. They didn't recognize me because I was in character, but they seemed to know perfectly well who Diane was, and they were not at all surprised by this episode. I just had to convince her not to blow my cover by always introducing me as "the movie star that is playing me."

Matthew had made me several sets of prosthetic teeth, which we both thought would last for the entire show. From the first time I met Diane, I wore my "movie teeth." I didn't want to hurt her feelings by letting her know I was wearing fake teeth to play her, so whenever she took me to the fast-food hamburger place, I would have to eat with my prosthetic teeth in place. Unfortunately they weren't made for eating. Matthew had to make quite a few extra pair for me before the filming was over.

To help me transform into the character, David Lynch also talked me into cutting off my hair. That was traumatic, and, trust me, I'd only do it for David. We had both wanted to work together for years, and this turned out to be the perfect project. Jack and David hadn't worked together since *Eraserhead*. Now they were like schoolboys again. They would walk around inspecting locations. David would mention to Jack that he thought the kitchen of Alvin's house was a little too small, and before he could blink, Jack would pick up a sledgehammer and start demolishing a wall. Then David would take out a crowbar and join him. David and Jack worked harder than any of us, and always with enthusiasm. I would often find them sweeping the sidewalks before the day's filming. As a director, David was a dream: a kind, calm person, with a wonderful inventiveness. It made us want to do anything for him. I had one scene where I hauled big sheets of plywood while talking

nonstop to Richard Farnsworth, who played Alvin Straight so beautifully. We did that scene all morning, until David said, "You know, Sis,
this doesn't feel right. Let's change it." So we reshot it a different way
for half of the afternoon, until David announced, "No, it was better the
other way." My arms were about to fall off, but in the end he was right,
and the scene was perfect.

It was fun watching him with the other actors, too. There was a
scene in a hardware store, where one of the elderly actors was supposed
to get something from behind a counter, say a line, then turn back
around. He kept mixing it up, and he was getting upset with himself for
doing it wrong every time. David was so patient. He told him, "I'm gonna
get a little string, and I'm going to tie it on to your belt loop. And every
time you start to go the wrong way, I'm gonna give that string a little
tug, and you're gonna know it's time to turn around and put that box
back on the shelf . . ." He had everybody laughing, and it calmed the actor down and made him laugh, too. He did the next take just right.

It was easy to see why David has such loyal friends who will drop
everything and work with him for minimal pay when he makes a film.
Freddie Francis, one of the greatest cinematographers ever, who had
worked with David on *The Elephant Man* and *Dune*, was director of photography for *The Straight Story* (and always wore pink cashmere socks).
Most of the crew had worked with David for years. We were like a big,
happy family on location, all staying together in a shabby little motel in
Laurens, Iowa. With Jack there, it reminded me so much of filming
Badlands out on the Colorado prairie, when I first realized that filmmaking could be art. Twenty-five years and thirty films later, I still felt
like I was at the center of the universe.

LIVING ON A FARM, surrounded by animals and weather and hay-
fields, our whole family was bound to the natural rhythms of life and
death and birth and renewal. Our girls watched as foals were born and
pets died and grandparents became frail. They grew up understanding

we are all a part of the grand and sometimes heartbreaking pageant of being alive. It was something I had learned as a child, with the loss of my grandparents and the death of my brother Robbie. I have always understood how precious and fleeting life can be. But one time, shortly after Jack and I moved to Virginia, the universe gave me a tap on the shoulder to make sure I remembered.

It was a lovely summer evening, that magic hour right before dusk when the light covers everything like honey. Jack and I were driving along the highway leading out of town when we passed the scene of an accident. Just minutes before, an old man had been riding his bike along the edge of the road when he was hit by a car. The police and ambulance hadn't arrived yet, although I could hear sirens in the distance. A few people were standing around the injured man, who lay sprawled on the ground. While I was looking out my window, the man died right in front of me. I watched as the life left his body. One moment he was pink and alive and the next he was gray and dead. It was the most incredible thing, because the life didn't drain out from him, but rose up from his body like a bright shadow, then was gone.

I knew I had witnessed something profound and mystical, and also strangely intimate. I kept thinking that I had watched a man die, but no one in his family even knew he was dead. They were expecting him to walk through the door any minute after his pleasant evening bike ride.

The experience has stayed with me all these years, and I still haven't fathomed its full meaning. Although it was a tragedy for the man and his family, for me it was an indelible reminder that life can be taken from us in an instant, without warning. It was like a mid-course adjustment, to remind me not to take anything or anyone for granted, to live without regrets and enjoy every minute of the time we have.

MY FATHER CAME to live with us on the farm when he was eighty-six years old. The house in Quitman had become too much for him to keep up, and he was already spending months at a time with us. We set him up in the front bedroom of the house, on the first floor, and turned the library across the hall into an office for him. There he would spend hours reading through a dozen or more newspapers, mostly the *Wall Street Journal*, and clipping articles that interested him. He saved all his papers, piling them in stacks on the floor. (That's probably why I only read newspapers online—to offset all the trees sacrificed for him!)

Our girls called him "Poppy," and I was happy that they got to know each other better during the years when he lived with us. Whenever we visited him in Texas, it took a while for them to settle down. They were out of their "normal" routine and sometimes ran wild around the house. "Sissy, I'm afraid these girls are gonna grow up to be criminals," he would tell me, shaking his head. But once he was able to know Schuyler and Madison in their own environment, where they were much calmer and their personalities could shine through, their relationship blossomed.

Madison followed Poppy everywhere. He took her for rides in the golf cart, and helped her with her homework. Both of the girls would sit with him on the porch while he made them applesauce by scraping a fresh apple with a spoon. He told them it was the same thing his grandfather, who had come from Moravia, had done for him when he was a boy.

My dad loved the history of this place, and he was beside himself when he discovered that Robert E. Lee's soldiers had camped in our front field during the Civil War. Even better, the large neighboring farm, of which we were once a part, had played a role in the Revolutionary War. In 1781, British troops stopped there on their way to capture Thomas Jefferson at Monticello. According to legend, the farm's owner, Dr. Thomas Walker, ordered up a fine, leisurely breakfast for the soldiers to delay them long enough for a rider to warn Jefferson. The future president escaped with minutes to spare, and the rest, as they say, is history. My dad was thrilled by these kinds of stories, and he often said how fortunate we were to live in the cradle of democracy. It was all we could do to keep him from putting historical markers up all over the farm.

My dad always liked to hunt. When he came to live with us, one of our neighbors told him that she had a lot of Canadian geese on her place, and he was welcome to come over and hunt them. So he woke up early one day and got into all his hunting gear and set out on his hunt. Our neighbor's farm manager drove him over to a pond where there were about 150 geese swimming peacefully.

"Okay, Mr. Spacek," said the manager. "You say when, I'll scare 'em up and you shoot 'em."

My dad just started laughing and said, "You've got to be kidding me. Where's the sport in that? That's not hunting, that's slaughter!"

We have loads of deer on our farm, and he was excited to learn that you can shoot deer on your own property without a license. He made himself a little blind in the woods, and he would drive up there in his golf cart, toting his rifle. He'd wait for hours for a deer to appear, but when he had one in his sights, he couldn't shoot. He decided he just wanted to watch them. From then on, he left his gun at home and took his binoculars instead.

That golf cart was great for Daddy. He'd take it up to the end of the long driveway and pick up the mail and the paper. Then he'd stop by Gerri's house for a cup of coffee. My dad made big breakfasts for himself and the girls—which they loved, since Jack and I weren't enthusiastic cooks. We were more into free-range grazing from a stocked refrigerator. But Daddy was a great cook, and he loved to make eggs and sausages. He would appear every morning fully dressed in pressed trousers and a button-down shirt. As I watched him carefully slip the eggs onto plates laid out on the kitchen island, the morning sun slanting through the blinds, I thought of that picture of him as a young agricultural agent, wearing his white linen pants and two-toned shoes, standing out in a cotton field. Whatever my dad did, he did it with style.

When he was feeling well, Daddy would take long walks along the farm road. I would always find little piles of sticks that he had gathered along the way. Just like in Quitman, where he couldn't seem to walk in the front door without pulling weeds from the lawn, my dad kept our pathways free of branches, just to be helpful. Even when he started using a walker to get around, we never ran out of kindling on the farm.

Daddy always loved making fires, but we never had a fireplace in Texas. To save money on construction, he had put in a fake gas hearth. He spent years with a pent-up desire for crackling flames. When we bought a small lake house with a fireplace outside of Quitman, Daddy spent all his time out there, building fires. When he moved in with us in Virginia, he kept the fireplace in his bedroom going day and night, three seasons of the year.

One night we came home from an evening out and looked down the long, dim hallway to see his walker tipped over in front of his room and a dark, still shape next to it. Jack and I raced down the hall, calling, "Poppy, are you all right?" He poked his head out of the doorway and said, "Well, I was collecting firewood and . . ." The dark heap was a load of logs that didn't quite make it through the door.

As the years went by, my dad's health started to fade. We replaced the four-poster bed in his room with a hospital bed that was lower to the ground and could help him sit up. But after a few days he wanted his regular bed back. The new one just reminded him that he was sick. So Jack hauled the disassembled four-poster back into the bedroom and started setting it up. Daddy could see he was having a terrible time trying to hold it and screw it together, so he asked, "Jack, can I help you?"

"I tell you what, Poppy," said Jack, struggling to keep the posts upright. "Can you get Sissy so she can help me set this up?"

Daddy turned his walker around and shuffled down the hallway. It took a long, long time and Jack could hear every turn of the wheel. I was in the family room, building a fire. When I heard him come in, I called out, "Hey, Poppy!"

"Hey, Sissy!" Jack heard him say from down the hall.

There was a long pause. And then my dad said, "Where's Jack?"

JACK'S MOTHER and my father died within months of each other. When Gerri was in hospice care at home, Madison made herself a pallet of blankets on the floor next to Gerri's bed and read aloud to her from *Harry Potter*. Gerri was buried in Ipava, Illinois, where a plot was waiting for her next to Jack's father, the pilot who had died when they were all so young.

About three months later, in late December 2000, my dad went into the hospital and never made it home. He was clear as a bell most of the time. We could tell he was reliving his past because he kept calling me Mother's pet name. "Sugarbunk!" he said. "I need my britches and a fresh shirt." Then he pointed to the clock on the wall. "I've got to go onstage in fifteen minutes, Sugarbunk . . ." He was back in college, performing with his band. Another time he looked around the room and said, "This is a nice cabin. Whose is it, anyway?"

I knew the end was coming, but when my father died that night, I was still shocked.

He was so young! I thought. And then I remembered: He was ninety years old.

IT WAS HARD to believe that our daughters were growing up and ready to start their own lives. It seemed like we'd never get them past that first three months. And when were they ever going to sleep through the night? Then suddenly they were walking and talking and starting school and driving and dating. And if you haven't taught them everything you want them to know by the time they're twelve, you can just forget about it. By then it's all over; they've stopped listening. Then you send them out into the world, and suddenly you think of all the things you've forgotten to tell them: Don't talk to strangers. Don't park in a loading zone. You lie awake at night thinking, "I've got to get 'em that Mace!" Actually, that was my gift to Madison when she went away to college. Jack got her a dog.

JACK HAD GONE THROUGH art school with Five, and he wanted to get a dog just like her for Madison. But we could never figure out her breed, or if she even was a breed. We checked out every shaggy dog that we could find, with no luck. After years of looking, Jack almost gave up. Then one day he opened up a new book we'd gotten about dog breeds, and found her. Five was a schapendoes, a Dutch sheepdog, a breed so rare in America that it's still not registered with the American Kennel Club. When he showed me the picture, I nearly fell off the couch.

We had to jump through hoops to convince the Canadian breeder that we were worthy owners for such a special dog. Finally, we got her, a beautiful brown and white fur ball, the most adorable puppy imaginable. As soon as we saw her, it was instant love.

In the Fisk tradition of naming dogs after numerals, Madison called her Zero. Like Five had done for Jack, Zero took great care of Madison for nearly four years. But every time Madison brought her home, Zero followed Jack around like a long-lost relative. It was clear to Madison that Zero was Jack's dog. She belonged with him. So on Madison's twenty-second birthday, she officially handed Zero over to her dad.

Jack took Zero everywhere with him, but she had a tough act to follow because Five was such a remarkable dog. One time a guard at a studio tried to stop us from taking Five into a screening.

"No dogs allowed," he said.

"Oh, really?" said Jack. "The invitation said 'cast and crew.'"

The guard leaned forward and whispered, "Is that a trained dog?"

"Oh, yeah," said Jack. "She's a trained dog."

"Well, then! You follow that yellow line, it goes around the corner, and it will lead you right to the screening room."

With that, Five put her nose to the yellow line, followed it to the corner, made the turn, and disappeared. The guard was amazed. A few moments later, Five looked back around the corner, as if to say, "C'mon! What's the hold-up?"

It didn't take long to realize that Zero had the same talents. While he was designing Paul Thomas Anderson's *The Master*, she came with him on location and even attended production meetings. We have a picture of her sitting in a chair at the table next to Jack. Once, when he was looking at a location, he and Zero had to walk a long way from the parking lot to the set. There were a lot of kids running around, and Zero was not used to small children, so Jack said, "Zero, get in the car." The location scouts were amazed when she just turned around, ran all the way back to the car, jumped in, and waited patiently for him to return.

Zero was the latest in a revolving cast of animals who had lived with us at the farm. There were always dogs and cats and ponies; sheep, chickens, and a donkey named Elvira. We had a pet songbird for a while. It must have fallen out of its nest, because when one of our cats brought it to the door, it was a tiny naked bundle of bones, so young it didn't even have feathers. Madison fed it mashed worms out of an eye dropper, and amazingly, it survived. The bird grew feathers and lived out on the second-floor sleeping porch. We named it Twerp 2. When it heard us laughing and talking outside, it would squeeze through a hole in the screen, then fly down and land on our heads.

We also adopted a stray dog we named Quitman. We found her shaking and soaked to the bones outside my father's house one morning. There had been terrible thunder and pounding rains all night, and she had huddled under the eaves, trying not to drown. When Jack discovered her, he blessed her. "May you have a long and happy life," he said. Then I came around the corner and said, "Look, a puppy! We have to take her back to Virginia." For the rest of her life she would quiver and run for cover whenever it rained, which, in Virginia, is a lot. And here she's been for almost fifteen years, with all her phobias intact.

Sometimes we'd have half a dozen or more dogs in our family. For many years, the leader of the pack was a miniature dachshund named Patch. Sometimes she reminded me of me: small but mighty. And bossy. Like many small dogs, Patch lived a long time, and she was a big presence in our lives. On the last day of her life, she walked outside to her favorite spot and sat down under a tree. I'll never forget how she looked around the farm, just taking it all in. It reminded me of the day my mother left home to go to the hospital and paused to drink in the sight of the world she was leaving. That's just what this little dog was doing.

There are valuable lessons everywhere, if you are willing to receive them. It's amazing when a small brown dog can teach us so much about how to live in this world, and then how to leave it.

AFTER ATTENDING THE University of Virginia, Schuyler moved to Los Angeles. She continues to act in films, but almost all of her energy for the past few years has gone into her music. She has already written countless songs and released two CDs, the latest, recorded in Virginia, in a little studio just a few miles down the road from our farm. I am in awe of her musical talent, which goes much deeper than my own. Every once in a while I'll sing backup on a song, or she'll bring me up onstage to put on a harmony while she's performing. One of the best moments of my life was performing with Schuyler during a huge concert at Wolf Trap National Park in Virginia. But most often I am happy just to sit in the audience, watching her live out my old fantasies of being a rock star.

Schuyler lives in a cozy house near the ocean with her fiancé, Chapman Bullock, a motion-graphics artist, and their rambunctious yellow lab, Rigby. There always seems to be something delicious bubbling on her stove or baking in her oven, and a crowd of grateful friends at her table. (I don't know how she learned to cook so well—it couldn't have been from watching me!)

Madison studied painting and sculpture at California Institute of the Arts and Virginia Commonwealth University with a yearning to become an artist and filmmaker. She's written and directed several short comedies; in one I have a funny cameo, playing myself as an out-of-work actor. Since then, she's been busy paying her dues and is on her way to becoming an art director, which is what she wants to do. She's moved to Texas, where there's a booming independent film industry and where she's surrounded by family and feels right at home.

The walls of her house are covered with her paintings: her adopted dachshund mix, Maude, who reminds me of Patch; a painting of me in a dress I wore in *Badlands*; and a study of her grandmother Gerri. I love her use of color and the way she captures the spirit of her subjects. Madison's paintings are expressions of the world around her.

It looks like the whole family is destined to live the "art life."

Like the first Spaceks who made that leap of faith and sailed across the ocean to settle in Texas, we depend on one another, and our lives are deeply intertwined. We like each other's company. Madison lives a short drive away from my brother Ed, his wife Tannie (who often tutored Madison on location), and their computer-enthusiast teenage son, Austin. Ed's eldest son, Stephen, is an artist's manager who lives near Schuyler in Los Angeles, and Mark is a filmmaker who lives near Madison in Texas. All of Ed's boys are like brothers to our girls.

Jack and I have also stayed close to his family. His sister, Mary, still lives nearby in Virginia. She runs our office, manages our business, and keeps things working smoothly on the farm. Although she and David Lynch have parted ways, they are still friends. Their son, Austin (did you notice we have a lot of Austins in the family?), grew up with our girls and is also like a brother to them. He's an artist and filmmaker, like his father and uncle, and his wife, Nancy, is a sculptor. Nasif Iskander, the son of Jack's older sister, Susie, is dean of faculty at a highly regarded school in San Francisco. Susie is remarried, to a rancher named Richard Francis, and lives in South Dakota. They tried moving to Virginia for a while, but they quickly returned to the western prairie. The East Coast didn't sit well with Richard.

"Too many trees," he said.

THE PART OF VIRGINIA where we live has grown over the years. We no longer have to rely on the combo platters at La Hacienda when we want to dine out. There is a bustling downtown open-air mall filled with fine restaurants, and theaters that attract some of the best musical artists in the world. Best of all, for me, a Whole Foods supermarket has opened. I still think it's the best way to be well fed at home (without actually having to cook). I've been shopping there for years, and the clerks all know me well.

Not long ago, I was coming back from a trip to California, and I was bringing Schuyler's chocolate lab, Cassidy, back to live on the farm. I had the dog and her huge shipping crate, so I asked the car company that always picks me up at the airport to bring a large SUV. We were going to need extra room. No problem, they said. And when my flight arrived, the driver was there with a Yukon, and he helped me get the dog into the seat next to me, and the crate into the back of the car. It was great!

On the way to the farm, the driver said, "You know, you've been gone a long time, would you like to go to the grocery store and get some food?"

"Oh, that's so nice of you. But you don't have to stop."

"Really, it's no problem! I know you'll be hungry when you get home, and Whole Foods is on the way."

"Well, okay! That's wonderful. I won't be a minute."

We pulled up in front of the store, and as I was stepping out, the driver said, "I just got a call. There's a football game at the university, and they need an SUV. Do you mind if we switch out cars while you shop?"

"Oh, no problem," I said. "Just take good care of Cassidy!"

The regular customers are so used to seeing me at Whole Foods that usually nobody pays any attention. So I thought it was odd that people kept coming up to me and asking for my autograph and taking pictures. Then I thought, "Oh, there are probably a lot of strangers in town for the ball game." But it kept happening. It was so weird! When I checked out with my groceries and walked outside, I found the longest white stretch limousine I have ever seen in my life, parked right in front of Whole Foods. The chauffeur was standing next to the car in his uniform, holding the door open for me. And there was Cassidy sitting up in the backseat, looking like Mrs. Astor's plush horse. Everybody was staring at me and taking pictures with their cell phones. They must have thought I was the most stuck-up thing east of the Blue Ridge. I laughed so hard I thought I would cry. I called Jack from the car. "You're not going to believe this, Jack," I said. In thirty seconds, a reputation that had taken me thirty years to build was dashed.

I THOUGHT I'D BE SHOCKED when I turned sixty, but it was easy—a lot easier than turning twenty, when I was nearly panicked that I was getting too old to make it in the music business. It helped that my friends, the producers Helen Bartlett and Tony Bill, threw me the best and certainly the biggest birthday party I'd ever had, at their home in LA. Being a Christmas baby, I'm not used to celebrating my birthday and being the center of that kind of attention. I was overwhelmed, and I hardly noticed that someone kept filling my glass with champagne. When the time came for me to thank my friends and family for their beautiful tributes, I looked out at the lovely crowd and thought, *Who are all these people and why are they staring at me?* Jack had to get me home early that night, but Schuyler and Madison told me the last half of the party was wonderful!

Other than a diminished tolerance for champagne, and occasionally losing my car in a parking lot, growing older hasn't been so bad. I try to approach it as gracefully as possible and I welcome all good advice. I think Sophia Loren said it best. When asked how she managed to appear so young, she replied, "I try not to make any noise when I get up out of a chair."

One of the best things I've done in my life came late: Harper Lee, the author of *To Kill a Mockingbird*, asked me to read the audiobook version of her masterpiece. I spent weeks wrapped up in her gorgeous prose, like a comfortable old quilt. I reexperienced all that I'd felt when I first read that book and saw the film that made me fall in love with movies.

I continue to be offered roles in rich, nuanced films, like *Get Low*, with Robert Duvall and Bill Murray, and most of them I've been smart enough to accept. I can hardly believe I almost didn't do *The Help*.

When Tate Taylor sent me the script, I kept flipping through the pages, looking to see if my character had any memorable scenes. Tate wanted me to play Missus Walters, the batty mother of the film's villain, but she only had a few lines of dialogue. When I read the novel to see if I could learn more about her, I discovered that Missus Walters played an even smaller role in the book. Still, I loved the Civil Rights–era story of how a misfit Junior Leaguer and a group of maids secretly wrote a book together in Mississippi. So I met with the director.

"Tate, I love the script," I said. "But I don't think there's enough there for me to make this character work."

"Oh, don't worry," he said. "You can improvise."

Now, many directors say that, but very few follow through. Tate Taylor was the exception. I created my Missus Walters from memories of my father's sisters, the eccentric, colorful aunts I grew up with in Texas, and then I added some red lipstick, cat-eye glasses, and cocktails. I'm afraid I shamelessly upstaged the other actors in all my scenes, and I don't regret a minute of it!

We filmed on location in Greenwood, Mississippi, located a couple of hours north of Jackson. To get there from the airport I drove within a few miles of the small town where my grandmother Elizabeth Holliday Spilman, was born. When people asked where I was from, I was able to tell them I was a Holliday, from just down the road. "Oh, that's a fine family!" I'd hear again and again. A few long-lost relatives even tracked me down while I was filming, and I learned even more about my Mississippi family. It felt like a homecoming.

One morning I was walking through the hotel lobby, on my way to the set, when a tiny blond woman introduced herself as Kitty Stockett, the author of *The Help*. I told her how much I loved her book, and we visited for a few minutes. I was wearing little round sunglasses and my typical summer uniform—Oxford shirt, knee-length shorts, and Chaco sandals—and I noticed that Kitty was looking at me intently.

"You don't look old enough to play Missus Walters!" she said.

"Oh, just you wait!" I laughed I'd like people to think it took hours to make me look that old. But the truth is, it didn't.

I enjoyed playing an older character in *The Help*. It was fun and liberating not to have to worry about looking youthful and attractive—although Missus Walters was plenty attractive to her boyfriend at the nursing home. He was played by Tate's father, John Taylor, who also was put to work as a driver. In fact the whole production felt like a family affair. Tate had grown up in Jackson with Kitty Stockett and had been good friends with Octavia Spencer and Allison Janney for years. We had a wonderfully diverse cast and crew, and many of the extras were friends and relatives.

The film used a light and comedic touch to explore a shameful era in American history, when the races were so segregated that the collaboration between a white writer and a black maid was dangerous for both of them. But at its heart, *The Help* is a story about love and friendship that transcends class and race. We certainly felt that on location, on what had to be one of the most integrated sets in the history of filmmaking. We all blended together and got along so well that nobody seemed to dwell on the ghosts of the past that still linger in Mississippi. As a nation, we still have a way to go before we heal the division between races. But to me, being able to make a film like *The Help* seemed like a reward for how far we have managed to come.

NOT LONG AGO I was walking through an old historic downtown mall in Virginia when a teenage girl came running up to me, all excited. "Sissy Spacek!" she squealed. "You're Carrie! You're Carrie!" She pulled back her sleeve to reveal a full color tattoo of me as Carrie in her prom dress, holding a bouquet of red roses. It was a beautiful tattoo, all pink and gold—it apparently captured the moment just before the bucket of pig's blood was dropped on my head—and I had to admire it, but I was still shocked that this lovely young girl would do such a thing.

"Do your parents know about this?" I asked her. And more important: "Do they blame me?!"

Early in my career, I thought that making it in the business meant appearing on the Johnny Carson show. These days, a mark of success is having one of your characters tattooed on someone else's body part. But nothing beats getting your star on Hollywood Boulevard.

I had been acting in films for more than forty years, but there was one milestone I hadn't crossed. Oscar on the mantel? *Check.* Handprints in the sidewalk at Universal Studios? *Check* Golden Globe? *Check, check, check.* Yet tourists were still unable to stroll over my name on the "Boulevard of Broken Dreams." I only realized what a big deal it was when, in the summer of 2011, the Hollywood Chamber of Commerce honored me with my very own star on the Walk of Fame. There I was, on the sidewalk outside the El Capitan Theatre, in the company of Tinker Bell, Winnie the Pooh, and Steve McQueen. It's a great piece of real estate right across from the Kodak Theatre, home of the Academy Awards.

My family was there, along with so many friends that I felt like it was an episode of the old TV show *This Is Your Life*. I was so thrilled to see everyone that I forgot to be nervous about the dozens of cameras pointed at me, and the hundreds of fans yelling my name. And I had excellent company on the podium that day. Two of my dearest friends, Bill Paxton and David Lynch, had agreed to say a few words about me.

When Bill spoke it was funny and heartfelt. I was reminded how important he has been in my life, and how far back we go. He talked about meeting me when he was a young set designer, and then acting with me on *Big Love* (although for some reason he never mentioned Twerp). Then it was David Lynch's turn. "You owe me, Sis," he said with a smile as I gave him a hug. David never attends ceremonies if he can help it. He rarely leaves his property up in the Hollywood Hills, where he works on his art, music, and film projects day and night, and his uniform never varies: khaki pants and white shirt, buttoned at the neck. Today he was wearing a stylish suit and looked very handsome and polished as he stepped to the podium.

This, with his permission, is the speech, delivered in the clipped, nasal twang that one writer described as sounding like Jimmy Stewart on acid·

"Good morning, ladies and gentlemen. It is a real honor and pleasure for me to speak about Sissy Spacek. This is perfect. Sissy is a star. Stars are mostly in space, and Sissy has the word 'space' in her name.

"I've known Sissy for a long time. Her husband, Jack Fisk, is my best friend since high school. On the set of *The Straight Story*, a film that I directed, Sissy played Alvin's daughter, Rose. Her performance is so beautiful and tender. Jack was production designer on this film as well. One night, Jack called just as we were finishing the day's shooting. He was a half-hour drive away, just finishing a set for the following day. He wanted to know if I would drive over to see the set right away. Sissy wanted to go over to be with Jack, so I took her, and we drove together through the night on small, two-lane highways— all dark, passing miles of cornfields. It started to rain.

"Now, a lot of the following story Sissy and I can't talk about. The United States government has told us not to. But this part I can say: I thought it was a bolt of lightning, a tremendous white light, and suddenly Sissy and I were inside a giant alien spaceship. Thousands of aliens were around us. The commander floated up in the air and told us a spectacular story. He told us that in many, many galaxies in our universe, on so many planets, Sissy Spacek is revered. All know of her films, and even her songs, and all the beings love the fact that Sissy works both with the studios and the independents. He even told us that from now on he's calling his ship a 'Spacek ship.'

"The commander told us that this day had long ago been predicted: Sissy getting her star on the Hollywood Walk of Fame. He told us that this very day, millions of beings around the universe will celebrate Sissy getting her star. The commander asked that I thank all those who made this honor possible, and to thank Hollywood for being Hollywood. And for creating the Hollywood Walk of Fame. After Sissy signed hundreds of autographs for the aliens in the spaceship, like a snap of the fingers Sissy and I were back on Earth, standing in front of Jack and his finished set.

"He jumped and said, 'How did you get here so fast?'

"Ladies and gentlemen, on behalf of the beings here on Earth that can't be here today, and beings in galaxies across the universe, please join me in congratulating, for her great work, for this honor of a star on the Hollywood Walk of Fame, the great Sissy Spacek!"

I was laughing so hard I could barely read the short speech I had prepared. I told the story of my first time in Hollywood, when I was pulled over by the police after hitching a ride with a van filled with hippies, and the cops pulled guns on us. Okay, maybe I changed a few minor details, but at least I didn't spill the beans about the space aliens, like David did. But what I really wanted to say was how amazing it was for me to come up in films with the likes of David Lynch and Bill Paxton, and how lucky Jack and I were to have them all to ourselves in the beginning, before we had to share their talent and bad jokes with the rest of the world.

·   ·   ·

JACK AND I BOUGHT a place near the ocean, so our family could have a home base in LA. It's only a coincidence that our living room overlooks the football field at the local high school. Sometimes I lie in bed and hear the sound of a marching band practicing in the stadium. It reminds me of my childhood home, where we could sit in our backyard and hear the band and the roar of the crowd at Quitman High on game nights. The sound folds over me, like the waves out on the Pacific, and rocks me back to that time and place in Texas, the source of everything that I am.

AFTER A LONG HIATUS, Terry Malick came back to filmmaking with a surge of creative energy. Jack has worked with him on each of his films, including *The Tree of Life*. To me, it's a masterpiece. Schuyler and I watched *The Tree of Life* together in a big theater in Westwood. I knew the film was very personal for Terry, and it was shot outside of Austin, in a town reminiscent of his childhood home. What I wasn't prepared to see were scenes from my own childhood, growing up in Texas in the 1950s, which has become a part of the language and history that Jack and Terry and I share. Jack had crafted a world for Terry's film so familiar and haunting that I watched in awe, struggling to control my emotions. There was the DDT truck, spraying clouds of fog for the children to dance in. There were the trails where my brothers and I used to run, the neighbors' house that I slipped inside of to explore, and the brother that I had lost. By the end of the film, when the family is reunited in what might be heaven, I was moved beyond words. Schuyler was probably starting to wonder if I'd lost my mind. I don't know how it would have been for me if I had seen it when I was younger. Maybe I wouldn't have been as moved. But that film, a collaboration of two of the most important people in my life, spoke to me on a level so deep and powerful that I wept. I saw the world with fresh, new eyes, and I was grateful.

· · ·

NOT LONG AGO I was on location, and I was sitting beside a young actress in the makeup trailer. I asked her what she was interested in, what kinds of things she wanted to do.

"Oh, I want to fly a jet plane," she said. "I want to skydive! And helicopter ski! And take a boat down the Amazon!" Her eyes lit up as she talked about all the things she wanted to experience. Then she turned to me and said, "And what do you want to do?"

I thought for a moment and smiled. "I just want to go home," I said. I couldn't think of anything I wanted to do or any place I wanted to be more than home. Where I can walk around the yard, sweeping leaves off the slate paths to my heart's content. Where I can spend all day in my pajamas puttering around the house, or curled up in my favorite chair in the family room next to the big stone fireplace. The walls are papered deep red, hung with Madison's paintings and lined with our favorite books. The furniture is comfortable and inviting. Our house is made to be lived in; we use every inch of it and don't mind the signs of wear and tear. There's a deep dent in the floor next to the hearth, a memento from one Christmas when the girls were given geodes—hollow stones lined with crystals—which they cracked open with a hammer on the heart-pine boards. It's part of the story of this house, where a family has left its mark, and where it continues to grow and evolve.

Jack and I love to watch the sun come up over the pond while we drink our morning coffee. It's these simple routines we miss most when we're working away from home. But we're grateful we have this place to come back to, a place to hold the treasures we've collected over the years. I like to keep my favorites out where I can see them: a piece of polished driftwood shaped like the head of a duck; a gray river stone cut through with a thin streak of quartz; a miniature dresser filled with drawings and letters from our girls, notes to Santa Claus and the Easter Bunny, and from some of the great actors I've admired: Lillian Gish, Gregory Peck, Jack Lemmon, Meryl Streep. In the entry hall there's a tall cabinet with glass doors filled to bursting with reminders of who we are and where we come from. This is where I keep the gifts that Jack left for me to find on the set of *Badlands*: the three-legged horse and rider, the butterfly door knocker, the horned toad, all stacked on the crowded shelves along with old family portraits, my parents' wedding cake topper, and clay pottery the girls made in grade school. Sometimes I find myself wandering from room to room, just taking in all these things that I love.

Our girls come home for birthdays and holidays or whenever they just need a breath of fresh air. Schuyler fills the farm with musicians who camp out in the guest cottages and play music in the living room, working out songs on the piano and on some of the same guitars I played during my early years in New York. Madison, like her dad, always has art projects under way—building, welding, painting, and creating in every corner of the farm. Both girls bring their friends and pets, and the house buzzes with energy. Our home is a living, breathing thing, and it keeps us busy and on our toes (if only to avoid tripping over the extra dogs).

Both Schuyler and Madison plan to move back to the farm one day, to raise their own families. Each has already picked out the spot where she wants to live. It makes me happy to imagine that kind of continuum: our grandchildren walking down the same farm roads our parents did, our lives growing new layers, like the rings of a tree that tell the story of each passing season.

Like my father and grandparents and the long line of Moravian farmers before them, I love to plant things and watch them grow. The maple trees that we put in when the girls were babies now tower over the cottage where Gerri lived. For years we've grown vegetables in raised beds, but lately it's flowers that delight me. The perennials I planted in the serpentine garden outside the dining room have matured like old friends. I planted irises around the pond with the spade my father gave me. And this spring there will be hundreds of new Moonstone peonies and tulips around the house.

· · ·

OUR FARM IS IN THE SHADOW of the Southwest Mountains, one of the oldest mountain ranges in America, where we ride along the same trails that Thomas Jefferson had traveled, and rest in the shade of the same majestic trees. One of them is a massive oak so old I can only imagine all it has seen. When I run my hand along its rough bark, I think of how deep its roots have grown to keep it standing through all the windstorms and heavy snows it's endured over the years. I feel rooted like that tree in this soil.

IN SUMMER, I WEAR my biggest hat and walk beneath stately linden trees that line our road, sent by boat from Europe a hundred years ago so ladies in their buggies would have shade on their way to and from the train station. Soon the leaves will turn deep auburn and gold, and winter will come again and sing its lonesome song. I'll bundle up against the cold and go to ground, like the fox that makes his home here. Then before I know it, spring will come and blooms will peek through thawing earth and new green will grace the hills. And it will start all over again.

I've walked and jogged thousands of miles up and down this road, and I never seem to tire of it. Most days, the dogs and Nigel, the cat that thinks he's a dog, follow me on my walks with sticks and bones, chasing one another around, happy for the daily ritual. I see something new every day—a piece of fool's gold glinting in the gravel, a blue damselfly skimming across the pond, a perfect heart-shaped leaf. I count my blessings.

··· Acknowledgments ···

Thanks to my husband, Jack Fisk, for helping me through every stage of this book. Our life together proves the old adage: Always marry your best friend.

Thanks to Schuyler for filling my life with music, and for her grace, her sparkle, and her wonderful cooking.

Thanks to Madison, for her creative mind and tender heart, and for taking us on an amazing trip through Texas.

To my brother, Ed Spacek, who inherited all of our parents' best qualities, thank you for helping me remember clearly and for being such a wonderful brother.

To Mary Fisk, the hub of the wheel, thank you for keeping things running smoothly.

Thanks to Maryanne Vollers, for turning this book into an adventure. Your talent is inspiring and your work ethic exhausting. Thanks for keeping me on the straight and narrow. I am lucky to have worked with such a dear friend.

To Courtney Kivowitz, Steve Tellez, and Jim Stein, for steering a steady ship.

Thanks to the folks at Hyperion: Elisabeth Dyssegaard, Kerri Kolen, Kiki Koroshetz, Samantha O'Brien, Leslie Wells, and Sarah Landis.

And thanks to Weiman Seid for absolutely everything. I don't know what I would do without you.

Thanks to these friends and relatives for sharing their memories and filling in the holes in my own:

Terrence Malick, David Lynch, Bill Paxton, Brian De Palma, Pat Torn Alexander, Janit Baldwin, Kathy Holliday Browne, Rose Byrd, Jack Carone, Susan Merritt Cummings, Sean Daniel, David Fender, Jane McKnight Fender, Dan Johnson, Mary Kalergis, Michel Kicq, Sue Kramer, Kenny Laguna, Meryl Laguna, Alberta Mahanes, Stephanie Mansfield, Ulna McWhorter, Hugh Motley, Winkie Motley, Cindy Owen, Andy Pearce, Clint Perkins, Monica Podell, Ed Pressman, Sr. Elizabeth Riebschlaeger, Aggie Rives, Barclay Rives, Jane Robinson, Alice Passman Schwartz, Judy Simpson, Stephen Spacek, Arlette Spilman, EJ Strmiska, Leah Rae Strmiska, Dr. Beverly Waddleton, Jan Spacek York, and the staffs of the Quitman Public Library and the Wood County courthouse.

For their love and support on the home front: Diane Bloom, Nanette Derkac, Sarah DuPont, Colleen Gibbons, Julann Griffin, Mary Kalergis, Aggie Rives.

Thanks to my friend Helen Bartlett for "planting the seed" for this book and for the wonderful notes when I finally got it written. And to my friend Lynne Brubaker, who dropped everything to produce the fabulous cover photograph.

Thanks to Bill Campbell and Jamie Meyer for helping with the photo inserts, and to Gene Bright, Lynne Brubaker, Joseph Burchfield, Aldo Filiberto, Sue Kramer, Barbara Colley Locke, Jean Pagliuso, Monica Podell, Douglas Randall, the Riker Brothers, the Spacek Family Reunion, and Pamela Wise.

Thanks to those who believed in me when it mattered:

Rip Torn, Geraldine Page, Bill Treusch, Rick Nicita, and Marion Dougherty.

Thanks to all my family, in this world and the next.

And thanks to a lifetime of four-legged friends.

Above all, thanks to Mother and Daddy, Robbie and Ed, and Schuyler, Madison, and Jack, who helped make this extraordinary, ordinary life possible.

Credits

Lower middle: Courtesy of Universal Studios Licensing, LLC. All Rights Reserved.

Lower right: BADLANDS © Warner Bros. Entertainment Inc. All Rights Reserved.

PAGE 3:

Upper left: Michael Ochs Archives/Moviepix/Getty Images

Upper right: Courtesy of Universal Studios Licensing, LLC. All Rights Reserved.

Middle: Photograph from "The Good Old Boys" provided by TNT Originals, Inc.

PAGE 4:

Upper left: Courtesy of Universal Studios Licensing, LLC. All Rights Reserved.

Upper right: Associated Press.

Middle left: Courtesy of MGM Media Licensing. CARRIE © 1976 METRO-GOLDWYN-MAYER STUDIOS INC. ALL RIGHTS RESERVED.

Middle right: HEART BEAT © Warner Bros. Entertainment Inc. All Rights Reserved.

Lower left: Courtesy of Universal Studios Licensing, LLC. All Rights Reserved.

PAGE 5:

Upper left: Courtesy of Jean Pagliuso

Lower middle: Courtesy of Douglas Randall

Lower right: Courtesy of Joseph Burchfield

All others: Spacek Family Collection

PAGE 6:

Middle: Courtesy of The Riker Brothers

Middle right: Brian Killian/Getty Images

All others: Spacek Family Collection

PAGE 7:
Middle: Courtesy of Aldo Filiberto
Lower right: Courtesy of Sue Kramer
All others: Spacek Family Collection

PAGE 8:
Middle left: Courtesy of The Riker Brothers
Middle right: Courtesy of Lynne Brubaker
All others: Spacek Family Collection

For all photographs not credited, every effort has been made to trace and contact copyright holders. The publishers will be pleased to correct any mistakes or omissions in future editions.